Advance Praise for *Surrendering to Utopia*

At a time of contrasting narratives about human rights, from irresponsible triumphalism to cynical pessimism, here is a book that masterfully guides us into the complexities of contextualized practices of human rights across cultures and national boundaries. It does this by powerfully engaging anthropology, a discipline that has been marginalized by conventional human rights scholarship to the latter's greater loss. Thanks to Goodale's very persuasive argument, the record is finally being set right.

—Boaventura de Sousa Santos,
Universities of Coimbra, Warwick, and Wisconsin-Madison

This fluid and compelling book draws on a broad intellectual tradition to highlight how the relationship between anthropology and human rights developed and what it could and should become in the future. An engaging and thought-provoking read!

—Marie-Bénédicte Dembour, University of Sussex

This is a sophisticated, brave, and ultimately successful attempt to bridge the gap between anthropology and normative theory. By taking on the intricate relationship between anthropology and human rights, Goodale shows clearly why anthropology should matter, not only academically, but also in the wider world of policy and politics. It is a timely book which moves beyond the relativism-universalism dichotomy and thereby demonstrates what anthropological theory in the 21st century ought to look like.

—Thomas Hylland Eriksen, University of Oslo

Goodale's meditation on human rights through the prism of culture pulls off a compelling discussion of the ways universalism and relativism continue to define international human rights. He offers a fascinating history of the political deployment of the term culture, as well as its use and abuse in national and international human rights struggles.

—Victoria Sanford, City University of New York

Stanford Studies in Human Rights

Surrendering to Utopia

An Anthropology of Human Rights

Mark Goodale

Stanford University Press
Stanford, California

Stanford University Press
Stanford, California

Printed in the United States of America on acid-free, archival-quality paper

Appendix 1: Originally published in *American Anthropologist* 49 (4): 539–543. www.anthrosource.net.

Appendix 2: American Anthropological Association (1999). http://www.aaanet.org/stmts/humanrts.htm.

Library of Congress Cataloging-in-Publication Data

Goodale, Mark.
 Surrendering to utopia : an anthropology of human rights / Mark Goodale.
    p. cm. -- (Stanford studies in human rights)
 Includes bibliographical references and index.
 ISBN 978-0-8047-6212-0 (cloth : alk. paper) -- ISBN 978-0-8047-6213-7 (pbk. : alk. paper)
 1. Human rights--Anthropological aspects. 2. Political anthropology. I. Title. II. Series.
 GN492.2.G66 2009
  306.2--dc22
                              2008054818

Typeset by Bruce Lundquist in 10/14 Minion Pro

For Isaiah, Dara, and Romana

There is no substitute for a sense of reality.

Isaiah Berlin

Table of Contents

Acknowledgments   xi

Prologue: The phenomenology of human rights at 35,000 feet . . .   1

1   Introduction: A Well-Tempered Human Rights   5

2   Becoming Irrelevant:
The Curious History of Anthropology and Human Rights   18

3   Encountering Relativism:
The Philosophy, Politics, and Power of a Dilemma   40

4   Culture on the Half Shell:
Universal Rights through the Back Door   65

5   Human Rights along the Grapevine:
The Ethnography of Transnational Norms   91

6   Rights Unbound:
Anthropology and the Emergence of Neoliberal Human Rights   111

Conclusion: Human Rights in an Anthropological Key   128

Appendix 1: Statement on Human Rights (1947)   135

Appendix 2: Declaration on Anthropology and
Human Rights (1999)   141

Notes   143

Bibliography   157

Index   171

Acknowledgments

I WANT TO FIRST ACKNOWLEDGE the role that my students at both Emory University and George Mason University have played in the shaping of this book. They have allowed my human rights seminars over the years to serve as an important space in which ideas and provocations have been tested, modified, debated, and, at times, found wanting. I have learned much from their critical perspectives and have been encouraged by their willingness to consider human rights in an anthropological key.

Funding for the research and analysis that inform different parts of this book was provided by a number of institutions and fellowships over a period of time, including the National Science Foundation, the Fulbright Scholar Program, the Organization of American States, and the Irmgard Coninx Foundation, as well as several internal university grants at George Mason University. A sabbatical during the early stages of writing was especially useful.

My wider thinking about anthropology and human rights has benefited from dialogue and different kinds of critical engagement with too many generous colleagues to mention here. Nevertheless, I must acknowledge, in particular, the following individuals: Sally Engle Merry, Kamari Maxine Clarke, Richard A. Wilson, Laura Nader, Hans Joas, Ari Kohen, Eva Erman, Kurt Shaw, Abdullahi Ahmed An-Na'im, Michael Likosky, Shannon Speed, Scott Newton, Kevin Avruch, Sara Cobb, Solon Simmons, Jane Cowan, Marie-Bénédicte Dembour, Sari Wastell, Shalini Randeria, Balakrishnan Rajagopal, Alain Pottage, Martha Mundy, John Dale, Upendra Baxi, Mauricio García Villegas, and Anne Griffiths. I also benefited from the close and critical readings of the book by two anonymous reviewers at Stanford University Press.

The development of this book has been much enriched by the opportunity to present ideas during invited lectures and presentations at a number of institutions over the last few years. In particular, I would like to thank my hosts, faculty colleagues, and students at the following: University of Oxford (Centre for Socio-Legal Studies), University of Helsinki (the Erik Castrén Institute of International Law and Human Rights and the Centre of Excellence in Global Governance Research), University of Sussex (Department of Anthropology and the Law School), Brandeis University (the Heller School for Social Policy), Georgia Institute of Technology (Ivan Allen College of Liberal Arts), Max Planck Institute for Social Anthropology, University of Zurich (Institute for Social Anthropology), University of Edinburgh (Faculty of Law), Chr. Michelsen Institute, University of Oregon (School of Law), University of Bucharest (Institute for Public Policy), University College London (Department of Anthropology), London School of Economics (Department of Anthropology), Humboldt University (Social Science Research Center), University of Amsterdam (Institute for Metropolitan and International Development Studies), University of Erfurt (Max Weber Center for Advanced Cultural and Social Studies), and Harvard University (Department of Anthropology).

Finally, I was fortunate to have Kate Wahl as my editor at Stanford University Press. Kate's support, expert guidance, and wisdom were much appreciated during the writing and production of this book.

Surrendering to Utopia

The phenomenology of human rights at 35,000 feet . . .

I T IS UNSETTLING how an experience can rapidly shift from the incongruous to the profoundly moving, from a moment of surprise to the realization that one's frame of reference, which has been put in place only with great difficulty, is no longer quite so adequate.

So there I was, halfway through a whirlwind sequence of lectures at European universities that was supposed to give many of the ideas in this book one final critical public airing before they were forever committed to the permanence of print. I found myself standing in line waiting to board a small regional jet in one of the outer terminals at Heathrow. My fellow passengers bound for Copenhagen looked to be mainly business travelers; already busy working their cell phones in several languages, they were oblivious to the world around them. Ever the anthropologist, I couldn't help but observe this sleepy early-morning ritual, marked as it was by its sheer mundaneness and rational efficiencies.

My hosts had sent me off the night before with a typically generous *despedida*. I was not exactly worse for the wear, but as I stood there waiting to hand my e-ticket to the Lufthansa agent, it occurred to me that the demands of daily early-morning international travel stood in some tension with the rhythms and idiosyncrasies of the academic life.

Suddenly the eerie quiet and sense of routine anticipation in that outer terminal at Heathrow were jolted by a din: from around the corner, still out of sight, came a multitudinous jumble of voices of the kind that is usually attached to a throng of people. This urgent sound snaked around the curved wall and hit the waiting masters of the universe like a thunderbolt. Cell phones

1

dropped from ears to well-clothed sides, and all heads turned with a collective gasp in the direction of a sound that we could now hear clearly included the crying and insistent pleas of very small children.

There was also something else, at least for me. As an ethnographer I have come to rely on all of my senses during what I can describe without too much irony as data collection. Indeed, early-modern scientific epistemologists like David Hume would have had no difficulty understanding how the complicated process of ethnographic observation demands the focused application of touch as much as sight, smell as much as sound. So as I waited to greet the incongruous in what would be a matter of seconds, my sense of smell was confronted with the odors of dust, the countryside, and, above all, fear.

From around the corner came a long line of African men, women, and especially children: older children carrying younger children, younger children holding crying babies. I estimated the group to be at least forty people. They walked right past us and boarded the plane. Their leader, a middle-aged woman with reading glasses around her neck, handed a packet of papers to the gate agent, but no tickets were scanned. The Lufthansa attendants simply stood aside to allow the clearly exhausted and bedraggled group to pass.

The one-hour flight was filled with screams, crying, shouts, unanticipated movements in the aisle, and, for me, the sudden realization that all of my critical engagements with human rights, my analytical desires, even my emerging ethical commitments, must be bracketed in ways that paradoxically underscore their tentativeness at the same time their urgency is reinforced.

It was my good fortune to sit among the group of Africans and even more to sit next to their leader. I learned from her that they were precisely forty-three—to approximate here would be obscene—refugees from camps in Zambia who had been granted the extraordinarily rare opportunity to resettle in the Human Development Index–topping social democracies of Western Europe. They were primarily Congolese, and I later learned that the current nationalist and conservative government of Denmark—which has maintained its power primarily on a not so subtly racist anti-immigration platform—only agrees to accept refugees from Africa whose vulnerability and victimization have been so clearly established that not even the high priests of Danishness in the Dansk Folkeparti can resist extending to them the hand of charity.

Yet this also meant that my worst imaginings in that moment—different from theirs but no less acute—were realized: the old man with the sad eyes sitting across the aisle, these small children at my feet who looked up at me with a mixture of terror and fascination on what was surely the second airplane ride of their lives (the first being the one that brought them from Lusaka to London), and that young teenage girl who patrolled her siblings from time to time with a stern look that told me she was probably now the head of her family on this journey had all just emerged from a maelstrom of human suffering. Had that old man been forced to watch while his sons were massacred and his daughters were taken away to be brutalized? Were these children at my feet war orphans, their parents among the hundreds of thousands of victims of the DRC's multiple paroxysms? And the proud teenage girl . . . I could not bring myself to look her in the eye and imagine her trauma. And yet there she was, a survivor, the pure embodiment of human dignity, with her whole uncertain life ahead of her. Perhaps, I thought, someday she will find a way to leave the ghost of King Leopold behind.

As the plane descended over the waters off the coast of Copenhagen, which arc filled with a phalanx of ecologically progressive wind turbines, the critic in me forced his way to the surface, if only for a brief and unwanted moment. I knew enough about the contradictions and hypocrisies of contemporary Western Europe to know what likely lay ahead for the refugees. Their years will be filled with struggles over language, employment, culture shock, and, for the adults, nostalgia for life in their equatorial homeland. But the children, like children everywhere, will adapt rapidly. They will enter a neighborhood public school in one of Copenhagen's immigrant districts, they will quickly learn a fluent and colloquial Danish, and they will grow up with all the protections and benefits to be found in a modern EU nation-state. They will always be hybrid Europeans, never quite accepted by some, but their life chances will be relatively expansive and they will never again cower in terror in an isolated village while rebel soldiers come for their parents, their aunts, their sisters. . . .

Even though I continued on to the next lecture, the next chance to describe what it means to consider human rights in an anthropological key, the encounter with those survivors—those *human beings* whose normative value is precisely equal to that of the pilots who flew them to safety, to mine, to the rebel soldiers roaming at the very moment through the forests of eastern Congo, to the president of the Finnish university where I would soon appear, to the winner of this year's Nobel Peace Prize (who also happens to be Finnish), to everyone who has and will ever live in the world—washed over me like a great existential wave. This is the phenomenology of human rights, that experiential dimension that lies well outside the boundaries of both the conceptual and the practical, all those intellectual puzzles that never-endingly fascinate scholars of human rights and all those bureaucratic and institutional challenges that occupy the energies of the legions of officials whose job it is to actualize the different facets of the international human rights system.

Everything that is to follow here must be read retrospectively in terms of this phenomenology. We must be brave in our critical engagements with the neo-Kantian aspirations of the postwar human rights project. But I, for one, will never forget that proud, beautiful, frightened Congolese teenager who had to flee her home with a world on her shoulders. It is for her, in the end, that this book was written.

Chapter 1

Introduction

A Well-Tempered Human Rights

A T THE END of his typically penetrating essay on the relationship between human rights and poverty, John Gledhill issues a version of what has become in recent years the standard anthropological expression of theoretical modesty. After a series of interventions that, among other things, reconfigure our understanding of the role of nongovernmental organizations in promoting rights in the developing world, suggest a dialectical framework for explaining the way hegemonic and counterhegemonic forces structure rights practices within emerging transnational legal and ethical regimes, and, finally, show how Anthony Giddens's apparently progressive vision of modern subjectivity is actually a "regime of truth" that denies agency to precisely those social actors whose lived experiences seem to most demand the protections of *some* effective framework, Gledhill goes on to explain that "anthropologists are not social and political philosophers, and our role is largely one of *observing* how . . . developments manifest themselves in practice" (2003:225; emphasis added).

Likewise, John Bowen, at the beginning of his study of the intersections of law, religion, and the constitution of political discourse in Indonesia, explains—after asserting the irrelevance to Indonesia of much leading political and social theory—that his "intention is not to offer a competing version of political theory, a reconstruction of society from first principles. Rather, I offer an anthropological account of such reasoning, the ways in which citizens take account of their own pluralism of values as they carry out their affairs" (2003:12). Yet despite developing a series of arguments that amount to an innovative theory of contemporary political and legal identity—one that makes value-pluralism the foundation for political community—he reminds us that his study should not be confused with an attempt to "formulate a systematic, principled account of how (some) societies ought to organized"; rather, his is merely an "account of the issues, institutions, and stakes for actors in a particular social setting" (267). He then goes on to conclude that his book is also "an anthropological account of the *reasonableness* of the ways in which citizens can take account of their own pluralism of values in carrying out their affairs—an account which might, in its turn, inform new versions of political theory" (268; emphasis in original).

In other words, his study of normative pluralism and citizenship in Indonesia both highlights the supposedly stark differences between "liberal political theory and comparative social scientific inquiry"—the former quixotically directed toward envisioning social and political life from first principles, the latter modestly and quietly documenting social and political life in all of its comparative diversity—and manages to "inform new versions of political theory" at the same time. Yet Bowen's anthropology of public reasoning *does* articulate a set of general theoretical principles that explain similar processes in other plural societies. Are we to believe that it is only in Indonesia where the four dominant "general features of public reasoning"—which Bowen insightfully describes as "precedent, principle, pragmatism, and metanormative reasoning"—are to be found? (258).[1]

Gledhill and Bowen are not to be faulted for their theoretical reticence. Since at least the mid-1980s, two trends have emerged within especially British social and American cultural anthropology: the first—which has been on the wane since the early 1990s—reflects an enthusiastic embrace of a series of (mostly) Continental social and critical theoretical influences, in which social theory is not necessarily derived from the application of scientific methods calculated to uncover the cause of things, but rather exists in a much more tenuous, even intentionally problematized, relationship with the practices of everyday life. The other trend, which Gledhill's and Bowen's work evokes, expresses a re-entrenchment, or perhaps rediscovery, of the advantages of anthropology's unique version of science, in which the anthropologist fulfills her purpose *only* to the extent that she gives an "adequate account of the issues, institutions, and stakes for actors." By "adequate account" what is meant at the very least is accurate observation and documentation; an even better "account" would, like Bowen's does, frame observed events and social interactions in relation to a series of meaningful cultural and historical contexts. Yet an account goes too far, becomes unanthropological, when it generalizes beyond even the richest study of a particular time and place and either aspires to a "regime of truth" (Gledhill) or evolves into a search for "first principles" (Bowen).

But here's the rub: just because many anthropologists have rejected the formal study and formulation of social theory does not mean that it is not being studied and formulated, often, as Bowen rightly argues, in a "skeletonized" way, through systems of ideas that are grounded in an entirely abstracted account of legal, social, and political practices. There is actually nothing logically inconsistent about pursuing social theory in this way, even if the goal is to pass particular systems of ideas about social life through the crucible of lived experience. That is to say, the anthropological critique of liberal political and legal theory on the grounds that it claims to describe "first principles" is not really a critique of the *manner* through which theorists like Will Kymlicka and Joseph Raz and John Rawls crafted systems that purport to explain the relationship between the subject and social values. What this critique is really pointing to is the fact that this particular constellation of theories was never intended to be embedded in, let alone derived from, the different types of experience that matter—legal, religious, political, economic. So we are left with either a philosophically rich but phenomenologically thin set of explanations for social life on the one hand or, on the other, a set of general ideas of real importance that are nevertheless kept frustratingly incipient—the social theory that dare not speak its name.

This dichotomy is of course a false one. There is no reason why anthropologists or others interested in making sense of contemporary social practice in a way that resonates beyond the mere case study, the mere collection of disconnected human exotica, should be forced to *either* observe and faithfully record *or* drown in a sea of theoretical foundationalism. The costs of this false choice are never simply, or even primarily, academic. It is perhaps too obvious to emphasize that ideas, and systems of ideas, have a tremendous impact across any number of social and regional planes. Ideas become quickly politicized, especially ideas that claim to affect basic economic or legal or cultural realities. Systems of ideas are products of intellectual histories, and their influence on people and institutions can be tracked within broader historical trajectories. Some ways of finding order in—or ordering—the legal, social, and political are more powerful than others. And systems of ideas, like other systems, both express and constitute broader alignments within which knowledge, money, political capital, and other resources are unequally distributed within any given assemblage, global or otherwise (Ong and Collier 2005).

For example, the entire bundle of liberal political and legal theory to which Bowen either refers or alludes expresses, despite obvious internal nuances, a set of unifying assumptions about both the nature of things—including social things—and the types of knowledge of them that are legitimate.[2] And this bundle, this system of ideas, is one that establishes the only permissible framework within which a whole set of current political and social processes can unfold, from European Union expansion and consolidation, to the establishment of transitional justice operations in post-conflict settings, to the proliferation of international human rights instruments and models of rights-based normative practice. But if Bowen is right, and this system of ideas is structurally deficient and thus inapplicable to contemporary Indonesia, not in this or that legal or political context, or in light of this or that set of historical circumstances, but per se, then its presence in Indonesia—through international and transnational political institutions, networks of economic relations of production, or even within academic or expert analysis of the country—reflects much more than simply the poverty of this particular theoretical bundle; it is the expression of power *through* ideas.

Yet the alternative—the development of compelling ideas about certain times and places that are formally contextual but that actually speak to more widely observable patterns of legal, political, and social practice—is the expression of a different kind of power, the ability to restrict the scope of ideas, to force them into prefigured modes of acceptable discourse, even though they are potentially much more transformative. If Bowen has demonstrated the social fact that in Indonesia value-pluralism is itself a value that is both the empirical and the normative basis for a sustainable political community, this fact turns the history of dominant political theory as it has evolved over the last three hundred years on its head. And although Bowen does not allude to it, his analysis of Indonesia also challenges several popular—and, in certain political and academic circles, influential—antitheses of foundationalist social and political theory, most obviously work indebted to pragmatism and neo-pragmatism.

I am thinking here of the line of critique of foundationalist liberal political and legal theory—including human rights—represented most clearly by the work of Richard Rorty and his European interpreters (e.g., Zygmunt Bauman). In his essay "Human Rights, Rationality, and Sentimentality" (1993), Rorty argues that no foundationalist theory of values can ever be the best framework for ethical and political practice; rather, the main objective for intellectuals or politicians, or anyone else in a position to influence others, should be to foster solidarity across cultural, national, and historical boundaries.

Now Rorty could very well be correct; it could very well be true that "nothing relevant to moral choice separates human beings from animals," or (I would add) one group of human beings from another. But this fact (if true) would unfortunately tell us nothing of importance about value-pluralism in Indonesia, in particular the way it appears to be foundational in a very traditional (though not metaphysical) sense and, even more, the way its foundationalism is the basis for its legitimacy or, as Rorty might say, its effectiveness.

If value-pluralism in Indonesia has indeed developed into a metavalue, a normative framework that urges, or demands, or facilitates the coexistence of multiple values or systems of values—legal, political, and, in this case in particular, religious—then there is, in a very important sense, at least one "first principle" in terms of which contemporary Indonesia must be understood. And what is even more critical to recognize is the fact that a researcher and analyst like Bowen does not create this first principle by describing the ethnographic or historical data that reveal it, or by formally articulating it in a way that gives it a certain amount of structure by contextualizing it in relation to other similar—or dissimilar—first principles, or by making claims about its cross-cultural relevance.

Rather, the "first principle," and the social theory that it implies, is simply a fact of ethical, legal, and religious life in Indonesia. To say this is not to claim that this particular first principle is either objectively universal (explanatory and present in all places at all times) or ontologically foundational (immanent to a particular place or group of people, in Indonesia or elsewhere). But it is to leave open the possibility that this first principle—value-pluralism— either is, or might someday become, "locally universal," that its *subjective* transcendence is precisely what makes it such a compelling ordering principle for social actors and institutions and political parties and religious leaders. In other words, *foundationalism* and *universalism* are themselves ideas that can become particularly meaningful in social practice, and the anthropologist (or other researcher or cultural critic) does a valuable service by making their importance and power topics for close engagement and critical scrutiny.

.   .   .

AT THE MOST GENERAL LEVEL, this book is a sustained argument for a type of engagement with human rights that combines the empirical with the conceptual in a way that avoids the strained opposition between intentionally ungrounded and deductive political and social theory on the one hand and intentionally grounded and carefully circumscribed case studies on the other. This approach can be understood as an "anthropology of human rights," but I must underscore the fact that although I will draw from particular intellectual histories in order to develop the book's propositions, I do not intend this to be an argument for disciplinary prerogative. Indeed, it will strike some as immediately odd that anthropology would form part of the foundation for an alternative approach to human rights, particularly in light of anthropology's marginalization from most of the dominant developments in human rights since the late 1940s. This story of marginalization, which will be explored in chapter 2, provides a window into the underlying political and intellectual currents that have shaped the emergence of both the international and the transnational human rights regimes. This history is also one that reveals a reservoir of potential, one that I will draw from throughout this book as I suggest ways in which an anthropology of human rights opens up several new spaces for research, analysis, and political action.

There are two broad developments that make the argument for an anthropology of human rights both timely and justified. First, the last twenty years have revealed something essential about contemporary human rights. Despite the end of the Cold War (a key event for my purposes) and a set of economic and political developments that have both accelerated preexisting forces (the consolidation of a multinational corporate capitalist mode of production) and initiated new ones (the emergence of midsize transnational political actors), human rights theory and practice remain static.

The constellation of Western liberal legal and political theories that formed the foundation for the 1948 Universal Declaration of Human Rights—and most of the follow-on instruments—remains the dominant intellectual resource within the international human rights system, even if this fact has led to a series of fissures or points of tension, particularly with the emergence of what I will describe in chapter 6 as neoliberal human rights. Even if one can make an argument on simple political grounds that the United Nations committee working on the Universal Declaration was, despite the rhetoric of inclusiveness, compelled to choose between competing philosophical worldviews, it is less obvious why liberal (or neoliberal) legal and political theory should continue to prove so foundational when this political choice is no longer necessary.

This is a particularly charged dilemma, especially since the "global community" that ratified the Universal Declaration was a much more constricted, colonial, and provincial place, a time when the diversity of the ethical, the political, and the legal was either unknown or known only to a small group of relatively obscure scholars or colonial officials, whose interests compelled them to deny, suppress, or work to destroy it. What this means is that contemporary human rights theory—if not "practice," which has a unified meaning only in certain broad international frames of reference—is vestigial, a tangled set of ideas and philosophical assumptions about human nature, the ontological status of the individual, and the possibilities for ordering collectivities through reason, which remains entrenched even though the contexts of its emergence—though not, perhaps, its purposes—have disintegrated.

But there is a second reason why a book like this is appropriate at this time. Since about the late 1980s, anthropologists have re-engaged with human rights on a number of different levels: first political, then ethnographic, and now—but only incipiently—conceptual. The arguments in this book are grounded in this recent period in anthropology's relationship with human rights. The growing body of ethnographic research on human rights constitutes, among other things, an expanding database on how human rights are actually becoming transnational and increasingly hegemonic, which makes it an excellent resource to draw from in developing a set of critical tools for understanding the relationship between human rights and local ethical practice. I will examine the reasons why anthropologists reoriented themselves toward human rights in the next chapter; suffice it to say here that the narrative is a complicated one, in which the process of engagement on the political level was initiated without any real theoretical guidance from within mainstream anthropology itself, while the later transformation of human rights practice into a topic for ethnographic and reflective inquiry was in part a response to the rapid expansion of human rights discourse after the end of the Cold War.

Essais and Interventions

In order to give the reader a firm sense of what to expect in this book, it would be more accurate to describe the chapters that follow as a series of interconnected critical essays. This is a signal that in building toward a broader anthropological account of human rights, I do so through a number of pointed, bounded, and admittedly idiosyncratic interventions that are not meant to serve as comprehensive surveys of, or definitive introductions to, the different topics that form the grist for the book's mill (think Montaigne rather than, say, Sir James Frazer). These *essais* also do not add up to a grand theory of human rights. Indeed, as we will see, an argument that threads throughout the book is that our understanding of human rights theory and practice in the postwar period has been impoverished by the dominance of just such theories, and the epistemology that they reflect.

Instead, the book's chapters are meant to bind together a series of arguments that, taken together, constitute an anthropological orientation to human rights, one that is anchored in, though not restricted to, the recent ethnography of human rights practices that was made possible by the rapid expansion of human rights after the end of the Cold War. Even here, my treatment of this body of research and analysis is illustrative and instrumental; as elsewhere in the book, in order to make my own interventions as direct as possible I do not burden the reader with extended intertextual debate, leaden lists of citations, or lengthy intellectual genealogies. A full accounting of the ethnographic and theoretical background to the chapters can be found in the extended bibliography. This is not to say that I do not make every effort to position these interventions in relation to points of similarity and difference within contemporary human rights studies. But this positioning is narrowly tailored within what is one expression of a wider project to rethink both the grounds and the potential of human rights through anthropology.

A Well-Tempered Human Rights

If the chapters that follow, taken together, point toward an anthropological orientation to human rights, one that both coheres with and in places radically diverges from different existing theoretical, political, and ethical approaches, then it would be helpful to give a concise overview to the book's major arguments. This overview is not meant to stand in for a full development of the arguments themselves; rather, it is a fingerpost to the book's main claims.

First, an anthropology of human rights is both an argument for an essentially and thoroughgoingly synthetic approach to human rights and, in a sense, an example of such an approach (however emergent). As we will see, contemporary human rights theory and practice have been consequentially structured by the opposite of a synthetic approach, what might be understood as the paradigmatic. Distinct categories—of meaning, of knowledge, of experience—have worked to obscure or elide the different dilemmas that remain at the heart of the postwar human rights project. Even so, a synthetic, anthropological orientation to human rights does not yield new and definitive solutions to these dilemmas. Indeed, the recent ethnography of human rights practices has demonstrated, among other things, that the problems that continue to bedevil human rights are, to greater or lesser degrees, existential, the inevitable consequence of the most profound and earnest contemporary effort to forge something straight from what the intellectual historian Isaiah Berlin (invoking Kant) called the "crooked timber of humanity" (1990).

Second, like much of contemporary anthropology itself, an anthropology of human rights reveals the potential in engaging in a critical intellectual history of different human rights genealogies, in this case the one in which anthropology as a discipline was for different reasons marginalized from the major developments in postwar human rights theory and practice. This kind of backward-looking interrogation, which Foucault (1972) described as an "archaeology of knowledge," is not so much an effort to reestablish the past on more solid, or more truthful, grounds, regardless of the importance of acknowledging just what did happen at *this* place at *this* time (a kind of historiography that is especially important in the area of human rights).

Instead, the critical intellectual history of at least one small slice of the postwar human rights project is concerned with the ways in which human rights meanings *can*—and, because of the dominance of paradigms, *cannot*—exist, those "conditions of existence" (Foucault 1972:117) that have underpinned the international community's most profound efforts to come to terms with, and ideally transcend, the consequences of what Kleinman, Das, and Lock (1997) describe as "social suffering."

If the orientation toward human rights that I develop across the book's chapters can be described as *anthropological*, this obviously does not mean that the account here reflects anything like a consensus within contemporary anthropology. Indeed, in my treatment of the problems of "culture" within human rights, I argue that anthropologists have played a significant role in both overly complicating the concept of culture and obscuring the prevalence in practice of what might be described as culture-in-the-world, the ways in which collectivities continue to self-identify in a manner that reflects an exclusionary, and not a unifying, social ontology.

To argue for a clear-eyed reckoning with culture-in-the-world, despite the unsavory and essentially anti-cosmopolitan implications, is also to argue for the importance of understanding human rights in what Sally Engle Merry (2006a, 2006b) has described as the "vernacular," those many sites in which ethical theory and social practice are mutually constitutive. And to prioritize human rights in the vernacular is to make yet another argument: that "human rights" (understood diffusely) must be both theorized and legitimated *in terms of* the groundedness of social practices, those mundane (yet often transformative) occurrences of what de Certeau (1984) called the "practice of everyday life."

This is not to deny the importance of legal and political institutions—international or otherwise—for human rights implementation, enforcement, and adjudication. But it is to re-order the hierarchy of significance and acknowledge the fact that *if* an enduring, effective, and legitimate transnational (or, perhaps, postnational—see chapter 5) human rights system is to be established, it will have to somehow be derived from these spaces of vernacularization, which do reveal certain cross-cultural patterns or modes of normative engagement (see, e.g., Cowan, Dembour, and Wilson 2001; Goodale and Merry 2007).

Further, a critical intellectual history of the postwar human rights project leads to a certain amount of skepticism about the utopianism that hangs over both the discursive construction of "human rights" and, more crucially, the political economies of human rights that postcolonial scholars, in particular, have examined with such force and insight (see, e.g., Anghie 2005; Baxi 2002; Mutua 2002; Rajagopal 2003). Nevertheless, an anthropology of human rights provides at least some measure of both theoretical and empirical support for the kind of cosmopolitan optimism that informed the worldview of those visionary elites who took it upon themselves to build a framework for perpetual peace from the ruins of mid-century last.

This is not to say that an anthropology of human rights suggests a *particular* cosmopolitanism—rooted (Appiah 2005), vernacular (Bhabha 2001), minoritarian (Breckenridge et al. 2002), indigenous (Biolsi 2005; Goodale 2006d), or otherwise. But contrary to the caricatures that have portrayed contemporary anthropology as a hotbed of naive relativism, social and ethical constructivism, and a kind of Continental nihilism, in fact, the recent ethnography of human rights practices has documented both the power and the cross-cultural resonance of what might be described as an emergent cosmopolitanism, a rough sense of inclusion within wider and wider categories of identity that can come, in certain instances, to approximate the Hierocletian ideal (see Nussbaum 1997).

Another of the book's major arguments begins by drawing a distinction between human rights *universality* and human rights *universalism*, a grounded theoretical distinction that likewise emerges from the growing database of information about human rights in practice. Human rights universality refers to the claims at the core of the modern idea of human rights: that everyone at all times is the same because they share a common human- ness (which can be usefully thought of as a biological sameness invested with a moral quality); that this common humanness has normative implications; and that these implications take one specific form among many possibilities— rights. Human rights universalism, by contrast, refers to the complicated dis- cursive presence of these claims as they are acted upon within existing legal, moral, and political practice. When a transnational human rights NGO, for example, introduces the idea of human rights to rural populations in Bolivia, and the transcendent universal claims associated with this idea are later taken up by local leaders and used within ongoing social struggles, this is human rights *universalism* (see Goodale 2009a).

In a sense, to understand human rights in part through the practices that revolve around, or are transformed by, the particular set of universal claims that can make the idea of human rights so consequential is to productively circumvent the set of intractable philosophical problems that have occupied so much of the debate within human rights studies: What are (or can be) the sources of human rights? How are (or can) human rights be legitimated? How do (or can) human rights relate—theoretically, not in practice—to other nor- mativities? What is (or should be) the role of the state in relation to human rights? What is (or should be) the relationship—again, theoretically—between the international human rights system and the regime of transnational human rights actors that has emerged over the last twenty years? And so on.

This is not to deny the importance of these problems—and others—in their own terms. But the ethnography of human rights-in-the-world over the last fifteen years has shown that the claims of human rights are invested with meaning and importance that transcend anything that can be said about them conceptually in the restricted and abstracted terms of several dominant human rights epistemologies.

Finally, as the international legal scholar and anthropologist Annelise Riles has argued (2006b), what is needed by both human rights scholars and human rights practitioners, more than anything else, is a greater sense of humility. This is not the kind of humility that leads to quietism in the face of profound human suffering. Instead, it is a willingness to recognize that the ethical log- ics, discursive power, and institutional machineries of human rights must exist in a world marked by disjuncture. The unifying and centripetal aspirations of human rights must exist in a kind of permanent tension with the essential centrifugality of human relations, the essential multiplicity of our troubled species. The "pendulum," as Marie-Bénédicte Dembour (2001) describes it, between the centripetal claims of human rights and the centrifugal reality that confronts these claims, is one that in different forms and in different ways has swung back and forth for centuries.

But if the intellectual histories of Western Europe have proven so consequential in the development of the modern idea of human rights, we can say, following the Norwegian anthropologist Thomas Hylland Eriksen (himself drawing on the Bulgarian-French intellectual Tzvetan Todorov), that what human rights needs is more humanist restraint and appreciation for particularity and less Enlightenment triumphalism. Eriksen (quoting Todorov) describes this balance as a "well-tempered humanism" (2001:143), a worldview that puts the human—conceived in the multiple, not the universal—at the center even as it recognizes, with Yeats, that this center cannot hold, at least not for long. At its core, this book is an argument for a human rights that is tempered by the same sense of humility, the same kind of appreciation for the disorienting fact of multiplicity, and the same willingness to make the mundaneness of social practice a source of ethical inspiration.

The Plan of the Book

In the next chapter I establish the historical context for what is to follow by considering the curious history of anthropology's engagement with—and disengagement from—human rights over the last fifty years. This narrative reveals much more about the development of human rights than about a particular disciplinary legacy, and the telling of this intellectual history is also a way of grounding the alternative approach to human rights that will emerge over subsequent chapters. Chapters 3 and 4 narrow the focus to what have been the two most recognizable contributions to wider human rights debates from within anthropology: the research and theorizing that have explored the problem of relativism and, more recently, the attempts to use research on human rights processes in order to reformulate our understanding of "culture." A fresh look at the problem of relativism and the contested meanings of culture in relation to human rights demonstrates, among other things, that both of these topics open up into debates that are far from resolved. These chapters make new analyses of these topics important parts of the book's more general argument about human rights.

Chapters 5 and 6 move from what are considered the more traditional anthropological topics within the broader human rights community to wider frames of analysis. Chapter 5 suggests that an anthropology of human rights has something innovative to contribute to our understanding of the transnational dimensions of human rights, and, in particular, the way in which human rights have become one disproportionately powerful vector within a normative universe that, while not "global" or even "globalized," is nevertheless unfolding beyond the nation-state.

In chapter 6 I examine the link between anthropology and the emergence (or reemergence) of what can be understood as "neoliberal" human rights, which include the class of rights that are framed at the collective level (ethnic and linguistic minorities, First Nations, indigenous peoples) and several other candidates for human rights status, including the rights to social and economic development. It is often claimed that anthropology has played an important role in legitimizing neoliberal human rights, and I explore these claims in order to gauge whether or not this area is evidence of anthropology's potential to transform human rights theory and practice more generally. Finally, the concluding chapter recapitulates the major arguments and implications of the book, not as a substitute for a full engagement with these as they were developed at different points and in different ways but in order to leave the reader with a holistic sense of both the book's most far-reaching claims and its necessary limitations.

Chapter 2

Becoming Irrelevant

The Curious History of Anthropology and Human Rights

I T IS NECESSARY to examine anthropology's ambivalent relationship to human rights for at least two reasons. First, this history illuminates certain basic dilemmas associated with the emergence of the postwar human rights project and the ways in which particular political and philosophical approaches to human rights became more powerful than other alternatives. Indeed, there is a distinct irony in the fact that a legal and ethical regime that was conceived in order to prevent or redress the violent assertion of illegitimate power within international relations itself came to be defined by subtle forms of power. The study of anthropology's exile from the early and formative development of human rights reveals how this shift in function was possible. Although this is not widely appreciated, either within the wider human rights community or in academia, the exclusion of anthropology from the critical moments in the emergence of the postwar human rights system would have lasting consequences. As we will see, at mid-twentieth century anthropology had established itself as the preeminent source of scientific expertise on many empirical facets of culture and society, from law to kinship, from religion to morality.

Yet it was at precisely this moment, when anthropology as a discipline was reaching the peak of its legitimacy and self-confidence, that it was blocked from contributing in any meaningful way to the development of understanding about what was—and still is—the most important putative cross-cultural fact: that human beings are essentially the same and that this essential sameness entails a specific normative framework. It was as if everything we know—or think we know—about the evolution of *Homo sapiens* included contributions from every discipline *except* biological anthropology, which, despite having been excluded, nevertheless continued to produce knowledge that spoke directly to the problem. In examining the history of anthropology's relationship to human rights, therefore, we will be able to better understand both how and why human rights developed as they did and, by extension, the ways in which they *might* have developed had the insights of anthropology played a role.

But the examination of this intellectual and political history is not only, or most importantly, retrospective. It is also a necessary backdrop for the arguments I make in this book about a reconfigured account of contemporary human rights. As I have already described in chapter 1, one of the basic assumptions of this book is that anthropological forms of knowledge and practical engagement can and should be used as part of a wider project of reconceptualizing the meaning and potential of human rights. The justifications for this assumption are to be found both in the historical absence of anthropology from the development of contemporary human rights and in the more recent attempts by individual anthropologists and the discipline's largest professional association to re-engage with human rights as both an object of study and a vehicle for emancipatory political practice. Although some aspects of this history have already been related in different places (see, e.g., Engle 2001; Goodale 2006b, 2006d; Messer 1993; Wilson and Mitchell 2003), this chapter provides a full and critical accounting.

If the wider engagement of anthropology is a necessary precondition for the transformation of contemporary human rights, that is true in part because anthropology as a discipline is committed to the systematic and comparative investigation of social practices, including normative practices. Nevertheless, as I have already indicated, this is not a book *about* anthropology. Rather, the examination of human rights in terms of anthropology's troubled history is meant to reveal both profound potential and basic limitations—not necessarily within anthropology but within a reconfigured human rights.

A Curious History

In 1947 the United Nations Commission on Human Rights, which was chaired by Eleanor Roosevelt, sought statements on the draft version of what would become the 1948 Universal Declaration of Human Rights. These statements were solicited in a variety of ways and through a variety of institutional channels, but perhaps the most important were the efforts of the United Nations Educational,

Scientific, and Cultural Organization (UNESCO). UNESCO solicited statements on a proposed declaration of universal human rights from different academic, cultural, and artistic institutions and individuals.[1] Although the essentially colonialist milieu within which the United Nations emerged after World War II made any attempt to achieve universal consensus through its working bodies utopian at best, the outreach efforts by UNESCO prior to the adoption of the UDHR were intended to gauge the diversity of world opinion about what Johannes Morsink describes as the "aggressive" push to forge an "international consensus about human rights" (1999:12).[2]

Within anthropology, it has become conventional wisdom to say that the American Anthropological Association (AAA) was one of those institutions that was solicited by UNESCO (see, e.g., Messer 1993). This is because the *American Anthropologist*, the flagship journal of the AAA, published something called the "Statement on Human Rights" as the lead article in the October–December number of the journal (vol. 49, no. 4, 1947; for the full text of the statement, see appendix 1). The statement was prefaced by a note that indicated that it was submitted to the UN Commission on Human Rights by the executive board of the AAA. And it was not surprising that this statement appeared in 1947, or that UNESCO had apparently turned to the AAA for an advisory opinion from anthropology on a proposed declaration of universal human rights.[3] By mid-twentieth century, all three major anthropological traditions—"schools" is perhaps too strong a description—had, taken together, established themselves as an important source of scientific knowledge about the range of both diversity and unity in human culture and society.[4]

But the evidence indicates that most of the conventional wisdom about the Statement on Human Rights is wrong. For example, there is the question of the actual relationship between UNESCO, the Commission for Human Rights, and the AAA. As I've said, the common understanding is that the AAA—as *the* representative of anthropology—was asked to write an advisory opinion on human rights, which it (through one or more of its members) did in 1947, after which this official AAA "Statement on Human Rights" was simultaneously published in the *American Anthropologist* and submitted to the Commission for Human Rights by the AAA executive board on behalf of its membership.

Yet according to documents in the U.S. National Anthropological Archives,[5] there is no record of UNESCO making a request to the AAA for an advisory opinion on a declaration of human rights. Instead, it appears that one anthropologist, Melville Herskovits, was approached by UNESCO in his capacity as chairman of the Committee for International Cooperation in Anthropology of the National Research Council (NRC), a post that he assumed in 1945. Herskovits was a prominent American anthropologist, a member of the AAA's executive board during this time, and chairman of the Department of Anthropology at Northwestern University. Herskovits had been a student of Franz Boas at Columbia University, where he earned his Ph.D. in anthropology in 1923. Although his research and writings present a more complicated theoretical and political picture than has been supposed, there is no question that Herskovits's orientation to culture and society was shaped by his training in what is known as American historical particularism, an anthropological approach developed by Boas that placed the emphasis on studying the evolution of particular cultural traditions within their historical contexts (see Stocking 1989).

In focusing so intensely—and ethnographically—on particular cultures within what was believed to be their unique historical trajectories, American cultural anthropologists like Herskovits became associated with a distinct outlook toward social phenomena. Two aspects of this outlook are relevant to the history of anthropology's relationship with human rights. First, the detailed study of cultures within history revealed the ways in which particular dimensions of culture—law, politics, religion, morality—were the result of a process of situated evolution, one that could not be understood in general terms or through the use of universal analytical categories. There might be "patterns of culture," as Ruth Benedict, another Boasian, described them, but such patterns were only rough outlines, ways of describing the fact that all cultures are in fact patterned in their own terms. The content of these patterns, however, the features that made a particular culture "Japanese," say, and not "Norwegian," was the result of the entire range of historical contingencies that could never be either reproduced again or predicted for other places and times.

And it was only a short step from this essentially empirical approach to culture to something more normative: if each culture was unique, the result of a particular and contingent history, then it was not possible to evaluate or measure cultures in terms of a set of standards that could be justified in a way that was itself not part of a particular cultural tradition, or interplay between cultural traditions. This normative implication of American historical particularism is what is usually described as "cultural relativism." Although I will devote a full chapter (chapter 3) to the dilemma of cultural relativism and its relation to human rights, it is enough here to simply note that Herskovits's reaction to the idea of a declaration of universal human rights cannot be understood without locating it within this longer theoretical and ethical tradition in American cultural anthropology.

Second, there was a political dimension to American historical particularism and the kind of anthropology pursued by the Boasians. Although Boas believed anthropology to be the "science of mankind," he also believed that it served a valuable social function by documenting the richness of cultures that were either under threat of destruction, or tragically misunderstood, or both.[6] American cultural anthropology at mid-century—less so British and French social anthropology—was concerned with the condition of what today would be described as marginalized or subaltern populations, and this concern was the result of both epistemological and political imperatives within American anthropology and of individual anthropologists.[7] So when Melville Herskovits was approached by UNESCO through the National Research Council's Committee on International Cooperation in Anthropology, he also considered the ways in which a declaration of universal human rights would affect the cultural traditions and political standing of those populations that seemed to stand apart from the confluence of legal, political, and social forces that were behind the "aggressive" drive for an international human rights system.

Although Herskovits was contacted by UNESCO by virtue of his position as head of an influential NRC committee dedicated to fostering both international collaboration between anthropologists and other scientists and the development of what today would be called "public anthropology" (i.e., the use of anthropological knowledge in consequential public debates[8]), it is historiographically important to acknowledge that this NRC committee acted as a de facto committee of the American Anthropological Association, or at least coordinated its activities with the AAA executive board.[9] Most of the members of the NRC committee during the mid-1940s were also members of the AAA, including (in 1946, the year before Herskovits drafted the Statement on Human Rights) one past and one future president of the AAA (Robert Lowie, 1935, and Frederica de Laguna, 1967).[10]

Nevertheless, the documentary record shows that the AAA was *not* first contacted by UNESCO; rather, Melville Herskovits's committee at the NRC was the entity solicited for a representative anthropological opinion on a declaration of human rights.[11] Herskovits worked on his Statement on Human Rights in early 1947 and began communicating with the AAA leadership about its intentions regarding it. By June 1947, Herskovits had already sent the statement to UNESCO on behalf of both himself and the NRC anthropology committee. At the same time, Ralph Beals, an AAA executive board member, was writing to Clyde Kluckhohn, the AAA president, with a recommendation that Herskovits's "rights of man" statement be adopted by the executive board and published as the lead article in the forthcoming *American Anthropologist*.[12] To underscore the importance given to the statement by the executive board, Beals recommended that the AAA order 1,000 reprints (with special covers) of the statement for public relations purposes.

Although the statement was published in *American Anthropologist* in late 1947 with a note indicating that it had been forwarded to UNESCO, this must be seen as a post hoc ratification of what Herskovits had already done some four to six months earlier.[13] Although Herskovits was pleased that the AAA chose to *resubmit* the Statement on Human Rights on its behalf, there is very little evidence that the statement was considered by the Commission for Human Rights during its deliberations. Further, despite the fact that the AAA was a much smaller and less representative organization at mid-century, it still functioned as a democratic association, in which major initiatives were voted on by the membership.[14] With the Statement on Human Rights, however, no such vote took place, and except for correspondence between several high ranking AAA members, there is no indication that association members had any knowledge of the statement until its publication in *American Anthropologist*.

This brings me to a second way in which the relationship of American anthropology—as a representative of anthropology more generally—to human rights has been fundamentally misconstrued. In Morsink's otherwise excellent history of the "origins, drafting, and intent" behind the UDHR, he foregrounds the 1947 AAA Statement on Human Rights in a way that gives a distorted impression of its—and, by extension, anthropology's—impact on the emergence of human rights after World War II. In fact, he begins his history with a detailed discussion of the statement's content; the implication is that the Commission on Human Rights went ahead with its work *despite* the objections and criticisms made in the statement. As he says, in "1947 the UN Human Rights Commission that wrote the Declaration received a long memorandum from the American Anthropological Association (AAA)" (1999:ix). And then later, after reviewing different parts of the statement, he observes that the "drafters of the Declaration . . . went ahead in spite of these warnings" (1999:x). But as

Morsink's own comprehensive account of the drafting process makes clear, it is more likely that even if received in some technical sense—either on behalf of the NRC or, later, the AAA executive board—the Statement on Human Rights played almost no role whatsoever in the drafting of the UDHR.

Morsink provides a detailed analysis of the seven stages through which the UDHR was drafted and then adopted by the UN Third General Assembly in December 1948. The seventeen members of the Commission for Human Rights were exclusively member-nations; a drafting committee of eight members was then created from within this group of seventeen. Morsink divides the individuals who played a key role in actually drafting the document into two groups, which he calls the "inner core" and the "second-tier drafters." There were only six members of this first group: John P. Humphrey, a law professor from Canada and the UN Secretariat's first human rights director[15]; René Cassin, an international lawyer and diplomat from France; Peng-chun Chang, a Chinese scholar (with a Ph.D. in education from Columbia University); Charles Habib Malik, a philosophy professor at the American University in Beirut (with a Ph.D. from Harvard); Hernán Santa Cruz, a military judge from Chile and a former professor of what could perhaps be called "military science"[16]; Alexie P. Pavlov, a lawyer from the Soviet Union who was the USSR's ambassador to Belgium during the time the UDHR was being drafted; and, finally, Eleanor Roosevelt, former first lady of the United States and chair of both the commission and the drafting committee.[17] And among this small group, Humphrey was the person who produced the crucial first draft of the declaration.

If we look at the composition of this group of key drafters, therefore, we begin to understand a little more about how the eventual declaration of universal human rights took the shape it did: three jurists, professors of philosophy and education (both trained at U.S. institutions), and a saintly daughter of an American dynasty. And given that Humphrey, the "primus inter pares" of this inner core of drafters, was the Gale Professor of Roman Law at McGill University at the time of his appointment to the UN, it is not surprising that the NRC/AAA Statement on Human Rights, which—as we will see below—expresses an understanding of the world that is almost diametrically opposed to the one reflected in the UDHR, is never mentioned among the sources that Humphrey (or anyone else) drew from (even if simply to negate its claims) during the drafting of the Universal Declaration of Human Rights.

If the Statement on Human Rights played a limited or (more likely) no role in the deliberations around the drafting of the UDHR, its status among anthropologists has also at times been misconstrued. With the exception of my own recent writings on the relationship between anthropology and human rights (see, e.g., Goodale 2006b, 2006d, 2009b), there were two earlier extended attempts to characterize this history, one by an anthropologist (Messer 1993) and the other by a law professor (Engle 2001). Both leave what I would suggest is the wrong impression about both the events surrounding the production of the Statement on Human Rights and, more importantly, the impact of the statement on anthropologists who might have participated more actively in the development of human rights theory and practice in the early post-UDHR period.

Although Messer and Engle have different agendas and approach the issues from different vantage points, they both tend to read the early history of anthropology's relationship to human rights in terms of its much more recent history. So, for example, Engle says that anthropologists "have been embarrassed ever since" the publication of the statement in 1947 (2001:536). And she is even more direct in characterizing the impact of the statement on the AAA itself. As she writes, "For the past fifty years, the Statement has caused the AAA great shame. Indeed, the term 'embarrassment' is continually used in reference to the Statement" (541).

The problem is that with the exception of three brief comments on the statement published soon after (Barnett 1948; Steward 1948; Bennett 1949), both the statement and, more important, human rights vanish from the anthropological radar for almost forty years. It is difficult, in other words, to demonstrate that the Statement on Human Rights caused widespread shame or embarrassment after its publication. Indeed, there was very little reaction at all, either in the period immediately after publication or during the decades in which the international, and eventually transnational, human rights regimes emerged. Why and how this happened will be described in more detail below, but the fact remains that American anthropology, not to mention the wider discipline, played almost no role in the formal development of human rights theory or institutional practice in the important first decades of the postwar period.

Melville Herskovits's Statement on Human Rights

I have said that the conventional wisdom about the Statement on Human Rights, not to mention the early relationship between anthropology and human rights more generally, has been largely wrong: in the details surrounding the origin of the statement; in the impact of the statement on both anthropology and key figures in the early postwar development of human rights; and in the supposed dark shadow that the statement cast over anthropology in the decades since those early, formative, post-UDHR years. But what about the statement itself? Regardless of the details of its production, or its impact, what about its content? Here too, perhaps most critically, it has been poorly understood. The most common way in which the statement is construed—especially by scholars who have rewritten the early history of anthropology's relationship to human rights in order to make a clean break—is as an example of cultural relativism run amok, something made all the more unpardonable by the events that led to the founding of the United Nations and the "aggressive" push to create an international political and legal order based on universal human rights.

The intellectual historian Isaiah Berlin has written in several of his essays on the nineteenth-century Russian intelligentsia that what characterized the group of disaffected young people who would eventually become revolutionaries was their proclivity to borrow ideas from Western Europe and then take them to their logical, absurd, and violent extreme. This is how Herskovits's Statement on Human Rights is usually characterized: yes, he meant well; yes, cultural relativism was developed as an intellectual buffer against colonialism, racism, and all other systems that had the effect of oppressing some human populations while elevating others; yes, the principles of the Universal Declaration of Human Rights cannot be understood apart from the political and economic interests associated with its creation; *nevertheless*, what about the Nazis?[18] How could anthropologists employ their services against the Nazis during the war (as they did in considerable numbers, in different capacities), yet lack a legitimate moral basis for doing so? Shouldn't the contrarian Statement on Human Rights simply be dismissed as either the misapplication of certain ideas about cultural diversity, or a piece of bad logic, or both?

But Herskovits's (and then the AAA's) Statement on Human Rights is much more complicated, and thus revealing, than the caricature of it would suggest. The statement makes three distinct critiques of a proposed declaration of universal human rights. These can be divided into the epistemological, the empirical, and the ethical. First, Herskovits made the observation that because the Commission on Human Rights was interested in gathering opinions on human rights from different perspectives and approaches to knowledge, he was required to consider the idea of universal human rights *as a scientist*. And because the "sciences that deal with human culture" (AAA 1947:539) had not developed methods for evaluating a proposed list of human rights in relation to the many other moral and legal systems that exist in the world, many of which would appear to conflict with the set of human rights emerging from the commission, anthropology was unable to provide the tools necessary for proving—or disproving—their scientific validity. Although he doesn't mention him by name, in highlighting what seemed to be an epistemological barrier to anthropology's full endorsement of human rights, Herskovits was gesturing toward a much older critique, one associated with Jeremy Bentham's utilitarian rejection of natural rights.[19]

Yet Herskovits also played both sides of the problem, assuming, for the sake of argument, that the anthropological evidence *could* be used to make claims about the validity (or not) of a proposed declaration of human rights. As he quite sensibly explained:

> Over the past fifty years, the many ways in which man resolves the problem of subsistence, of social living, of political regulation of group life, of reaching accord with the Universe and satisfying his aesthetic drives has been widely documented by the researches of anthropologists among peoples living in all parts of the world. All peoples do achieve these ends. No two of them, however, do so in exactly the same way, and some of them employ means that differ, often strikingly, from one another. (AAA 1947:540)

This has been taken as a rigid and dogmatic expression of cultural relativism, which all but guaranteed that Herskovits would reject the idea of universal human rights. But what is ignored is what comes soon after. The real problem, he argues, is not with the idea of human rights itself; rather, the problem is that for political and economic reasons, proposals for human rights (so far) have always been conceived for the wrong purposes and based on the wrong set of assumptions. As he says, "Definitions of freedom, concepts of the nature of human rights, and the like, have . . . been narrowly drawn. Alternatives have been decried, and suppressed where controls have been established over non-European peoples. The hard core of *similarities* between cultures has been consistently overlooked" (540; emphasis in original). In other words, he seems to be suggesting here that the empirical question is still open: a declaration of universal human rights *might* be drafted that is legitimate across cultures, one that codifies and expresses this "hard core of similarities." But the Anglo-European proposals of 1947, which became the UDHR, did not speak to this "hard core of similarities"—whatever these might be, Herskovits doesn't elaborate—and so they should be rejected.

Finally, and arguably most importantly, Herskovits raised a number of ethical objections to the proposal for a declaration of human rights by the United Nations. This critique, more than any other, has been ignored in the subsequent rush to pigeonhole Herskovits as the anthropological equivalent of one of those Russian revolutionaries who couldn't wait to take abstract principles to their logical, if absurd, conclusions.

Apart from the substance of the ethical critiques in the Statement on Human Rights, taken together they underscore a basic fact about the statement that is rarely acknowledged: that it was, above all else, an act of moral and intellectual courage. Imagine the context: the horrors of the Holocaust and the violence of World War II were being fully exposed (through the ongoing Nuremberg trials, among other sources)[20]; there was broad consensus among the major powers around at least some kind of international legal and political order based on some version of human rights; and, behind all of this, scholars, experts, political leaders, and influential public figures across the range were hurrying to lend their services in order to bring this new legal and political order to fruition.

Despite all of this, Herskovits (and then the executive board of the AAA) forcefully dissented. Instead of serving as a bulwark against fascism and the oppression of the weak, a declaration of human rights would, eventually, no matter how well intentioned, tend toward the opposite: it would become a doctrine "employed to implement economic exploitation and . . . deny the right to control their own affairs to millions of people over the world, where the expansion of Europe and America has not [already] meant the literal extermination of whole populations" (AAA 1947:540). And this concern was not only, or most importantly, prospective; Herskovits drew from history in making the argument that declarations of human rights were often legal smokescreens for the oppression of one group of humans by another. For example, the "American Declaration of Independence, or the American Bill of Rights, could be written by men who themselves were slave-owners," and the revolutionary French embrace of the rights of man became legitimate only when extended "to the French slave-owning colonies" (542).

And regardless of the growing international consensus, regardless of the stated intentions of what claimed to be a diverse and representative Commission on Human Rights (and, more generally, United Nations), and regardless of the democratic nature of the UN charter, Herskovits refused to see the proposed declaration of human rights as anything other than a set of aspirations "circumscribed by the standards of [a] single culture" (543).[21] Such a "limited Declaration," Herskovits argued, would exclude more people than it would include, *because of*—not despite—its claims of universality.

Throughout this book, we will have the chance to examine the thrust of Herskovits's arguments in retrospect. As we explore alternative approaches to human rights, we will see that his objections were both prescient and limited. But for now I must return to the narrative of anthropology's broader relationship with human rights.

The Wilderness Years

After 1948 the international human rights system emerged only haltingly, in part because the imperatives of the bipolar Cold War world imposed a whole series of constraints—political, ideological, cultural—on the realization of what was clearly a competing vision for international affairs. So even though Eleanor Roosevelt had hoped that the idea of human rights would be carried along what she called a "curious grapevine" behind the walls of repressive states and ideologies, to reach those most in need of its protections, her dream would have to be deferred (Korey 1998). In the meantime, anthropologists *were* participating in the development of postwar institutions and knowledge regimes, but not those that were framed in terms of human rights. A good example of this public anthropology during the 1950s and early 1960s was the formative role played by anthropologists—in particular Alfred Métraux, Ashley Montagu, and Claude Lévi-Strauss—in the series of UNESCO statements on race, which called into question the biological concept of race and described in some detail the ways in which race should instead be seen as a social construct (UNESCO 1969). This was a provocative and progressive reframing of the race issue at a time when, in the United States for example, the traditional biological understanding of racial differences was still codified in law and reflected in patterns of political and social inequality.

Yet human rights did not frame this work on race, despite the fact that the basic idea of human rights assumes that human beings are essentially the same, both biologically *and* morally.[22] Even more telling, anthropologists were active in the civil rights movement in the United States throughout this period, including Melville Herskovits himself (Gershenhorn 2004).[23] But civil rights were understood in a quite different way than human rights, within a different system of political and legal legitimacy, and anchored in a different set of assumptions about human nature and the foundations of citizenship.[24] And apart from the fact that anthropologists during the 1950s and 1960s did not frame their different *political* interventions in terms of human rights, the anthropological voice was equally absent from developments in the *philosophy* of human rights, especially to the extent that such evolving ideas influenced the content of the important instruments that followed the UDHR.[25]

For anthropology, these were the wilderness years, the period in which the international human rights system was established as a set of ideas, practices, and documents, despite the fact that the actual protection or enforcement of human rights by nation-states and international institutions was often minimal throughout much of the world. The emergence and eventual transnationalization of human rights discourse after the end of the Cold War would not have been possible without these preexisting institutional and philosophical foundations, which were laid without contributions from anthropological forms of knowledge and methods of studying social practices.

Social Justice and Other Universalist Projects

The political and culture climates changed dramatically during the mid- to late 1960s, and anthropologists were again active participants in these changes. But a major difference between the mid-1950s to early 1960s and the late 1960s through the 1970s was the fact that the anthropological contributions to the political and cultural movements of the latter period were fueled, in part, by correspondingly dramatic intellectual shifts within the wider discipline.

Nevertheless, the idea of human rights was still not used by anthropologists in their writings to justify their participation in these political and cultural movements; rather, the most common intellectual (and political) rationale for the anthropological participation in anticolonialism, or protests against the war in Vietnam, was some version of Marxism or neo-Marxism. What is important for my purposes here about the incorporation of the Marxist critique in anthropological writings on social justice issues is that it offered an alternative universalizing framework for addressing these pressing political and social problems, one that, at least theoretically, was as hostile to the cultural relativism of the 1947 Statement on Human Rights as the competing claims of the UDHR itself.

That is, during the 1960s and 1970s anthropology underwent a profound shift—one mirrored in other academic disciplines, both in the United States and elsewhere—that had the effect of creating formal *epistemological* links between scholarship and political activism. The Marxist (or neo-Marxist) emphasis on the inevitability of conflict, the role of intellectuals in political movements, and the importance of understanding structures of inequality within broad historical contexts, among others, made it an ideal source of inspiration for anthropologists desperately seeking a way out of the box created by the dominant theoretical approaches of earlier generations, which either ignored the dynamic interplay between cultures (American historical particularism), downplayed the wider historical, economic, and political forces that shaped particular cultures and societies (British functionalism and structural-functionalism), or denied the influence of history altogether (French structuralism). So although human rights did not figure into the profound shift in the way many anthropologists justified their participation in movements for social justice, an opening was inadvertently and ironically created by the influence of Marxism through which another (and essentially liberal) universalizing project could pass. By the end of the 1970s, anthropology was ready for human rights. But were human rights ready for anthropology?

The Prodigal Son Returns

Although it wouldn't be until the 1980s that anthropology as a discipline took a sustained interest in human rights for the first time, there was an earlier event that foreshadowed the shape of this new interest. In 1972 the anthropologist David Maybury-Lewis and his wife, Pia Maybury-Lewis, cofounded Cultural Survival, Inc. Cultural Survival was not established as a research institution, but rather as a nongovernmental organization dedicated to the survival of indigenous cultures through political advocacy, education, and public awareness programs. There is some question, however, about whether Cultural Survival was founded initially as a human rights organization or as an indigenous cultures organization that only later made indigenous rights a centerpiece for education and advocacy. Although Cultural Survival now makes "indigenous peoples' rights" the basic framework through which it works to ensure the survival of indigenous cultures in different parts of the world, this focus apparently did not emerge within the organization until the 1980s.[26] Nevertheless, the plight of indigenous peoples eventually became *the* issue on which anthropology staked a claim within human rights; it was a small claim at the beginning, to be sure, but as an indigenous rights discourse took on greater importance later in the 1980s, anthropology's involvement suddenly became more noticeable and politically consequential.

The 1980s were turbulent times for anthropology. Especially in the United States, the epistemological shifts of the 1960s and 1970s, in which scholarship and political action were connected within one of several variations of Marxist/neo-Marxist social theory, came home to roost in the form of a period of intense disciplinary self-critique and eventual fragmentation. By the mid-1980s, anthropology as a discipline was in a state of crisis, with clear lines forming between anthropologists who wanted to reaffirm the scientific foundations of the discipline and those who saw these same foundations as a symbol of a longer history of Western colonialism, orientalism, and the assertion of technocratic power against vulnerable populations. The critics of scientific anthropology (see, e.g., Fox 1991; Marcus and Clifford 1986) came close to dismantling American cultural anthropology in particular; at the very least, they made a series of arguments about research methods, ethnographic writing, and the nature of anthropology as a neocolonial encounter that had the effect of painting anthropology into a corner.[27]

There were two major ways out of this corner, one theoretical and the other political. For some anthropologists, the period of intense critique was both revelatory and liberating. Finally, here was a public debate within anthropology about the basic questions of scientific legitimacy, the relationship between science and economic and political exploitation, and, even more abstractly, the questionable assumptions about the nature of social reality on which the "science of mankind" depended. But if this public debate was a revelation for many anthropologists, the path toward liberation quickly became highly theoretical and disconnected from the concerns with social practice that figured, at least symbolically, in some of the earlier critical writings. Instead, the earlier discussion of the problematic nature of the great object/subject divide within social science evolved into an extended debate about subjectivity itself (Spiro 1996); the critique of ethnographic writing was transformed into a debate over the politics of writing genres (Sanjek 1990); and concerns over the way anthropologists chose places to conduct fieldwork evolved into an excursus into the definitions and implications of "space," "place," and "the field" (Amit 1999).[28]

But there was another response to the disciplinary crisis within anthropology in the 1980s and early 1990s. Since much of the critique of anthropology focused on the ways in which anthropologists were unwitting actors in larger political and economic projects, some anthropologists reacted not by trying to eliminate the political from anthropology but by making anthropology *more* political. The idea was to put anthropological knowledge to work at the service of specific groups of people struggling against specific forms of systematic oppression and violence. For anthropologists working with indigenous peoples this was an obvious move, since many indigenous groups found themselves suffering under a range of new or intensified constraints as the era of neoliberalism took root in places like Latin America.

And parallel to the politicization of anthropology and the increase in violence against indigenous peoples as a result of neoliberal political and economic restructuring during the mid- to late 1980s, there was another development that made the anthropological embrace of human rights possible: the advent of "indigenous rights" as a distinct and recognized category within the broader human rights system. This is a complicated history in and of itself—one that I will examine in detail in chapter 6—but suffice it to say here that the controversy over the 1992 500 Years Observances in many parts of the world, the adoption in 1989 of the "Indigenous and Tribal Peoples Convention" by the UN International Labor Organization, and the approval of the Draft Declaration on the Rights of Indigenous Peoples in 1993 by the UN Working Group on Indigenous Issues, among other moments, contributed to—and symbolized—the emergence during this period of an indigenous rights discourse.[29]

For some anthropologists, an indigenous rights discourse provided a means through which their understanding of an essentially political anthropology could be put into practice. What eventually became a transnational indigenous rights movement provided a way out of the human rights wilderness for anthropology. The discipline that embodied the most promise as a source of knowledge about the meanings and potential of human rights in 1948, but which had spent the intervening decades in exile as the idea of human rights was refined conceptually and elaborated institutionally, could now return home. The problem for anthropology was that this way home, while creating new openings for political and institutional action, had the effect of obscuring other possible ways in which anthropology might contribute to human rights theory and practice. But as we will see, this narrowness in anthropology's (re-) engagement with human rights would prove to be only temporary.

The new orientation of anthropology toward human rights can be symbolized by major shifts within the American Anthropological Association. In 1990 the AAA established a special commission, chaired by Terence Turner, to investigate the encroachments on traditional Yanomami territory by the Brazilian state.[30] The creation of this commission and its subsequent report

(1991) led to the establishment by the AAA executive board of the Commission on Human Rights (1992), which was charged "to develop a human rights conceptual framework and identify relevant human rights issues, to develop human rights education and networking, and to develop and implement mechanisms for organizational action on issues affecting the AAA, its members and the discipline" (AAA 2001). In 1995, the Commission on Human Rights was converted into a permanent standing committee of the association—the Committee for Human Rights (CfHR). Among other activities, the members of the CfHR began working on a new statement of principles that would have the effect of definitively repudiating the 1947 Statement on Human Rights. These efforts culminated in the 1999 "Declaration on Anthropology and Human Rights." This declaration, unlike the Statement on Human Rights, *was* formally adopted by a majority vote of the general AAA membership (for a full text of the declaration, see appendix 2).

The declaration's most important assertion is that "people and groups have a generic right to realize their capacity for culture" (AAA 1999). Far from expressing any doubts about the cross-cultural validity of human rights instruments like the 1948 Universal Declaration of Human Rights, the 1999 declaration locates a putative human right to realize a capacity for culture within a set of as-yet-to-be-articulated human rights that actually go well beyond the current rights recognized within international law. As the declaration states, its new position "reflects a commitment to human rights consistent with international principles but not limited by them" (1999). The declaration was thus a clear reversal by the AAA of its earlier position on human rights. But it also signaled something else: the conversion of at least a subset of the world's largest association of professional anthropologists into a human rights advocacy NGO focused on vulnerable populations and emerging rights categories.[31]

Finally, in 2000 the Committee for Human Rights augmented its original set of guidelines and objectives, and this list remains the current (as of 2008) set of operating principles for the committee: (1) to promote and protect human rights; (2) to expand the definition of human rights within an anthropological perspective; (3) to work internally with the membership of the AAA to educate anthropologists and to mobilize their support for human rights; (4) to work externally with foreign colleagues, the people and groups with whom anthropologists work, and other human rights organizations to develop an anthropological perspective on human rights and consult with them on human rights violations and the appropriate actions to be taken; (5) to influence and educate the media, policymakers, nongovernmental organizations, and decision makers in the private sector; and (6) to encourage research on all aspects of human rights from conceptual to applied (AAA 2001).

Toward an Ecumenical Anthropology of Human Rights

After the ratification of the 1999 declaration by the AAA, the association continued to transform its orientation toward human rights. The Committee for Human Rights became one of the most visible and active of the association's working bodies through a series of high profile investigations and interventions, a Web site dedicated to human rights activism and education, and collaborations with other human rights bodies embedded within other professional associations. For example, as it did in 1990, in 2001 the executive board of the AAA created a special task force, in this case to investigate allegations in a sensational book published in 2000 by a French investigative journalist, Patrick Tierney. The book, *Darkness in El Dorado*, contains a number of provocative claims about research conducted among the Brazilian Yanomami, including allegations that the geneticist James Neel and the anthropologist Napoleon Chagnon—who brought the Yanomami to the attention of the world through his prolific writings (see Chagnon 1984)—participated in a study in which a measles epidemic was intentionally unleashed among the Yanomami in order to observe its effects in a genetically isolated population. The five-person task force, which was closely associated with the Committee for Human Rights, issued its report in 2002.[32]

Based on its own investigation, which took place in light of mounting critical attention from outside of anthropology, the El Dorado Task Force found that although many of the claims in the book were unsubstantiated, there had been a pattern of unethical behavior in the research conducted among the Yanomami by Chagnon and others.[33] The task force report was considered unsatisfactory by anthropologists on all sides of the issue. Some felt that the report did not go far enough in both condemning the actions of Chagnon and others and in using the controversy to continue to highlight the ways in which anthropology should reorient its research to protect and advance human rights. From the other side, there were howls of protest against what was believed to be a reckless attack—by both Tierney and then the task force—against well-regarded scientists, an attack that had its *real* roots in a fundamental set of disagreements about the nature of anthropology itself. Still other anthropologists ignored the murky underlying issues and focused on the more technical aspects of the process—not the process through which Tierney wrote his book, but the process through which the AAA buckled under the pressure of external public scrutiny, hastily assembled an ideologically slanted Star Chamber, and then sat back while the reputations of two eminent scientists (one of whom, Neel, was deceased) were tarnished.

After several years of acrimony, the El Dorado controversy took a dramatic and unexpected turn. In 2005 two members of the AAA (Thomas Gregor and Daniel Gross) succeeded in getting a referendum put before the membership. The association's members were asked to formally rescind the 2002 acceptance of the El Dorado Task Force report. Although the referendum made clear that it was "not [meant] to address the merits of the charges leveled against Neel and Chagnon," the often bitter debate that preceded the actual vote—much of which took place on the Web site www.publicanthropology.org—belied this assertion and demonstrated, among other things, that anthropology remained divided by a series of fault lines over such basic issues as the role of science in society, the ethics of social research, and most importantly for my purposes here, the proper relationship between anthropology and human rights. In any case, by an almost three-to-one margin, the AAA membership voted overwhelmingly to rescind the El Dorado report.[34]

The work of the Committee for Human Rights after 1995 was not simply political. Apart from the 1993 review essay by Ellen Messer that I have already mentioned—which was as much a programmatic call to action as a review of anthropology and human rights—several founding members of the committee brought their arguments for a robust engagement with human rights together in a special 1997 issue of the *Journal of Anthropological Research*. One of these articles, by Terence Turner, encapsulated both the importance and the tone of this period in anthropology's relationship with human rights. Turner, whose own activist scholarship on behalf of the Kayapo has come to embody anthropology's rediscovery of human rights and its repudiation of what are understood to be the mistakes of the 1947 generation, argued that anthropologists should contribute to an "emancipatory cultural politics." By this he meant that much of the emerging cultural rights discourse has been, and should continue to be, supported through a kind of anthropological research that is conducted *in terms of* specific projects for social change. And because human rights—for example, the "right to culture" that was described in the 1999 declaration (which Turner played a major role in drafting)—had become essential to these projects, especially those involving indigenous people, anthropological knowledge could prove useful in making legal and political claims in the increasingly dominant language of rights. This emancipatory cultural politics approach to human rights through anthropology remains the primary orientation for anthropologists interested in human rights, including those who work outside academia in high-profile roles within the nongovernmental and activist communities.[35]

Beginning in about 1995, another anthropological approach to human rights emerged, one that represents a major shift in the way some anthropologists understand human rights and, even more important for my purposes, provides much of the foundation for my own set of arguments about the ways in which an anthropological orientation can help transform the way human rights are understood and practiced in different parts of the world. Here anthropologists converted the practice of human rights into a topic for ethnographic research and analysis. Human rights were reconceptualized in part as a transnational discourse linked to the spread of neoliberal logics of legal and political control after the end of the Cold War. As such, anthropologists working in this analytical mode remained ambivalent, or even skeptical, about the use of human rights discourse by social actors in the course of struggles for social change. This research and analysis, which were made possible by the rapid rise in human rights talk and institutional development since the early 1990s, both documented the contradictions and contingencies that surround the practice of human rights and led to the creation of a cross-cultural database on the meanings of human rights.[36]

Finally, even more recently, yet a third approach to human rights through anthropology can be distinguished. To a certain extent, what can described as a critical anthropology of human rights synthesizes both the emancipatory cultural politics and the ethnographic approaches: it is committed at some level to the idea of human rights, though in some cases a radically reconfigured idea, and it makes information derived from the practice of human rights the basis for analysis, critique, policymaking, and political action (see, e.g., Clarke 2008; Cowan 2006; Eriksen 2001; Goodale 2006d). There are profound implications to making the practice of human rights both the conceptual source for understanding what human rights *are* (and can be) and the source of legitimacy for claims based on human rights, not the least of which is the fact that it calls into question many of the basic assumptions of postwar human rights theory and practice.

Moreover, to the extent that the international human rights system is a reflection of these assumptions, then it too must be reconsidered. There can be no doubt about the important contributions by the range of legal scholars, philosophers, ethicists, and others who were instrumental in creating the modern human rights system (and the ideas that supported and then flowed from it). Nevertheless, the ethnography of human rights suggests both a different human rights ontology and grounds on which a potentially global normative project like human rights can be justified. In other words, there is still a tremendous reservoir of untapped potential in the idea of human rights, even if there are also certain basic limitations that must be acknowledged and institutionalized.

.   .   .

THIS, THEN, brings the narrative of anthropology's relationship with human rights up to the current period. In relation to human rights, anthropology is at something of a crossroads. Over the last ten years, anthropologists have expanded beyond the emancipatory cultural politics or activist approach to human rights and have managed to build an important body of information about the complicated ways in which the idea of human rights unfolds within a wide range of social practices. Yet this information has not been taken up in large measure by members of the wider human rights community. Nor has it been adequately considered within the smaller world of academic human rights studies. For example, academic lawyers associated with the New Approaches to International Law movement, while critical of human rights institutions and the ways in which human rights discourse reflects a post–Cold War "moral imperialism" (Hernández-Truyol 2002), have given the findings of anthropologists of human rights little weight, in part because even strong critics within the international legal community have a difficult time reconciling the implications of the ethnography of human rights with the imperatives of legal reasoning and procedure (Riles 2006a). Proposals for human rights reform outside of anthropology tend to swing between two extremes, neither of which gives the social practice of human rights full consideration. One of the leading contemporary anthropologists of human rights, Richard A. Wilson, has drawn attention to this dichotomous tendency (Wilson 2006).

On the one hand are proposals for human rights reform that call for a strengthening of international institutions, the continued activism of transnational human rights NGOs within violator-states, and public education campaigns within developing countries on the importance of human rights (Claude and Weston 2006; Falk 2000; Mertus 2005; Waltz 1995). On the other hand, there are any number of critiques of human rights that emphasize the power inequities within post–Cold War human rights discourse (Mutua 2002), the way human rights law focuses on certain kinds of violence while ignoring others (Rajagopal 2003), and the way human rights language is taken up by political actors and put to strategic uses that go well beyond the original purposes of the international human rights system (Dunne and Wheeler 1999). But despite the differences, these various proposals for reform within contemporary human rights theory and practice all fall somewhere on what might be thought of as a continuum of optimism.

Supporters of international human rights feel that the post–Cold War world has created the first real opportunity for what is an otherwise sound set of institutions—and the ideas that they express—to be effective in meeting their stated goals (a reduction in conflict and human suffering, accountability for human rights violators, the emergence of a functioning international legal system, etc.). Critics argue that the end of the Cold War has only exacerbated a set of basic economic and political inequalities within the international system, which prevents human rights norms from being legitimately inculcated and enforced. Yet even in critiques of power within human rights processes there is an important subtext: although unlikely, *were* these economic and political inequalities to be eliminated, *then* an effective human rights system could be implemented, in part because of the unassailability of the assumptions underlying documents like the UDHR.

But as I show throughout this book, the anthropology of human rights suggests ways in which these basic assumptions should be reconsidered, and, in certain cases, dropped (or replaced), yet without having to leave behind the promise of human rights as a legitimate cross-cultural legal and ethical framework. This means that the kind of anthropology of human rights that I and others have in mind is *both* critical and optimistic, both attuned to the problem of power within the current international human rights regime and sanguine about the potential role a reconfigured idea of human rights might play in projects for social change across a range of cultural, legal, and ethical terrains. In chapter 3, I continue the process of tracing the outlines of an anthropological approach to human rights by taking a renewed look at the problem of universalism and cultural relativism.

Chapter 3

Encountering Relativism

The Philosophy, Politics, and Power of a Dilemma

T HERE IS A SPECTER haunting Europe these days, but the specter is not anything as passé as communism. As it turns out, what continues to cause so much distress, at least in certain circles, is the phantom of relativism. On the day before he was elected pope, Benedict XVI (the former Cardinal Joseph Ratzinger) identified the key challenge facing the Catholic Church as the "dictatorship of relativism" (Dionne 2005). This was not the first time the new pope had rallied the faithful to erect barriers against relativism: as early as 1996, for example, he had described it as the "central problem for faith today" (Ratzinger 1996). The denial of absolute truth is supposedly a main tenet of relativism, and this, according to Benedict, does not set people free—it binds them in invisible shackles. Having too many moral or epistemological or theological choices, without any guiding framework for choosing definitively between them, sets up a kind of tyranny, according to the new leader of the world's one billion Catholics.

But the renewed attack on relativism has not come only from what are, after all, the expected quarters. (Any world religion based on one Truth *would* tend to find the ambiguities of relativism, regardless of controversies over definition or meaning, to be anathema.) The idea and its perceived consequences have also suffered a backlash from the other flank, from neo-Enlightenment thinkers committed to the intellectual, political, and social frameworks associated with a different (though isomorphic) kind of Truth, in this case one derived from universal rationality and human dignity and not divine justice.

In his short book/long essay *The Defeat of the Mind* (1995), the French social thinker and intellectual provocateur Alain Finkielkraut engages in a bout of earnest counter-romanticism in an attempt to recover what remains of the Encyclopedists' reason after two centuries of perversion, prejudice, and—thanks to the anthropologist Claude Lévi-Strauss—what Finkielkraut calls the "second death of Man": the killing of the universal person in order to "return to a romantic notion of culture," not because of some nationalist or racist devotion to the *Volksgeist* but so that leftist Western intellectuals could "atone for past sins."[1]

Yet despite this earnestness, Finkielkraut is not sanguine about his mission. The mandarins of relativism have been at work for too long through too many of France's venerable institutions. In a bitter irony, even the Collège de France—the nation's citadel of free thought, which was born from humanism but came into glory during the Enlightenment (where Cuvier, for example, held the chair in natural history)—has lent its weight to the cause of relativism. A Collège report to France's president on the future course of public education in the country stated that the very first, and guiding principle, of a modern curriculum should be to "integrate the universalism inherent in scientific thought with the relativism of the social sciences . . . with disciplines attentive to the significance of cultural differences among people and to the ways people live, think, and feel" (quoted in Finkielkraut at 96).

What this means, as Finkielkraut laments, is that instead of "humbling Shakespeare, we ennoble the boot maker" (114).[2] Moreover, Finkielkraut continues, the "educators of tomorrow [must] follow Herder . . . and convert literature into folklore" (99). All of this makes for another kind of dictatorship of relativism, one in which "barbarism replaces culture" and the "life of the mind . . . quietly move[s] out of the way, making room for the terrible and pathetic encounter of the fanatic [supporters of Islamic headscarves in public schools?] and the zombie [all those French citizens who mindlessly flock to IKEA Paris?]" (1995:135).

If relativism is the specter that has returned to haunt Europe's intellectual and spiritual leaders, it also continues to hover close by human rights. And this ethereal metaphor is even more apt in this case, since the outlines of this apparition are difficult to discern; it comes and goes in the most unexpected times and places, and many refuse to believe that it exists at all, preferring, rather, to chalk relativism sightings up to the recalcitrance of small groups of philosophical primitives, political premoderns, and moral scoundrels. If the Holocaust was, in part, the murderous end result of a process of cultural and philosophical development in which Nietzsche triumphed over Voltaire, then the 1948 Universal Declaration of Human Rights was meant to dramatically refill the moral, legal, and political voids created by the forces of anti-universalism. Didn't the UDHR reestablish, one and for all, the manifest truth—and thus prerogatives—of the universal, the principle that all of the nations of the world must recognize a basic set of transcendent moral facts despite the equally manifest fact of cross-cultural and historical diversity?

And more recently, after the end of the Cold War unleashed the cultural and economic forces of globalization, hasn't the world become a still more homogeneous place, one in which a set of transnational values has emerged to replace—or, perhaps, suppress—all of those pre-UDHR normative artifacts, so that the sharp edges of cultural diversity have been blunted, making the problem of relativism even less relevant than at any time since the dark days of mid-century last? Hasn't the "flattening" of the world, to invoke the image popularized by the globalization guru Thomas Friedman, meant that the specter of relativism has nowhere to go, no deep reservoirs of cultural or moral alterity to draw from? And yet, and yet, despite all of this, relativism continues to vex human rights theorists and practitioners, whether or not they are willing to admit that it is the source of their problems.

Indeed, the continuing persistence of relativism as an explicit or, more commonly, implicit topic for concern within human rights can be seen in the ambivalent and even dismissive ways in which relativism is treated by theorists and activists across a range of perspectives. Before he describes relativism as "not plausible" (1998:63), before he even begins his analysis of relativism and its discontents (which I return to below), the legal philosopher Michael Perry "focus[es] the mind" of the reader with lurid newspaper accounts of torture, rape, and the mutilation of children during the conflict in the former Yugoslavia in the early 1990s. With the mind focused thusly, the moral equation becomes crystal clear: those who might raise the relativist challenge to human rights at this late hour must stand on the side of murderers, rapists, torturers, and all the other dark angels of our common human nature.

Michael Ignatieff argues that the best way for "Western human rights activists" to confront the relativist challenge to human rights is to "admit its truth" (2001:74–75). He also acknowledges that "there are many differing visions of a good human life, that the West's is only one of them, and that, provided agents have a degree of freedom in the choice of that life, they should be left to give it the content that accords with their history and traditions" (74). Yet despite anchoring his analysis of relativism and the problem of culture in what appears to be a framework that is sympathetic to the relativist challenge to human rights, Ignatieff declares relativism to be "the invariable alibi of tyranny" (74).

From a different epistemological and political vantage point, the postcolonial social theorist and legal scholar Upendra Baxi adopts Christopher Norris's description of relativism as a "coat of many colours" (2002:113). Perhaps the most basic of these colors is the idea that "different cultures and civilizations have diverse notions of what it means to be human and [thus what it means] for humans to have rights" (113). Baxi concedes that this idea is true that different cultures and "civilizations" do, in fact, express diverse notions of humanness—which would seem to pose something of a prima facie problem for a transnational moral-legal framework that is based on the truth—whether descriptive or prescriptive—of the exact opposite. But Baxi dismisses this form of relativism as "trivial." Other versions of relativism are likewise described as "logically or analytically flawed," "willfully ignorant," and "exercises in unconscious Realpolitik."

Jack Donnelly, who has been one of the most prolific writers on human rights over the last twenty years, someone whose publications can be justifiably credited with doing much to help develop a field of human rights studies (see, for example, Donnelly 1985, 1997, 2003), describes a "necessary tension" between the universality of international human rights and relativism. He gives as an example of this tension the fact that the names of many cultures can be translated to mean simply "the people," which implies that at least some cultures embrace a sociolinguistic ontology that excludes anything like a common human nature, indeed, the very idea of "the human" itself.[3]

Again, an excellent and perceptive point, and one not made very often, even by anthropologists and others who would be expected to be more finely attuned to both the fact, and the broader meanings, of such a culture-language nexus. Yet after making this point, Donnelly immediately sweeps away all the obvious and serious problems that flow from it. "Such views," he says—those that identify a collectivity in exclusionary, not inclusive, terms—"are almost *universally* rejected in the contemporary world" (2003:91; emphasis added). Rejected by whom? By those for whom this type of exclusionary ontology is embedded in language and reflected in group identity? When people in twenty-first-century Bolivia self-identify as *runa* (which can mean "the people" or "man" in the individual, not collective, sense), do they not mean what they say, or is it that they are not really *in* the "contemporary world"?[4]

As a final introductory sounding, we turn to the way anthropologists of human rights have treated the problem of relativism. As I explained in chapter 2, contemporary anthropology has had as much a troubled and ambivalent relationship with the idea of relativism as it has with human rights. This ambivalence is usually refracted through the eyes—and writings—of non-anthropologists, who expect the anthropological presence within particular debates to consist of strenuous arguments against foundationalism of any stripe; an epistemologically unhealthy obsession with ethnography (which is derisively taken to mean long periods of hanging out, not collecting "qualitative" "data"); and, above all else, the exaltation of Culture, which is suspected of being a cipher for all manner of political and ideological commitments (and which therefore can be either ignored or caricatured).

An illuminating example of this refraction can be found in the intertextual dialogue between Jack Donnelly and the Danish applied anthropologist Ann-Belinda Preis, who has worked for many years for UNESCO (Donnelly 2003:86–88). Donnelly must have been shocked to be taken to task by Preis (1996) for what he can only have assumed was his sympathetic, *anthropological* approach to culture and human rights. Who knew that anthropologists were no longer apotheosizing Culture, that all-encompassing body of beliefs and practices the study of which was supposed to form the basis of—and justify—their discipline? Instead, as Donnelly wryly notes, anthropologists like Preis were urging him and others concerned with the relationship between "culture" and human rights to understand the former as "fluid complexes of intersubjective meanings and practices" (Donnelly 2003:86).[5] In other words, anthropologists seemed to be saying now: no Culture, no problem between (cultural) relativism and human rights.

But despite the prevalence of this conceptual sleight of hand, scholars (including many anthropologists), practitioners, government officials, and activists continue to write, act, and think in terms of culture in the traditional (formerly known as the "anthropological") sense. Indeed, the American Anthropological Association's 1999 "Declaration on Anthropology and Human Rights" represents an attempt to radically reconfigure anthropology's relationship with human rights on the basis of a very conventional understanding of culture, one in which those static and bounded sets of ideas and practices give rise to a new *human* right—the right to culture, the very thing itself.

But this return to a neoclassical theory of culture in anthropology, which must be understood in terms of a much longer trajectory of activism, advocacy, and concern with "cultural survival," marks only one important strand in the discipline's recent reengagement with human rights. It was understood quite early on in the cultural survival movement that "culture" in the traditional sense was a clear, and generally accepted, ordering principle around which struggles against different agents of oppression (states, corporations, international financial institutions) could be waged. So even as other segments of anthropology were developing highly abstract (and abstracted) theories of culture as a way of coming to terms with the increasing transnationalization of social life—especially after the end of the Cold War—another segment was reinforcing a quite different notion of culture, although in this case for instrumental, rather than theoretical, reasons. (That is, it is difficult to envision how the cultural survival movement, or the activities of the AAA's Committee for Human Rights, could have developed as they did on the basis of a theory that sees culture as "fluid complexes of intersubjective meanings and practices.")

Anthropologists of human rights working within the ethnographic orientation have also grappled with the problem of culture in relation to human rights, usually with sophistication and conceptual nuance. Perhaps the best example of this can be found in Cowan, Dembour, and Wilson's collection of essays on culture and rights published in 2001. In their introduction, the editors do not necessarily dismiss the importance of the cultural relativist challenge to human rights. Instead, they attack the overly dichotomous nature of this "most serious and still ongoing debate," in which people are forced to choose between universal human rights and cultural relativism. They see this as a false choice, in part because binaries of this kind are always purely conceptual and not an accurate reflection of the way different ideas compete for attention within actual social practices. But also, like Preis (whom they list in their bibliography but do not cite), they problematize the meaning of culture itself in light of the ever-increasing interrelation between "global and local norms" (2001:6). This is not really a theory of culture per se but rather an attempt to balance the conceptual and empirical tensions created by the clash between different meanings of culture and, equally important, the clash between different categories of meaning.

.   .   .

I COULD CONTINUE to take the measure of relativism through a much longer introductory survey of the way the concept has been understood in different disciplines over time. But even so, we would still want to know at the end: What exactly *is* relativism? Why and how does it continue to create dilemmas for human rights theory and practice? And finally, what does the recent anthropology of human rights, apart from what I have already briefly indicated, have to contribute to the various debates? The rest of the chapter is my answer to each of these questions.

Thinking of Relativism

To begin with, it is important to recognize that much of the confusion within debates over relativism and human rights is categorical. What I mean is that approaches to relativism are shaped by a range of different analytical categories, which are associated with academic disciplines, political orientations, institutional affiliation, and so on. Is relativism a philosophical or conceptual "problem" to be solved according to the generally accepted standards of theoretical analysis, regardless of debates over which body of theory should be brought to bear on it, or how convincingly such analysis is undertaken? Is it a cynical rationale through which different political interests in different parts of the world can be advanced in the name of "culture"? Is it a code for Western elite guilt over several centuries of Euro-Atlantic imperialism and more recent projects of neo-imperialism in the form of international humanitarian development? Or is "relativism" in certain contexts something like an empty signifier, without any clear or discernible referent at all, no matter how deeply we penetrate its coded facade?[6]

Relativism is, we might say, all of these—and more—at different times and in different contexts. But it is not enough to simply recognize this multiplicity, the fact that relativism is a "coat of many colours," which is quite justifiably described as a "trivial" point. In order to work toward an alternative clarity about "relativism" and its multiple meanings, it is first necessary to identify these different categories through which questions about relativism are asked and answered. Even more important, we must examine the underlying contexts that compel the use of certain categories and not others, or that elevate some over others. As we will see, a contextual approach of this kind reveals parallel processes and discursive structures within human rights itself, even apart from the relativism–human rights debate.

Philosophy and the Mirror of Truth

In his wide-ranging attack on the reflective edifice of Western philosophy, Richard Rorty (1979) argues that over millennia of intellectual history philosophy has been characterized by a search for foundations, which reflects a trans-categorical "desire for constraint" that has allowed people in different times and places to establish "frameworks beyond which one must not stray, [identify] objects which impose themselves, [and make] representations that cannot be gainsaid" (315). What has united the different philosophical schools and traditions that are derived from—or at least heavily imprinted by—the ancients has been the belief that philosophy is a mirror of nature: that the results of philosophical "confrontation and constraint" have, in one way or another, to greater or lesser degrees, and with more or less accuracy, mirrored or represented reality.

Although the dominance of this epistemology within Western philosophy—or, as Rorty might say, the dominance of the idea of epistemology itself—was shaken by the "holistic, antifoundationalist, pragmatist treatments of knowledge and meaning . . . [found] in Dewey, Wittgenstein, Quine, Sellars, and Davidson [among others]" (317), it nevertheless persists and structures ways of thinking about things from law to political institutions, from the causes of war to biomedical ethics. With the exception of some key fields (for example, the jurisprudence of contemporary legal pragmatists like Richard Posner), there is no question that in the historic battle of the two D's (Descartes and Dewey), the framework of "knowledge and meaning" established by the first D continues to triumph.

Yet despite the fact that we can locate these profound struggles over frameworks of knowledge and meaning within philosophy and recognize—with Rorty and other historians of philosophy—the profound differences between them, for my purposes it is what they have in common that is important. In relation to the debate over relativism and universal human rights, we can identify what can be understood quite loosely as a "philosophical" approach, which would characterize (admittedly ironically) Rorty's own analysis of relativism and human rights as much as those of "natural law" (see Skeel 2007) scholars like Michael Perry. Regardless of whether a thinker is foundationalist or anti-foundationalist, committed to a correspondence theory of truth or one based on coherence (or verificationism, or behaviorism, etc.), those who use a philosophical approach share one thing in common: they see problems—social, moral, political, cultural, legal—as either conceptual in themselves or, if not, then they believe that the *solutions* to problems should, in the best of circumstances, be conceptual.

In order to see this philosophical approach at work—in this case in the context of the relativism and human rights debate—it is not necessary to define "problems" beyond saying that in each instance the problem is that thing that is felt to be behind the trouble (of whatever kind), the thing, or dimension of a thing, the resolution of which will lead to an artistic breakthrough, or the possibility of a new social structure, or a new insight into the human condition, or greater tolerance between peoples. To see problems (or solutions to problems) as largely conceptual is to locate them, first and foremost, in the sphere of ideas. It is to understand conflicts to be the result of the way ideas clash: because they are believed to be theoretically irreconcilable, or because certain ideas had their genesis within certain insidious forms of political or other forms of domination, or because particular ideas—or systems of ideas—have been shaped by intuitive or non-rational forces (like religion), and so on. In each case, the problem itself is not, primarily, in the way ideas are put into practice, or in the social or cultural contexts within which ideas emerge, important as these obviously are; rather, the problem is embedded in the abstracted spheres in which competing accounts of concepts clash. And conceptual problems call for conceptual solutions.

A common way in which this philosophical approach has been employed in the relativism and human rights debates has been to identify the source of the problem in the idea of relativism (instead of, for example, in the idea of human rights). Critics working in this mode argue that the idea of relativism should be subdivided into conceptually distinct subcategories. Without this analytical parsing, "relativism" remains merely a "vacuous word" (Baxi 2002:113), an empty signifier whose discursive presence hinders, rather than clarifies, discussions of human rights. Other scholars argue that these subcategories are actually implicitly present in many debates over relativism, but unacknowledged, confused, or "conflated," as Alison Dundes Renteln puts it (1990:68). The problem, in other words, lies in the way "participants have not used precise terminology" (1990:69). The solution, therefore, is to insist on the use of precise terminology after first bringing to the surface the conceptually distinguishable variations of relativism lurking within.

Dundes Renteln draws a distinction between epistemological, cultural, and ethical relativism and then suggests that the epistemological is a kind of meta-relativism, a conceptual category that encompasses the others. She then focuses on the relationship between cultural and ethical relativism after defining cultural relativism as the idea that "*some* evaluations are relative to the cultural background out of which they arise" (69; emphasis in original). Ethical relativism, however, is not conceptually coequal with cultural relativism, but rather is a subset of it. Dundes Renteln then subdivides ethical relativism itself into three further (sub)subcategories: apparent ethical relativism, ethical relativism as descriptive (factual) hypothesis (she borrows this subcategory from Schmidt 1955), and ethical relativism as prescriptive (value) hypothesis (again, adopting the concept/terminology from Schmidt).

So we have quite a conceptual matryoshka doll here: epistemological relativism—cultural and ethical relativism—then the three final subcategories of ethical relativism. Without denying the conceptual existence, or importance (in the abstract), of ethical relativism's first and third subcategories, Dundes Renteln argues that subcategory #2—ethical relativism as descriptive (factual) hypothesis—is most important for debates about human rights because it does not imply tolerance of particular cultural practices. In order to signal the importance of this (sub)subcategory, she says she will refer to it—somewhat confusingly, for me at least—as simply "relativism" (71).

The anthropologist Melford Spiro, in an article credited with reviving serious attention to the problem of relativism within the discipline, likewise employs a philosophical approach in order to "clear away some of the intellectual underbrush that has served to obfuscate some of the controversies surrounding this perennial debate," which has been beset by "conceptual muddles" and the conflation of "types" that are "not merely analytically *separable* but historically distinct" (1986:259; emphasis added).

For Spiro, "cultural relativism" denotes the general category of relativism, which—he hastens to add—should not be confused with the simple fact of cultural diversity or variability. The analytical category cultural relativism can be subdivided into three subcategories: descriptive relativism, normative relativism, and epistemological relativism. The first of these can be subdivided into three further (sub)subcategories (strong, moderate, and weak forms of descriptive relativism) and the second into two (cultural and social/psychological normative relativism). The third appears to be conceptually indivisible, although Spiro draws a number of different implications from it. Moreover, he describes epistemological relativism as taking its "point of departure" from the "strong form of descriptive relativism," which suggests that Spiro actually sees epistemological relativism as a subcategory of strong descriptive relativism, which would make it (stay with me here) a (sub)(sub) subcategory of the general category cultural relativism.[7]

Examples of this philosophical/conceptual approach to relativism could be given not quite ad infinitum, but certainly enough to give a sense of the epistemology that shapes them and some indication of whether for my purposes they have brought us any closer to understanding "relativism" and—by extension—its relation to human rights. The philosopher Rodney Peffer, for example, on whom Upendra Baxi relies heavily in his discussion of relativism and human rights, takes the conceptual approach to its most abstract conclusion in distinguishing four types of relativism through what Baxi describes as a "logical demonstration" (2002:113). Here the technique is purely analytical: the parsing of "relativism" into what Peffer believes are its four logically *distinguishable* (not distinct) types.[8] I emphasize "distinguishable" in this way in order to connect Peffer's analysis with Spiro's, who describes *his* (not "the") multilayered categories of relativism as analytically "separable."

In other words, both Peffer and Spiro are signaling something critically important: that the categories and (sub)subcategories of relativism that they catalog are not distinct or separate in some Platonic sense and embedded within the idea of relativism itself, simply waiting to be discovered by the conceptual explorer; indeed, prior to analyses by individuals, in the course of debates over "problems," these categories could not be said even to exist in any meaningful sense, except as figments of the analytical imagination. So when Spiro describes the categories of relativism as "separable," we should take this to mean that his analytical mind is capable of making these distinctions within the—equally subjectively construed—idea of "relativism" (or cultural relativism or ethical relativism, etc.), not that he believes he has discovered something "within" relativism, the discursive equivalent of gravity or irrational numbers.

This excursus into epistemology has a very specific purpose: to show how what anthropologists would call categories of meaning have shaped the course of debates over relativism and human rights. I have very little to say about the value of distinct categories in their own terms, or the extent to which certain scholars have navigated within these categories to greater or lesser degrees of persuasion—logical, rhetorical, or otherwise.

Nevertheless, it should be obvious that the use of a philosophical or conceptual approach to relativism can be quite exclusionary, something that can create all sorts of profound difficulties when it is employed within the epistemological cacophony of interdisciplinary human rights debates. Moreover, we might also ask why the conceptual has been the historically dominant approach to relativism, both in relation to human rights and beyond. As I will describe more fully below, there is a discursive power that shapes debates over human rights, one that compels certain modes of engagement and excludes others. Because the conceptual has, until very recently, been the approach that has dominated discussions of human rights—whether in their legal, ethical, or institutional dimensions—it is likely that those who have examined relativism in relation to human rights have been compelled to mirror the other side of the equation.[9]

Values in the Arena

In a December 2005 speech in Philadelphia, President George W. Bush discussed the upcoming Iraqi elections and elaborated on the reasons why the United States went to war. The location of the speech was carefully chosen and meant to signal a profound shift in justifications for the war. As Philadelphia was the cradle of American democracy, the place where Enlightenment notions of the rights of man were given pioneering expression, so too would Iraq—at some distant point in the future—serve this symbolic role for the Middle East. As President Bush explained, "I can think of no better place to discuss the rise of a free Iraq than in the heart of Philadelphia, the city where America's democracy was born" (Bush 2005).

Gone, of course, was any mention of weapons of mass destruction or even much in the way of the instrumental invocation of U.S. "national security." Instead, President Bush argued that the U.S. military was in Iraq as a kind of normative midwife, helping the Iraqi people during this "period of difficult struggle" give birth to a new political, legal, and moral vision, in which the universal human rights of Iraqis—which had always been present even as they were being brutally violated or suppressed—would form the foundation for a new society.

President Bush's speech is soaked with references to human rights, both as a general concept and in relation to those specific rights that most indelibly mark this "turning point in the history of Iraq, the history of the Middle East, and the history of freedom": minority rights, property rights, the right to freedom of assembly, the rights of free speech and the press, women's rights, and the right to vote. And the burden for ensuring that these rights flourish in Iraq does not, in the end, rest with the Iraqi people themselves, whose collective "desire to be free" is both unquestionable and "universal," found in all peoples at all times (as in Philadelphia in 1776); rather, the burden rests with the United States itself. As the president framed the issue: "The fundamental question is, do we have the confidence [in our] universal values to help change a troubled part of the world?" (Bush 2005). We have, then, a justification for American foreign policy wrapped in the language of moral philosophy. The human rights codified in the U.S. Constitution of 1789, the UDHR of 1948, and the Iraqi Constitution of 2005 are universal rights, minor variations expressed in the same normative key. And every Iraqi, as much as every American, is a bearer of these rights.

But more important, President Bush seemed to be saying, the existence of these universal rights implies a parallel, or perhaps underlying, normativity, which is expressed in terms of "values." Chief among these is the value to protect human rights in places where they are suppressed or denied, a value that *is*—not ought to be—universal and that should ideally be the basis of action in the world as a kind of catalyst to human rights. At least in relation to its continued prosecution of war in the Middle East, therefore (similar arguments have been made about the U.S. intervention in Afghanistan), we have a U.S. administration that has become a veritable hotbed of universalism. Even if the ultimate source of this universalism is the evangelical Christian God, and not human nature comprehended through universal reason, the implication is the same: the political (and military) actions of the United States are legitimate to the extent that they reflect a "confidence" in "universal values," including the value to "help change . . . troubled [i.e., human rights–deprived] part[s] of the world." As we will see below, whether or not this neoconservative jumble—which mixes orthodox social contract theory with a kind of apocalyptic Kantian ethics—can be taken seriously is another question. So too is what this type of double-barreled universalism means for debates over human rights and relativism.

In the early 1990s, however, the assertion of values within the international political arena cut in the opposite direction. Rather than appropriating the discourse of universal rights as part of wider geopolitical struggles, leaders of different Southeast and East Asian countries adopted a discourse of cultural identity in which "Asian values" were emphasized at the expense of what were believed to be "Western values" masquerading as cross-cultural universals.

Although the discourse of Asian values emerged as a response to particular events—the sanctions against China following Tiananmen Square are typically cited by commentators as a key moment (see, e.g., Bell, Nathan, and Peleg 2001)—it soon grew into something more complicated and far-ranging. As Lynda Bell explains, in an essay on the production of Asian identity, "as modern nation-states in East Asia have risen to international economic and political prominence in the last two decades, leaders and individuals within them have reacted to Western human rights discourse with their own brand of outraged cultural relativism." She identifies the "principal agents" of this counter-universalism as "state agencies and political figures from Singapore, the People's Republic of China, and Malaysia" (2001:23).

Most Western analysts of the Asian values debate have been extremely critical of the invocation of cultural relativism by political and social leaders, a kind of response that stands in almost inverse relation to how the Bush administration's invocation of universal human rights has been received. Donnelly, for example, devotes a whole chapter to the Asian values debate in his 2003 book. He describes the positions of different leaders and states with a heavy dose of skepticism, which is symbolized by his refusal to remove the quotation marks from the phrase "Asian values." The suggestion that there *are* Asian values, he seems to be telling us, is essentially spurious, a sham. Although he appreciates studies of the debate that "seek to separate politics and cant from legitimate concerns and insights" (2003:107 n. 1), it is clear that he believes the invocation of Asian culture or values during the early 1990s was 98 percent politics and cant, 1 percent confusion about relevant concepts on the part of certain Asian leaders, and 1 percent legitimate concerns and insights.

Like others writing on this issue, Donnelly views the opposition to human rights activism within Asia during this period as mostly political disingenuousness, a crude attempt to shield or justify authoritarian brutality in the name of cultural integrity and anti-imperialism. Despite his otherwise even-handed and deservedly influential examination of the complexities of human rights, he is a committed internationalist and advocate of a very traditional conception of human rights, which means his tolerance for alternative visions has its limits. As he explains, "Human rights, as specified in the Universal Declaration and the Covenants, represent the international community's best effort to define the social and political parameters of our common humanity. Within these limits, all is possible. Outside of them, little should be allowed" (2003:123).

Cowan, Dembour, and Wilson (2001) analyze the "concern with [Asian] cultural values" from a quite different vantage point. The authors track the way the "rhetorical invocation" of cultural relativism within the Asian values debate took on a life of its own, serving many masters and purposes at the same time, from "political opportunism" to what Bell would describe as a "counter-hegemonic" strike against the "already-powerful and prominent Western discourse on universal human rights" (Bell 2001:24).

Even more intriguingly, Cowan, Dembour, and Wilson show how the culturalist critique of human rights by Asian elites has forced human rights activists and international actors to "adopt the language of culture" *on behalf of* universal human rights.[10] And, as other commentators have done, they make a variation on the "who speaks for culture" argument. They show, quite rightly, that neither the concept of "culture" itself nor the "meanings and practices" that this concept is meant to describe in specific cases are uncomplicatedly static or monolithic within different Asian nation-states, which means that the relationship between cultural identity and international human rights can never be understood in the abstract, as a simple exercise in normative metrics. To illustrate the contested nature of culture and its relation to human rights within Asia, they cite language from the Asian Human Rights Charter, which firmly opposes any reference to Asian values and resists culturalist arguments against international human rights standards.

So in the case of the U.S. administration's embrace of universal human rights as part of a wider initiative to reframe its military interventions in the Middle East, and in the analyses of the invocation of culture by certain Asian leaders ostensibly *against* universal human rights, we have two examples of a categorical approach to relativism and human rights that is different in important ways from the philosophical or conceptual. Here the problem, the thing that leads to discord, misunderstanding, and what Cowan, Dembour, and Wilson would describe as "high[] suspicion," is located in what we can describe as the political sphere, by which I mean all of those material, structural, and social forces that are harnessed—or resisted—by actual groups of people in the course of struggles for power, broadly understood.

In other words, a political orientation to the problem of relativism and human rights is one that displaces the object of action from the conceptual—the sphere of ideas—to the actual, from the plane of the abstract, in which any number of contingencies that might qualify the analysis of relativism and human rights are intentionally ignored or denied, to the plane of the practical, in which ideas are only one among many dimensions of concrete lived experience and the practice of everyday life. So even if there is a superficial resemblance between these two different categories through which relativism and human rights are examined and understood, the political represents an orientation with its own rules of engagement, expectations, and, most important, purposes. This can be seen in the way relativism and human rights are approached by the same critic or analyst working from within both categories at different times.

Take Donnelly's analysis of relativism and universal human rights, which is frequently cited and influential within interdisciplinary human rights studies (and probably within international human rights practice, although this is harder to track).[11] Like Dundes Renteln, Spiro, Rorty, and many others, Donnelly relishes the opportunity to make a philosophical contribution to the debate, and he clearly sees this category as his strongest.[12] And like others who are committed to a philosophical approach to relativism and human rights, Donnelly appears to bring a number of analytical categories and subcategories into being from within the idea of relativism itself through the kind of Cartesian parsing we have seen before.[13]

Instead of concentric analytical circles, Donnelly uses the metaphor of the continuum to illustrate the different dimensions of relativism that are (for him) distinguishable. At one end is "radical cultural relativism"; at the other end is "radical universalism." In between "these end points," the "body of the continuum . . . can be roughly divided into . . . strong and weak cultural relativism" (2003:89–90). He then describes the "furthest extreme" of both "strong cultural relativism" and "weak cultural relativism," which implies that he envisions something like two sub-continuums on (or within) the general continuum/category. He also notes that weak cultural relativism "might also be called strong universalism." And since the question of judgment or evaluation is also important to the more general problem of relativism and human rights, Donnelly distinguishes analytically between types of "culturally relative practices," types that are, moreover, *categorically* in conflict.

But when Donnelly turns to the Asian values debate, he asks and answers questions, describes problems, and otherwise frames an understanding from within what is clearly a different category of knowledge. He dispenses entirely with conceptual typologies, continuums, or any other methodological tool that indicates he believes the core problem within the Asian values debate to be conceptual. He does not, for example, examine the arguments of Asian political and social leaders on their own terms in order to evaluate the truth-value or coherence or legitimacy of the ideas that give rise to them.

Instead, his analysis is directed toward a whole range of political problems, which include the "record of Western (and Japanese) colonial rule" and its relation to assertions of sovereignty, the relationship between the economic "demands of development" and political resistance to international human rights standards, and even the way a "super-father figure like Kim Il-sung" of North Korea does or does not symbolize an Asian tendency to "defer to paternalistic political authorities" (2003:120). Again, the point here is not to criticize the way Donnelly examines relativism and human rights from within radically different categories of knowledge at different places, or to evaluate the comparative value of either the philosophical or the political approach. Rather, I draw out these differences in order to show that responses to relativism and human rights are profoundly shaped by the categories of knowledge and meaning through which they are apprehended.

The Power of a Dilemma

In making the argument that debates over the relationship between relativism and human rights are influenced by categories of knowledge and meaning, which have the effect of compelling certain modes of engagement, certain expectations of analysis, and even certain purposes toward which such approaches are directed, while excluding other possibilities, I am also making a related argument: that it is not necessary, or even possible, to say that one category is more analytically comprehensive than the other, or more realistic, or less dependent on unstated stereotypes, or better able to penetrate to the heart of the problem. Instead, the position I have implicitly developed so far has been what we might describe as "discursive": I am interested in the way patterns of discourse shape, compel, and negate ways of approaching the problem of relativism—in its "many colours"—in relation to human rights.

This way of framing the relativism and human rights debate can also be described as anthropological, a way of examining the main claims of a problem like this through the multifocal lens of cross-cultural experience, epistemological flexibility, and a thoroughgoing skepticism toward even the most apparently benevolent systems (political, ideological, moral), not to mention the nefarious ones. In returning now to the broader anthropology of human rights in order to step away from both the philosophical and the political approaches to relativism and human rights—which, taken together, nearly exhaust the way the issue has been examined—something interesting happens: a third dimension to the problem of relativism and human rights comes into view.

This third dimension is much less easily illuminated than the other two, especially since it exists as a sort of residual category, or, perhaps even more accurately, as a negative key to relativism and human rights. Yet the persistence of this negative key in shaping the course of debates over relativism and human rights will continue to prove destabilizing for any international human rights system modeled on the current one. It is, therefore, the one we most need to understand.

To the extent to which relativism and its discontents persist in vexing different aspects of human rights theory and practice, I believe this is not because there are lingering philosophical problems to be identified and definitively solved or because of the way relativism has been used as a disingenuous front for different acts of political opportunism. Rather, it is because of the peculiar phenomenology that shapes the experience of both "relativism" and "human rights." What I mean is that there are basic, deceptively straightforward ideas that are associated with both human rights and relativism, not as these two concepts form the basis of critique or elite analysis or institutional action but as they are perceived by ordinary actors within different social practices in different times and places.[14] And perception perhaps gives the wrong impression of how these basic ideas should be understood. It would be more accurate to say that they are actually intuited by social actors as much through a kind of inarticulable emotional engagement as through what we would recognize as detached and formal contemplation.

On the side of human rights, there is the simply stated but world-shatteringly profound idea that human beings are all essentially the same and that this sameness extends well beyond the mere fact of human biology. The follow-on to this—again, something that most people intuit (however vaguely) rather than "know"—is the idea that this essential sameness suggests an entire moral and perhaps legal framework, one that is expressed in what is for many people around the world an unintelligible normative language (rights), yet one that either does, or ought to, supersede all of those political, religious, or other structures that work to oppress, restrict, or diminish.

And on the side of "relativism" (which is, unlike human rights, a word/concept that is meaningless for the vast majority of people in the world), the intuitions run in the opposite direction. Many people sense that they are essentially different from others. In certain parts of the world this sense of difference extends from one individual to the next; in other places, difference is intuited at a collective level, from one group—nation, ethnicity, "race," people—to the next. This intuition of difference begins from the same place as intuitions of human rights (the fact of *apparent* common human biology[15]), but the conclusion it draws (not logically or rationally but emotionally, phenomenologically) is that this commonness is trivial and pales in comparison with all of the many profound ways in which individuals and groups differ from each other: religion, political ideology, language, phenotype, life experience, caste, social class, and so on.

The essence of each intuition lies in the act of *going beyond* the observable, the immediately apparent, or the "self-evident." Within the phenomenology of human rights, which takes its departure from the idea of sameness, and within the subjective, intuitive experience of essential, irreducible difference (which I identity with "relativism," but see below), a leap of faith is needed to go from what is apparent but trivial to what is intuited and profound. In other words, the phenomenological process is more or less the same even if it leads in radically different directions. Nevertheless, the argument I am making here is that this leap cannot ultimately be made or understood in terms of what I have described as either the philosophical or the political approach to relativism (and, by extension, to human rights). This is the reason why an even longer gray line of conceptual analyses of relativism will not get us any closer to what we need to know, regardless of how nuanced or logically impeccable they are, no matter how many more categories and subcategories are extracted from the idea, no matter how many more colors are identified, no matter how many more species of the genus are classified.

And the phenomenology of relativism and human rights is complicated in yet other ways. For example, because the intuition of essential sameness and the intuition of essential difference are both subjectively experienced at that murky, emotional, non-rational level of consciousness, they can come together in ways that lead to bitter irony, paradox, a refusal to acknowledge the fact of human suffering, a refusal to acknowledge the fact of power within international humanitarian networks, and a host of other thorny dilemmas. Moreover, these are dilemmas that plague commentators, critics, and activists as much as ordinary social actors, whose encounters with human rights and intuitions of relativism are more likely to be fleeting and thus experienced as at inexplicable cross-purposes.

Take the problem of human suffering.[16] The experience of pain and cruelty can be both direct and vicarious, and the intuition that leads to human rights can also lead to a burning desire to employ them as a bulwark against human suffering. But at the same time, even in the presence—direct or vicarious—of tremendous human suffering, the intuition can pull in a different direction. Here the fact of *human* suffering is obscured by the intuition of essential difference and a sense that the denial of it in the name of "human nature" or a "common humanity" is due, in part, to a refusal to come to terms with it and its unsavory implications. Even more, the intuition that pulls toward relativism can burn with its own kind of desire, although in this case one that seeks to give political or legal or institutional effect to the fact of human diversity. Yet as it turns out, it is much easier to rationally derive a framework—intellectual, political, legal, moral—that is based on essential sameness than one that is based on essential difference.

So here we have yet another way of understanding the relationship between relativism and human rights, not as a debate in any formal sense—whether in the arena of conceptual analysis or as an expression of the imperatives of Real-politik—but through the way that certain core meanings are apprehended by people intuitively, emotionally, and implicitly. Now I should underscore that I am not making a prescriptive argument. I am not saying that there are certain dimensions to both relativism and human rights that are best left to the shadowy level of the intuitive construed in some naive sense or as a latter-day version of what Cowan, Dembour, and Wilson describe as the "'blood and soil' response of nineteenth century German Romanticism to the universalism of the French Enlightenment" (2001:4).[17] It is, instead, a thoroughly descriptive argument: these *are* the ways in which most people encounter sameness-as-human-rights and difference-as-relativism.

An anthropology of human rights recognizes this alternative way of understanding the range of problems associated with relativism and human rights since it is only through the close ethnographic engagement with the practice of everyday life that they become apparent. But more than simply recognizing and describing the way categories of meaning—philosophical, political, discursive-intuitive—shape the way the experiences of relativism and human rights are understood, an anthropology of human rights must also draw out the broader implications.

From the Universal to the Human

I said at the beginning of the chapter that I would ask and answer several questions, including the question "What is relativism?" But instead of engaging in yet another debate over definition, or proposing an analytical schema that finally, once and for all, breaks free of the accumulated "intellectual underbrush," I argued that it was more important to understand *how* this question is asked in particular contexts, and the way responses come to be shaped in radically different ways. In refusing to introduce my own conceptual matryoshka doll or to provide yet another cynical reading of the appropriation of the idea of cultural relativism within international politics, I am suggesting that the use of these influential approaches leads to a kind of analytical myopia. But a critique of this kind is never sufficient, no matter how necessary, no matter how much it reveals. For many critical scholars it is the act of shining a light into the interstices that comes most naturally, the act of showing supposedly airtight structures to be actually houses of cards, waiting to be knocked over. It is much more difficult to then go on to erect a truly airtight structure, especially when there are doubts about whether such structures even exist.

But despite these doubts, there are good reasons for thinking that an alternative structure or approach is possible in this case, and not just because we believe one *must* be possible in light of the underlying stakes involved. Yet in order to even begin to consider ways in which relativism and human rights can be reconciled in new ways, we must first acknowledge, as a precondition, that such a project requires a special kind of coalition. I do not mean a coalition of the willing, although its members must, of course, enter into it willingly enough, or at least with sufficient goodwill to see if it can work. Rather, I am referring to an alliance between those two groups that Isaiah Berlin famously described as hedgehogs and foxes. For a fundamentally different human rights framework to be envisioned and then—eventually— implemented in political, legal, and cultural practice, it is first necessary for those on both sides of the universality/relativism divide to reposition themselves, not in relation to universal human rights or cultural difference, but in relation to positions as such.

On the side of human rights, there are the hedgehogs, those who believe in the possibility of discovering, or creating, all-encompassing systems—of knowledge, of morality, of laws. On the side of relativism there are different kinds of foxes, those who are repelled by the very notion of an all-encompassing system and who spend their lives tracking—and relishing in—the forces that pull away from the centripetal tendencies of the system-builders. Foxes know (to invoke Yeats again) that the center cannot hold, and they must learn to find a kind of ironic pleasure in this fact. Hedgehogs, by contrast, have difficulty even envisioning a world without centers, even if it is clear that all existing centers are corrupted, unstable, or in desperate need of reform. In order for foxes and hedgehogs to come together around the problems of relativism and human rights, foxes must be willing to consider the possibility of a unifying framework, even if this means willfully ignoring any number of glaring contradictions or structural dilemmas. Hedgehogs, in turn, must be willing to acknowledge these contradictions and dilemmas and recognize contingency where they would otherwise see timeless certainty. So what would this rapprochement look like? And what would it mean for the future of human rights?

Incompleteness

It is important to first realize that the philosophical approach to relativism and human rights reflects an epistemological political economy in which the deduction of conceptual systems from first principles occupies the highest rung (of power, prestige, and lucidity), one well above the next lower rung, the much more internally diverse category occupied by theory derived from the empirical sciences (which arguably includes anthropology). Now there is nothing wrong with the philosophical approach to relativism and human rights in its own terms, or with the underlying epistemology that it reflects. The problem is that the privileged reliance on this kind of conceptual analysis creates a structural barrier to envisioning a more expansive framework and then translating this framework into different forms of intellectual, political, and social practice.

Consider again the different conceptual analyses of relativism that I describe above. What divides them are the qualitatively different outputs from what is essentially the same process of parsing the idea of relativism into *distinguishable* and *separable* (not distinct and separate) sub-parts. Each one is, to greater or lesser degrees, both coherent in its own terms and, to this extent, persuasive. But even if one were committed to the philosophical approach to relativism and human rights, how would one choose between what are distinct analyses that must jostle for the attention of those who would come to terms with the tension between sameness-as-human-rights and difference-as-relativism? And perhaps more significantly, any philosophical system that purports to resolve—or definitively clarify—the problem of relativism and human rights will be necessarily incomplete: one can always, with perfect logical consistency, extract yet more subcategories from within the idea of relativism or reorder the analytical relationship between relativism's different colors. Who knows—maybe *these* new subcategories are the really important ones, those whose discovery will create the *real* breakthrough?

I think all of this—and more—means that the role of the philosophical within debates over relativism and human rights (and within human rights debates more generally) must be reconfigured, beginning with the way it has been privileged. This does not mean, however, that there is no place for traditional conceptual analysis within the kind of anthropology of human rights I have in mind. Even so, the form this analysis takes will have to be different. It cannot simply be another version of the kind of Cartesian parsing that has dominated the landscape for so long. In fact, I would argue that a quite different strategy should be adopted. Relativism and human rights must be *simplified* conceptually, something that I have attempted to do above. This is because there are core ideas at the heart of both human rights and positions that reject the idea of human rights (whether they can be described as "relativism" or not), and it is at this core level that points of agreement, disagreement, and synthesis should be sought.

Even though there will inevitably be debates over what these core ideas are, or what they mean in practices of different cultural, legal, and institutional kinds, the focus on such intentionally simplified renderings of human rights and relativism would represent a key move, and not only because it is an admission on the part of hedgehogs that at least in this area greater knowledge is not created through more complete—and complex—analytical systems. It also signals that the problem becomes subject to the attention of a much wider circle of people and institutions, a circle that extends well beyond the typical cadre of professional scholars. This broadening through simplicity means that the intuitive appeal of cultural particularity, or the emotional (not rational) dimensions of universalism, among other previously disparaged or underappreciated issues, are suddenly invested with a new sense of urgency and importance.

Of Fashions, Academic and Other

In her essay on the movement of what she calls the "pendulum" that swings back and forth between universalism and relativism, Marie-Bénédicte Dembour makes a point that is hardly ever made, one that I want to build (and end) on here because it has important implications not only for an alternative approach to relativism and human rights but for the anthropology of human rights more generally. In the course of discussing Elvin Hatch's contrarian 1997 apologia on behalf of the "good side of relativism," Dembour decries what she describes as the "footnote 10 phenomenon": the fact that the problems of relativism are usually disdainfully relegated to the footnotes.

In the example she draws from, a "book from a leading law publisher which contained almost 800 pages of text and materials on international human rights" included only one reference to relativism, which it tucked into a "seven-line footnote" with the excuse that it was "an issue of such depth that it falls beyond the scope of this work." As she goes on to explain, "With this acknowledgement, the book is written as if the universality of the human rights provisions it reproduces raises no issues whatsoever. This is consistent with the dominant attitude in the field" (2001:73–74). With the exception of small groups of recalcitrants—she mentions anthropologists—who meet from time to time to discuss the relativism *rara avis*, "the rest of the world [acts as if it] could forget about this fundamental issue. It cannot" (74).

What I want to suggest is that the wider fortunes of relativism, cultural or otherwise, within human rights theory and practice have had more to do with the vicissitudes of cultural and academic politics than with anything we might have learned about relativism itself. How else to explain the "footnote 10 phenomenon," or the way in which the very real dilemmas of relativism have been treated derisively, ignored, and otherwise assigned to the intellectual savage slot? For many professional scholars relativism has never been simply another idea or concept to be pulled apart or reinforced; it has, rather, served as one of the main vehicles through which other battles have been fought. The response to relativism has depended on the broader cause it could serve, or disserve, from the struggle against unilineal evolutionism and eugenics in the prewar period, to the more recent international campaigns to prevent culture-as-nationalism from becoming murderous again, in which relativism is seen as nothing more than a thin curtain behind which lurks the heart of darkness (recall Perry's efforts to "focus the mind"). In both cases, relativism becomes what the anthropologist Sherry Ortner (1973) would describe as a "summarizing key symbol": an ambiguous discursive vessel into which all manner of meanings and interests are poured. Yet the turn to—or against—relativism in each of these moments did nothing to address a core problem like the tension between the centripetal allure of essential human sameness and the centrifugal power of essential human difference.

But if Dembour and I are correct, and "real" relativism remains a "fundamental issue"—indeed, "so fundamental that it is bound to crop up in places where we would not expect it" (she mentions the European Court of Human Rights; 2001:74)—then something must be done to shift it from the realm of the symbolic so that relativism can denote—once again? perhaps for the first time?—what remain key problems at the heart of the postwar human rights project. In order for that to happen, relativism cannot be allowed to simply wax and wane with the fate of academic and political fashions. In fact, relativism is only peripherally an academic issue, since what is at stake touches on the meaning of culture, the enduring specter of imperialism, racism, and the inequalities of power within the international system. Indeed, it is precisely at that moment when academics are declaring the problem of relativism obsolete, marginal to real issues, or logically absurd that we can be assured that the problem is most current, central, and intellectually challenging, and thus most in need of the attention of a wider range of critical voices.

Chapter 4

Culture on the Half Shell

Universal Rights through the Back Door

W HEN NICO JACOBELLIS took a chance and decided to screen Louis Malle's *Les Amants* at the Continental Theater in Cleveland Heights, Ohio, he must have thought he was doing the residents of the east Cleveland suburbs a favor. Only two years before, in 1957, the Continental had shown the film *And God Created Woman*, which launched the career of Brigitte Bardot and caused an uproar over the movie's eroticism, most famously symbolized by the so called table scene, in which Bardot's merry dance scandalized a nation and titillated a generation weighed down by the moral yoke of 1950s America. Jacobellis and the Continental had weathered the storm the first time, and anyway, Jacobellis must have thought, why should a place like Greenwich Village be the only center of the avant garde? Should Ohioans have to settle for *The Mickey Mouse Club* or the latest episode of *The Milton Berle Show*? So instead of Annette Funicello, Jacobellis brought Jeanne Moreau to the God-fearing moviegoers of the Buckeye State.

For his troubles, he was arrested under an Ohio statute for "possessing and exhibiting an obscene film." After a conviction in the lower courts, and failed appeals all the way through the Supreme Court of Ohio—whose members were apparently not students of the French New Wave, at least not publicly— this theater manager from Cleveland Heights took his case to the U.S. Supreme Court. In their infinite, but bitterly divided, wisdom, the men in black reversed the Ohio courts after what must have been an interesting private showing of the film in presumably a chamber of the Court itself. As Justice Brennan solemnly observed, "We have viewed the film . . . and we conclude that it is not obscene" (378 U.S. 184, 196, 1964).

In his one-paragraph concurring opinion, Potter Stewart expressed sympathy for the other members of the Court, who took up the "task of trying to define what may be indefinable": the meaning of obscenity, a class of speech not protected by the First Amendment to the U.S. Constitution. As for Stewart, he refused to offer his own definition of obscenity, writing instead: "I know it when I see it, and the motion picture involved in this case is not that" (197). Stewart's quip has taken on a life of it own, of course, and has come to represent a way of saying there are certain very important categories in life that simply cannot be adequately captured through the normal process of analysis, definitional or otherwise. But I take this anecdote to mean something else, something that, oddly enough, bears directly on several key problems at the heart of contemporary human rights.

Apart from its obvious First Amendment implications, *Jacobellis v. Ohio* can also be read as a states' rights case or, even more broadly, as a case that illustrates the tension between cultural norms and what look (and act) much like human rights—those fundamental entitlements guaranteed to all U.S. citizens irrespective of race, religion, gender, age, or political affiliation. Should local communities have to tolerate the kind of culture that they found abhorrent simply because "society at large," as the Court put it, had a different perspective? Wasn't "society at large" just a cipher for a much smaller—even if influential—group of people, those who could be found in the bastions of the economic and social elite of the northeast corridor? And wasn't the United States simply too diverse across its many regions for the Court to take a general measure of an abstracted "society at large," one that didn't trample on the expectations and traditions of wide swaths of the nation?

This battle was being fought by the Court in many different areas at the same time, and just as in *Jacobellis*, across the range of its jurisprudence it came down on the side of "society at large" as against particular *societies* at any one place in time, whether they were in Selma, Alabama, or in Cleveland Heights. In other words, local communities were not going to be allowed—legally, that is—to stand in the way of progress in the United States, progress toward realizing in practice the set of basic rights enshrined in the U.S. Constitution, rights that expressed the values that any civilized people *ought* to hold dear.[1]

So here we have the old clash between cultural particularity and universal—in the guise of American—values, with the armies of the universal marching triumphally across the land, backed by political authority, the force of law (in the form of court orders, and even the National Guard if necessary), and the more subtle powers of moral suasion. But even though there are many rich and suggestive parallels between the Warren Court's expansion of national/universal rights at the expense of community values and more recent struggles over the relationship between universal human rights and culture, these are not the links I want to develop here. Rather, I want to take Stewart's pithy observation in *Jacobellis* in a different direction. If "culture" continues to be a key topic—we might even say problem—for human rights theory and practice, this is partly due to the fact that, as in the case of obscenity, very few people seem to know what it is, although its presence is keenly felt in all sorts of ways. Compounding this puzzle is the fact that there are at least three distinct dimensions to it, all of which come together to make culture an ongoing thorn in the side of human rights.

First there is the problem of defining culture, which involves so much more than a simple debate over meaning. The accounts of these debates follow a traditional master narrative, which has become so standardized, so conventional, that it has almost become an analytical mantra. It begins with a brief foray into the intellectual history of the word itself, which takes us into different early origins, usually in the nineteenth century, and typically through either the English "culture" or the German "*Kultur*," or both. In many quarters the English culture stayed true to its Latin beginnings (via Old French) as "*cultura*," which meant the tending or nurturing of land (both "cultivation" and "cult" are derived from *cultura*).

Thus when Matthew Arnold writes in *Culture and Anarchy*, his treatise on the subject, that "the great men of culture are those who have had a passion . . . for carrying from one end of society to the other . . . the best knowledge, the best ideas of their time" (2006 [1869]:53), he is pointing to a sense of "culture" as both intellectual or artistic refinement and the willingness to "humanise [culture] to make it efficient outside the clique of the cultivated and learned." This meaning became dominant within the Anglo-American world during the Victorian era, and it is still a common way in which people understand "culture"—thus high culture, low culture, "John Smith is eminently *cultured*," and so on. Even though Arnold's work was meant, in part, as an argument for the moral benefits of culture for the greater number, in fact it was always a relatively small segment of society that had the time, ability, or desire to pursue "the best knowledge, the best ideas of [its] time." So "culture" became both elitist and socially programmatic.

The German "*Kultur*," by contrast, developed a different set of connotations. Although the word itself shares the same Latin root as the English "culture" (something that can be seen in a number of different German words—e.g., *Kult, kultivieren, kultiviert*), "*Kultur*" encompassed a much broader range of ideas and practices, so much so that it came to define Germanness itself, or at least an ideal version of it (one, it is important to note, shaped and promoted by the state). *Kultur* in this register complemented other ideas of the time, for example the Hegelian version of the *Volksgeist*, or "spirit of the people," which emphasized both uniqueness and the way in which a people's spirit, or culture, developed within history (a process that could be investigated scientifically and explained objectively).[2]

It was this idea of culture that formed the basis for the sciences that developed, in part, to explain how distinct groups of people emerged, how they differed one from the other, and how they related to each other within a broader evolutionary framework. Anthropology, especially as it emerged in the United States, is the best example of how this version of culture was taken up and systematized. Franz Boas, the "father of American anthropology," was a German heavily influenced—as most nineteenth-century intellectuals were—by Hegel's philosophy, which explains why a concern with culture became the centerpiece of the academic discipline he shaped so indelibly.[3]

All of this comes together—so the master narrative goes—to produce an anthropological definition of culture that has been taught to thousands of people through hundreds of textbooks, who have then introduced this understanding of culture into thousands of different contexts, so that by now it has become the dominant sense of culture around the world. A typical statement is the following: culture is "the system of shared beliefs, values, customs, behaviours, and artifacts that the members of society use to cope with their world and with one another, and that are transmitted from generation to generation through learning" (Bates and Plog 1990:7). Although popular media, artists, and others continue to use "culture" in the much more restricted sense, it is the *anthropological* version that most people adopt across the widest possible range of regional, linguistic, and other contexts (a version, by the way, that necessarily incorporates the Arnoldian).

But the twists and turns of intellectual history are nothing if not ironic, and at this point the culture master narrative goes in an unexpected and puzzling direction. The anthropological approach to culture was, in part, a way of democratizing the understanding of it: people might live in a range of circumstances within different kinds of collectivities around the world, but everyone had *culture*, everyone was born into a "system of shared beliefs, values, customs, behaviours, and artifacts." These systems occupied vastly different locations within broader global alignments of power, obviously, and it was a constant battle—as Boas and his students, for example, soon discovered—to prevent others (colonial administrators, religious missionaries, travel writers) from comparing these systems one with another and making unfounded and harmful judgments about their relative worth. But the anthropological definition of culture was developed, in part, to make such invidious comparisons more difficult. The key move here, in fact, was not the assertion that people shared beliefs, values, and behaviors with others. More important was the idea that these beliefs and practices were brought together within a discrete system, one that was transmitted from generation to generation. This was what made especially the American anthropological approach to culture so radical: it placed the emphasis not on the way specific collectivities differed from all others, but on the particular system through which collectivities emerged within history and changed over time.

Although the culture concept was developed, in part, as a critique of prevailing colonial relations of production that were based on a quite different framework for understanding and, even more, justifying, human diversity, it eventually became apparent that the culture-as-system idea had its own problems. First, when political conditions were right (or wrong, as it were), it was impossible to prevent states, particular interest groups, and others from viewing the diversity of cultures hierarchically, with predictable (and, at times, terrible) consequences. And more importantly (again, according to the culture master narrative), academics themselves began to notice that the culture concept was not doing the work it was, in part, designed for: to provide an alternative account of human diversity, one that would have the effect of destabilizing existing relations of global power. If anything, as the struggles against colonialism took on greater urgency during the 1950s and 1960s, it slowly dawned on at least some anthropologists that the idea of culture could not accommodate what was hoped would be a future of profound transformation in human relations on a global scale. The basic idea of the system pushed in the opposite direction: it was static, insular, and centripetal, everything that a revolution wasn't.

Several things happened next to "culture," but two are of particular importance for my purposes here. Some academics, including anthropologists, decided to respond to these problems by expanding the definition of culture, ironically by reinvesting it with a set of connotations that actually brought it closer to its Victorian associations with art, literature, and intellectual production, although not the high examples of these particular expressions of the human experience but rather their middle and low cousins (which had been suppressed by the nineteenth-century advocates of "culture" like Arnold).

Since the anthropological version of culture had, for historical reasons, come to be associated with only *certain* systems of shared beliefs, values, and behaviors, those to be found on the receiving end of Western imperialism, it was important, so the argument went, for "cultural studies" to be undertaken in the Western metropoles themselves in order to demonstrate the way cultures (and expression *of* culture) interconnected *across* political, geographical, linguistic, and other recognizable boundaries. Culture here was still largely a thing, a system. Its range of application might have expanded; the locations of culture might have grown to include the boardrooms of major corporations and the street corners of East London. But culture was still a noun, just one that was now never modified by "primitive."

Somewhat later—again, so the culture master narrative goes—came the cataclysmic year of 1989, which unleashed the forces of globalization, which in turn broke down those boundaries that had always been closest to human identity—the boundaries of culture. The result was the emergence of global or transnational cultures, perhaps best symbolized by cultures in diaspora, those hybrid and essentially dynamic cultures that were no longer connected to territory. It was a small step from the emergence of transnational cultures, a process that accelerated rapidly through the 1990s, to the withering away of culture itself. When the world is characterized by interconnected flows of information, relations of production, political ideologies, and aspirations for particular political (democracy) and legal-moral (human rights) conditions, what use is a concept that presupposes fixed social boundaries that serve to encapsulate distinct systems of shared beliefs, values, and behaviors?

The traditional anthropological account of culture had become a centripetal anachronism in a centrifugal world. And it wasn't even the problem that centers could no longer hold; it was that globalization had created a world of centers, or potential ones. And since "center" has meaning only in relation to other points of oppositional reference (like "margin" or periphery"), the center disappears when they do. So too with culture. The concept had emerged as a way to explain the many different systems within which human beings sought collective meaning and identity. But globalization was creating a *single* system, one with many different variations, to be sure, but a global cultural system nonetheless. So if "culture" retained any meaning whatsoever, so the master narrative continues, it was as a way of describing the many *processes* through which cultures around the world were dissolving into a single heterodox transnational culture, an interconnected network that was reconfiguring the way the global landscape was understood. Culture, that is to say, had become a verb.

For many anthropologists, this proved to be simply too much. Much better to let the idea of culture fade away than to try and bend and stretch it to the point where it no longer had any explanatory value whatsoever or where its use would have to be accompanied by a kind of wink and nod—No, I'm not really talking about *culture*, but I'm using the word simply as a heuristic, or because others—those who haven't been brought up to date—continue to use it, or because its use can stand in for a more time-consuming analysis of the *real* changes that mark these early-twenty-first-century times.

Eventually others caught on to these anthropological troubles with culture, something that was reflected by the sudden appearance of the dreaded quotation marks every time "culture" (QED) was mentioned. The concept of culture was henceforth officially problematized, under attack, subject to the sustained attentions of critical scholars across a range of disciplines and interests. Yet even with the ubiquitous quotation marks, the referent, that which culture was meant to denote, looked very much like those old systems of values and beliefs, modified of course to reflect current political, economic, and ideological realities. The anthropologists can't really be serious, these ambivalent quotation marks seem to be saying. Do they really believe that cultures are disappearing, and not just in certain parts of the world where cultural survival has always been tenuous? How to explain the fact that after the end of the Cold War group identity, framed in exclusionary—that is, *cultural*—terms, had become an apparently more, not less, significant dynamic? And if the anthropologists—those mavens of culture who identified with the marginalized and the excluded and who did their best to serve as a conduit for these excluded voices—abandoned culture, who would speak for "it" (and, thus, "them")?

Despite these rhetorical worries, anthropologists pressed ahead and in the process helped to create a new field of study in which the object was those "fluid complexes of intersubjective meanings and practices" (née Culture) that spanned national boundaries, were "contested" (another anthropological term of art), and avoided, above all, the horrors of "fallacious reductionism" that Preis alludes to in her 1996 article that we encountered in chapter 3. This vacating of the field has, among other things, led to ironic exchanges like the one between Donnelly and Preis, in which the political scientist, whose strength is "conceptual analysis," is forced to carry the banner of culture. After all, as Donnelly says, "There are undeniable differences between, say, Tokyo, Tehran, and Texas and the 'cultures' of which they are exemplars" (2003:88) (not to mention, we might add, the differences between, say, Las Vegas, Lhasa, and Lisbon).

So the uses and understandings of culture have themselves become "complex, variable, multivocal, and, above all, contested" (Donnelly 2003:86), the different implications of which for human rights I am going to explore at some length throughout this chapter. But I said above that there are three distinct dimensions to the problem of culture that bear on human rights. The second is equally acute but can be more quickly described. Assuming that an approach to, or definition of, culture can be agreed on for specific purposes, we quickly face an empirical question: how to decide what comes within a culture, however expansively we define it, or however fluid, contested, or porous it is. This problem becomes greater the further we move from the traditional understandings of culture, so that by the time we arrive at fluid and contested complexes and perpetually unfolding transnational ethnoscapes it becomes almost impossible to link culture to anything concrete enough to study empirically or apprehend beyond the analytical imagination itself. (Perhaps this is why the culture concept persists despite an earnest desire to see it transformed beyond all recognition.)

And scholars like Donnelly, who are sympathetic to the more recent anthropological critique of culture, are also understandably hesitant to offer up their own hardened cultural categories, whether in order to compare them with those suggested by international human rights law or otherwise. The result is that there is confusion about *both* what culture means in different contexts and what specific cultures—however defined—consist of. This second dimension to the problem of culture is even more pronounced outside of academia.

Take this example, chosen (almost) at random. In his review of a new biography of Henry Ward Beecher, the historian Michael Kazin (2006) commends the book's author for her "deep knowledge of 19th century culture and politics." At another point he (quoting from the book) refers to the impact of Beecher on "American culture." And in yet another passage Kazin discusses Beecher's "embrace of the new culture of mass consumption."

Here we have the full range of possible cultures, including one that has not made its appearance yet, all used as if they were unproblematically interchangeable. We have a version of the more limited Victorian approach to culture ("culture and politics," although it is not clear what level of art, literature, and intellectual production he has in mind); we have an example of *Kultur* as developed within (especially American) anthropology ("American culture," which would *include* politics); and finally we have yet a third type of culture, the most restricted, one that defines narrow types of ephemeral social practice (the "new culture of mass consumption"). But although this conflation of cultures does not stand up to even the most cursory analytical scrutiny, the odd thing is that one can read this book review and somehow *know* what Kazin means, even if one cannot explain it. Again, I come back to where I began: although Kazin—and apparently his readers—does not seem to be able to define culture with any consistency, he knows it when he sees it.

The third dimension to the problem of culture that bears on human rights is more complicated, and I will only describe it briefly at this point. This is the problem of legitimacy, and perhaps ethics: who speaks for culture? This rhetorical question embodies both the descriptive and the normative aspects of the problem—who *does* speak for culture and who *ought* to speak for culture. As we will see, this problem bedevils human rights in particularly intractable ways, since the field of discourse is often crowded with competing notions of what culture means conceptually and, even more, how values supposedly derived from particular cultures clash, or not, with those expressed in dominant symbols of human rights like the UDHR.[4] When leaders of an ethnic-political movement assert that their culture is under attack by international institutions, and then go on to describe the imperiled facets of this culture in great detail, are they wrong at some level?

But wait, the rootless cosmopolitan human rights scholar might be tempted to say in response to this assertion of culture—what you are describing does not exist, cannot exist, not in 2009, because what you are describing is a bounded, static, insular, conservative *culture*, and systems of values, beliefs, and behaviors of this kind have gone the way of the dodo. You don't actually have a culture in this sense (the cosmopolitan scholar continues); rather, your life is connected to many other lives in different parts of the world, people with whom you have just as much in common as you might *think* you do with the farmer or the factory worker next door. In fact, what you think of as uniquely Japanese/Iranian/Texan values (the alliteration has disappeared, but see Donnelly above) or patterns of behavior or customs has changed so quickly that it does not define you in any meaningful sense. That Coke bottle that fell from the sky changed everything, don't you know, and if you are watching CNN in Spanish instead of listening to the shaman describe the dangers of walking at night between villages, that is clear evidence that you are now living in a fluid complex, one in which you find meaning intersubjectively—and your fellow subjects could be anywhere.

The response from the fervent advocates of culture in its most rigid, exclusionary, rooted sense is likely to be a variation on two themes. The first expresses a complete lack of comprehension that something so obvious as the empirical fact of culture, and thus cultural difference, would for some reason need to be buried under so many layers of conceptual ambiguity. The second understands the impulse that might lead cosmopolitan intellectuals to react so strongly to the stubborn fact of culture but says, in effect, you are wrong and we are right and, by the way, we are willing to die for our culture. Are you for yours? But can both be right, either descriptively or normatively? Can the post-1989 globalized world have experienced a general withering away of culture for all the reasons I have described above, while at the same time experiencing the spread, or at least the re-entrenchment, of culture in the anthropological sense, the proliferation of those distinct systems that are "transmitted from generation to generation" and that therefore constitute the basis for collective meaning and identity?

Codifying Culture

It is understandable that the problem of culture would have been seen in a certain light in the immediate aftermath of the Second World War. The rise of fascism in Italy and Germany and its eventual metamorphosis into state programs of genocide and racial murder were directly connected to the same nineteenth-century philosophical and ideological ferment that produced and refined the notion of *Kultur*. Indeed, as Hannah Arendt has shown (1951), although the Nazis appropriated ideas like "nation" and "the people" when it suited their wider political and military purposes, these appropriations were not entirely instrumental; rather, for their brand of quasi mysticism to be so effective it had to be deeply rooted in a broader ideological framework that ostensibly reflected the deepest imperatives of the German people, of which politics was only one—albeit central—expression.[5]

So it was no surprise that although the committee working on what would become the Universal Declaration of Human Rights did its best to take account of different legal, moral, and religious traditions in forging a political consensus around human rights, most of its work was pulled in the opposite direction. In fact, what resulted was quite clearly and formally an attempt to construct a *trans*-cultural legal and moral framework, one that would serve as an ultimate check on the abuses of culture manifested as nationalism. At best, then, the advocates of culture in its most expansive register were ignored during the drafting of this most foundational of human rights documents; at worst they were seen as barbarians just outside the gates, to be intentionally ostracized by the circle of international lawyers and philosophers who were largely responsible for the development of human rights in the post-1948 period (as Messer has suggested, 2006).

Despite this, culture did manage to find its way into the Universal Declaration of Human Rights, although in a form that demonstrates how controversial it was from the very beginning of the postwar human rights project. It makes its first appearance in article 22, the UDHR article that perhaps most illustrates on its face (i.e., without any statutory interpretation) the essentially political nature of this quintessential symbol of international human rights. All of the compromises and complicated political alignments and negotiations are reflected in this torturously worded provision.[6]

> Everyone, as a member of society, has the right to social security and is entitled
> to realization, through national effort and international co-operation and in ac-
> cordance with the organization and resources of each State, of the economic,
> social, and cultural rights indispensable for his dignity and the free development
> of his personality.

Leaving aside the obvious problem of how a supposed human right, something that all human beings are imbued with "without distinction of any kind," including those made on the basis of the "political, jurisdictional or international status of the country or territory to which a person belongs" (article 2), can also be dependent on something as arbitrary as the "organization and resources of each State," the reference to "cultural rights" here is clearly not meant to invoke the earlier anthropological understanding of culture. Rather, the culture in "cultural rights" takes us back to the Victorian sense of "the best knowledge, the best ideas" of a particular *member nation-state*, which is a way of framing culture that immediately raises a whole set of questions. Assuming cultural diversity within nation-states, how can international cooperation and national resources be mobilized in ways that do not privilege some cultural expressions over others? What does it mean to "realize" a right to artistic, intellectual, or other creative expressions (i.e., "culture")? Which of these forms of expression are "indispensable," and who is to decide? The nation-state, on whose resources this right depends? Leaders of ethnic groups or other collectivities? Or, as article 22 seems to suggest, the individual herself?

In any event, the suspicion that a politically compromised version of culture made its way into the Universal Declaration is confirmed in the second, and last, place in which it appears—in article 27, which asserts that "everyone has the right to freely participate in the cultural life of the community, to enjoy the arts and to share in scientific advancement and its benefits." In his analysis of this article, Morsink (1999) focuses on two aspects: the way it frames the right to participate in culture as a kind of property right (something that is more clearly indicated in the article's second part, which refers to the "material interests resulting from any scientific, literary or artistic production of which [the right holder] is the author"); and that it recognizes a right that has both collective ("of the community") and individual dimensions ("everyone has the right").

But what Morsink does not discuss is the fact that what is meant by "cultural life" is left entirely to the imagination. If article 22 is compared with article 27, it is clear that culture is apparently distinct—according to the drafters—from economic and social activities. Moreover, the phrasing in article 27 can be read to either *distinguish* culture from the arts and science or see the arts and science as *examples* of culture. And why were economy and society left out of article 27, while science and art are not mentioned in article 22? Was this confused rendering of culture intentional? Although some measure of ambiguity inevitably creeps into the process of drafting legal documents, the puzzling invocations of culture in the UDHR cannot be explained so easily.

Yet Morsink does provide a clue to the likely source of this ambiguity, even if it cannot be extracted from the language of the declaration itself. We have already encountered John Humphrey, in chapter 2; it should be recalled that he was the Canadian law professor who is credited as the principal drafter of the declaration, the one whose personal imprint is most visible in its phrasing, jurisprudence, and style. As Morsink explains, "Humphrey had almost no clear constitutional precedents before him" in deciding to include a right to participate in culture (1999:217). Nevertheless, "the Humphreys" (John and his wife, Jeanne) "were deeply involved in the cultural life of Montreal and other places they lived" (218). This cultural life included entertaining "numerous intellectuals and artists"; helping to found the Contemporary Arts Society of Montreal; and in general (as related in his memoirs), taking time to attend "cultural events" like plays.

So the "culture" that was codified—however ambiguously—in the Universal Declaration of Human Rights was tantamount to what would have been known in Canadian polite society circa 1948 as "the arts": those activities that are sometimes described, and not only in parody, as "high culture" (see Bourdieu 1984). And although the meaning of "cultural life" is certainly susceptible to a broader range of interpretations, we can at least pinpoint fairly accurately what *Humphrey* understood by culture: those preeminent expressions of a very narrow sliver of fine and performance art, the kind befitting the patronage of McGill University's Gale Professor of Roman Law and his wife. We can be fairly certain, therefore, that article 27 creates (or recognizes) a human right to experience the never-ending mysteries of *King Lear*. But what about the paintings of Jackson Pollock? Would the Contemporary Arts Society of Montreal have considered *Number One 1948* to be art, and thus an expression of the kind of "cultural life" to which a person should have a right protected under international law?

The 1966 International Covenant on Economic, Social and Cultural Rights (ICESCR) was the international legal mechanism through which the so-called socioeconomic rights in the Universal Declaration of Human Rights were made legally binding on member-states through the treaty signature and ratification process. This was the next significant appearance of culture within a major international human rights instrument, and its circumscribed meanings had not changed from those of articles 22 and 27 of the declaration.[7] Indeed, with the exception of a few minor shifts in phrasing, article 15 of the ICESCR is identical to article 27: states parties recognize a (human) right to participate in "cultural life," benefit from science, and have a property interest in intellectual or artistic production of which a person is the author. Although a full discussion would take me too far afield, it is perhaps worth noting that the laborious process through which the ICESCR finally entered into force in 1976, almost twenty years after the Commission on Human Rights had finished its work on it, illustrates perhaps more than anything else the way political considerations have traditionally dominated the postwar international human rights system.[8]

The meaning of culture within international law was altered by the 1972 Convention Concerning the Protection of the World Cultural and Natural Heritage (the World Heritage Convention). Here "culture" was disassociated from living groups of people and linked to the past in the form of "cultural heritage." With the 1972 convention, and its subsequent oversight by UNESCO's World Heritage Committee, culture was differentiated on separate, but no less exclusionary, grounds than those implied in Humphrey's "cultural life" in article 27. And this was not simply because culture was here identified with only the most visible and remarkable symbols of the past. A competitive hierarchy of culture was created, one in which not all examples of cultural heritage were deemed worthy of protection under international law. As article 1 of the convention says, only those expressions of cultural heritage that are "of outstanding universal value from the point of view of history, art or science" will fall within the "effective system of collective protection . . . organized on a permanent basis . . . in accordance with modern scientific methods."

So the great pyramids of Giza are in; Pink's Hot Dog stand on La Brea Avenue in Los Angeles ("A Hollywood Legend Since 1939"), perhaps the most famous hot dog stand in the United States, is out. The Royal Botanic Gardens at Kew are in; the Mercado de Hechicería, or witches' market, in La Paz, Bolivia (where everything from coca leaves to llama fetuses is on offer), is out. In other words, the primary cultural organization of the United Nations passes cultural heritage, and thus culture, through a sieve, with the result that only a tiny portion of Humphrey's cultural life of communities remains. And since the legal and financial mechanisms of UNESCO have become the principal means through which culture and human rights come even remotely together within international law—that is, in the absence of any enforcement whatsoever of article 15 of the ICESCR—the real problems that culture (in the earlier anthropological sense) poses for human rights remain unacknowledged.[9]

·   ·   ·

THESE, THEN, remain the ways culture has been codified within the international human rights system. In relation to the different meanings of culture, we have seen that the UDHR and the ICESCR adopt a narrow—and at times confusing—construction, one that was shaped by an essentially Victorian understanding in which culture encompasses only a tiny and heavily normative slice of human artistic and intellectual expression. But if culture has traditionally occupied this narrow and ambiguous place within international human rights, there have been much more recent signs that its status might be changing.

Again, the impetus has come from UNESCO and can be best illustrated by the 2001 UNESCO Universal Declaration on Cultural Diversity (UDCD). Even though the declaration is not legally binding on member-states, its invocation of culture is startlingly different from almost all earlier—and existing—examples within the international system (and one that stands in stark contrast to UNESCO's own prior usage). The UDCD adopts a variation on the earlier *anthropological* definition of culture, one that dramatically expands its scope and raises the stakes for human rights. Culture "should be regarded as the set of distinctive spiritual, material, intellectual and emotional features of society or a social group, and that it encompasses, in addition to art and literature, lifestyles, ways of living together, value systems, traditions and beliefs."

This is culture as a bounded sum total, one that would seem to encompass economic, scientific, social—indeed, all possible—"ways of living together." Moreover, this new "universal declaration" (a framing that evokes the UDHR in its grandeur and sweep) pushes back against the unifying impulse that was so essential to postwar international institutions. Instead, the UDCD goes to great, almost ethnographic lengths to explain the ways in which cultures differ from one another and, even more, how cultural diversity—not the unity of the human experience *across* cultures—is an essential ingredient of human development and fulfillment.

Yet even as the UDCD extols the benefits of cultural diversity in a laundry list that includes everything from fostering creativity to facilitating "international cooperation and solidarity," dark clouds appear on the horizon as soon as the declaration addresses the relationship between culture and human rights. Here is what article 4 asserts (in part):

> The defence of cultural diversity is an ethical imperative, inseparable from respect for human dignity. It implies a commitment to human rights and fundamental freedoms. . . . [But] no one may invoke cultural diversity to infringe upon human rights guaranteed by international law, nor to limit their scope.

But as anthropologists and others have shown in great detail, the meanings of both "human" and "dignity" are themselves part of those "distinctive spiritual, material, intellectual and emotional features" of a group that form part of its culture. If this is true, how then can "human dignity" stand apart from "cultural diversity," as article 4 suggests? And if one may not invoke cultural diversity as an argument against complying with provisions of international human rights law that guarantee, say, social security or the equal treatment of men and women, then how can it be claimed that cultural diversity is coextensive with a "commitment to human rights"? In fact, the kind of anthropological cultural diversity written into the 2001 UDCD is prima facie violative of wide swaths of existing international human rights law. Now we can understand why the restricted version of culture codified in the UDHR does not—and cannot—lead to similar problems. When it is only *King Lear* that is at issue, there can hardly be a clash between culture and human rights.

In the next section, I direct the focus away from international human rights law to consider the way culture has been treated by human rights scholars and activists.

The Vanguard of Overlapping Consensus

In his 1993 book *Political Liberalism*, John Rawls argued that his earlier theory of distributive justice was not meant as a comprehensive replacement framework but was rather a way of establishing the means through which people or groups that held to *different* comprehensive theories could mutually guarantee minimum rights and freedoms through a kind of ethical compromise. Rawls called the achievement of this compromise the "overlapping consensus." The basic idea is that people who hold to quite different moral, legal, and political positions can find those points at which apparently divergent systems intersect or overlap. Rawls was interested in the way divergent political systems could nevertheless overlap at the point at which people living within them agree to respect and tolerate certain common minimum standards, which should be hardened into rights, including the standard that says differences should be respected and protected (which acts as a kind of precondition). This willingness to tolerate differences, while respecting the points of overlap, was for Rawls the essence of fairness and the foundation—or definition of—justice.[10]

I invoke Rawls here because within the field of interdisciplinary human rights scholarship the problem of culture has been approached quite similarly. A committed vanguard of scholars has arisen to resolve, in a sense, the tension between cultural diversity and the universalist program of international human rights by identifying those points at which cultural traditions overlap in a way that reconciles them to both the idea and the substantive content of international human rights. As with Rawls, this intercultural approach to human rights (it goes by different names) proceeds by describing *minimal* areas of normative congruence: for example, while something like a human right to paid vacation from work might not resonate with every cultural or legal tradition (yes in France, no in the United States), something like a right to life or bodily integrity would (even if these are qualified or modified in context). The techniques or arguments used to achieve an inter- or cross-cultural consensus on human rights span a wide range, from the diatopical and (eventually) dialogical hermeneutics of Raimon Panikkar (1979, 1982), to the empirical case-study method of Abdullahi Ahmed An-Na'im and the other contributors to the influential 1992 volume *Human Rights in Cross-Cultural Perspectives*, a work that perhaps best illustrates both the promise and the difficulties of trying to solve the problem of culture and human rights through intercultural consensus.[11]

The hermeneutic strand draws from a long tradition of exegesis and the comparative analysis of especially religious texts. And as with the orthodox hermeneutic tradition itself, the work of Panikkar and others employs nuanced interpretive strategies in order to elicit what is believed to be a set of core cross-cultural values, which have become burdened under the many layers of historical-cultural evolution. Nevertheless, the hermeneutic approach to human rights can do its work only if an underlying cultural unity of mankind is assumed a priori, as a first principle. (For Panikkar, this unity goes deeper, to include both spiritual and psychic dimensions.) Although a nod is given to the empirical dimensions of intercultural normative coherence, in the end the hermeneutic approach to culture and human rights remains essentially philosophical and, we might say, critical.

This is perhaps to be expected, since like the broader hermeneutic tradition from which it is derived, the object here is to achieve understanding through the study of different—and often clashing—structures of meaning. It is difficult to demonstrate empirically that the UDHR and the Qur'an, for example, are *actually* in agreement in particular ways. Rather, one must argue how, among a range of possible meanings, those that demonstrate intercultural or intertextual convergence lead to a deeper, more compelling, more humane understanding. It is, of course, also an intensely political claim that a major source of cultural values like the Qur'an (or the UDHR, for that matter) is *essentially* multivocal; nevertheless, as a matter of epistemology, the hermeneutic path through the thickets of cultural diversity toward human rights is not possible without it.

The case-study approach to intercultural consensus on human rights begins with the same set of basic assumptions about underlying cultural unity (expressed with greater or lesser degrees of certainty and framed in relation to wider political or ethical projects that are both acknowledged and unacknowledged). The difference is in the way cross-cultural agreement on certain aspects of international human rights is established. To a certain extent, the philosophical basis for this case-study framework was outlined by scholars like Alison Dundes Renteln, who argued quite rightly that the question of cross-cultural legitimacy for human rights was an empirical one. Even though Dundes Renteln remained agnostic about what such a cross-cultural project would yield, there was a supposition that cross-cultural legitimacy for human rights could, in fact, be established. With this supposition as a starting point, human rights scholars in the vanguard of overlapping consensus work to reveal the ways in which major human rights instruments like the UDHR can be harmonized with apparently divergent normative traditions.

One of the most able and dedicated scholars working toward cross-cultural understandings of international human rights is Abdullahi Ahmed An-Na'im, who has developed several important positions across a number of different studies, most of which focus on the relationship between human rights and Islam.[12] As Richard Falk has correctly observed, if a cross-cultural approach to international human rights requires "cultural rethinking, reinterpretation, and internal dialogue," these have been "powerfully and creatively embodied" in the work of An-Na'im (1992:49).

An-Na'im develops an explicitly pragmatic approach to the problems—what he calls "issues and concerns"—surrounding culture and human rights, one that unfolds along both vertical and horizontal axes. Both of these encourage "cultural re-interpretation and reconstruction" as a way of "enhancing the universal legitimacy of human rights" (1992:3). The vertical dimension is the process through which cultures change as a result of what he calls an "internal . . . discourse," one that is not unidirectional. Rather, reconstruction is nurtured through a kind of thoroughgoing cultural critique that ramifies up and down through all levels of society because of "intellectual and scholarly debate, artistic and literary expressions of alternative views . . . and political and social action furthering those views" (1992:4).

On the horizontal plane, scholars and activists seeking to foster the "authenticity and legitimacy" of human rights within the framework of cultural tradition must also engage in *cross*-cultural dialogue in order to "introduce into [cultures] some elements of a human rights agenda" (4). Like internal cultural discourse, cross-cultural dialogue on human rights is made possible by the fact that "cultures are constantly changing and evolving," in part "through interaction with other cultures" (4). This means that cultures are structurally receptive to those who might seek to "influence the direction of . . . change and evolution from outside" (4). This is a not a naive blueprint for moral or cultural imperialism, however, since the "process must be both mutual between cultures and sensitive to the needs of internal authenticity and legitimacy" (5). Nevertheless, it is a delicate balancing act that is difficult to achieve in the best of circumstances.

On the one hand, An Na'im says that "it should not be difficult" to influence cultural change in the direction of human rights consciousness from the outside. But on the other hand, he is adamant that external scholars and activists "must never even *appear* to be imposing external values in support of the human rights standards they seek to legitimize within the framework of [a particular] culture" (5; emphasis added). So although An-Na'im insists that global power imbalances should not drive the process of shaping cultural change on behalf of a human rights agenda, he also recognizes that inequality *will* at times find its way into the cross-cultural exchange.

Like other scholars working within the intercultural approach to human rights, An-Na'im bases his cross-cultural framework on a traditional—i.e., anthropological—definition of culture (see also An-Na'im 2006; An-Na'im and Deng 1990). As he explains in his essay on the cross-cultural meaning of "cruel, inhuman, or degrading treatment or punishment," he uses culture in its "widest meaning": to refer to the "totality of values, institutions, and forms of behavior transmitted within a society, as well as the material goods produced by man [and woman]. . . . This wide concept of culture covers *Weltanschauung* [worldview], ideologies, and cognitive behaviors" (1992:22–23).[13] Notice the ironies here. Intercultural human rights scholars take the fact of culture in its earlier anthropological sense as a given (that is, those distinct systems of "shared beliefs, values, customs, behaviours, and artifacts" that are transmitted from generation to generation). They then employ a range of different theoretical and methodological techniques in order to use preexisting cultural receptivity to at least some human rights as a way to open the door to the full spectrum.

At the same time, however, contemporary anthropologists and other specialists in the study and conceptualization of culture have been busy telling us that the post–Cold War global landscape has rendered the traditional meaning of culture—the one that anthropologists themselves developed and popularized—

problematic at best, meaningless at worst. How can scholars work to shape the evolution of cultural traditions in the direction of human rights if the existence of culture itself is in doubt? If the world is now characterized by transnational flows of people and information (including what used to be called "culture"), how can there be cross-cultural dialogue at all, on human rights or otherwise? In the next section, we consider yet other ways in which the problems of culture have been examined by human rights scholars.

Into the Rabbit Hole

In the introduction to her edited volume *Globalization and Human Rights* (2002), the political scientist Alison Brysk paints a picture of what the world looks like now, the type of place that has transformed the meaning of cultures—and the traditions that formerly constituted them—beyond all recognition. The contemporary world is dominated now by "transnational flows of people, production, investment, information, ideas, and authority (not new, but stronger and faster)" (2002:1). This description stands in symmetrical opposition to the notion of culture employed by intercultural human rights scholars and others: instead of discrete systems of values, knowledge, institutions, and behavior, we now have transnational flows of people, information, and ideas. Systems are static, bounded, identifiable, and rooted to place; transnational flows are dynamic, unbounded, difficult to locate at any one point in time, and translocal. Culture-as-system is, by definition, a fundamentally conservative way of envisioning human relations; the ethereal transnational flows evoked by globalization scholars like Brysk, by contrast, point to a future of never-ending change and limitless human potential.

If this implicit utopianism is read into much of the enthusiasm for globalization as a new paradigm for understanding contemporary processes, including human rights, we can begin to understand why globalization and the death of culture have become such common tropes. Brysk explains what globalization means for human rights by describing the new world order in a rush of alliteration: it is "simultaneously more *connected, cosmopolitan, commodified*, and influenced by *communication*" (2002:6; emphases in original). And what of culture in this era of the four C's, one that "surpasses previous eras in the breadth, scope, and intensity" with which irreversible change is occurring on a global scale? Brysk does not tell us, although she does argue that "globalization is most positive for human rights when it enables the exchange of information and the formation of new identities, and most negative when it reinscribes borders" (8). If by "new identities" she means the adoption of cosmopolitan liberal values at the expense of all those illiberal alternatives, and if by "borders" she means the range of boundary markers—language, dress, religion, etc.—that symbolize the division of one group of humans from another, then we can understand why "culture" is not the fifth C in her account of our globalized present.

A more nuanced consideration of the relationship between contemporary social change (or re-entrenchment), culture, and human rights can be found among the essays in Cowan, Dembour, and Wilson's 2001 edited volume, *Culture and Rights*, which reflected what was by then roughly ten years of qualitative research on different aspects of the international and transnational human rights regimes that had rapidly expanded after 1989. The meanings of culture are unpacked with subtlety and insight through case studies that illustrate the contingencies and contradictions in the practice of human rights, from Greece (Cowan) to Botswana (Griffiths), from Thailand (Montgomery) to Nepal (Gellner). The editors argue that both "culture" and "rights" should be studied and understood discursively.

If the meanings associated with each are derived from both the specific contexts and the wider political, economic, and ideological systems within which local contexts are necessarily embedded, then no fixed, final, or normative understanding of them is possible. Moreover, the editors are rightly concerned with what they describe as the "prevalence of 'culture' as a rhetorical object" within contemporary political and legal movements in which human rights discourse (itself conceived as a "rhetorical object") is deployed.

This way of conceptualizing the relationship of culture to human rights underscores an important point for my purposes here: that anthropologists and others who wish to understand this relationship must look to ordinary social actors whose practices of everyday life constitute culture, and for whom human rights discourse might (or might not) be useful, meaningful, relevant, life-changing. Yet in looking to the practice of human rights, can we really say that culture is merely a "rhetorical object"? Doesn't this way of conceptualizing culture do a kind of violence to what we might describe as culture-in-the-world, all those messy ways in which people both talk about it and struggle to reinforce it in all of its orthodox connotations?

In her book on the regulation of gender violence within the international human rights system, Sally Merry (2006a) shows just how much the stubbornly orthodox account of culture impacts the creation of human rights discourse in even the most transnational of settings. For example, during hearings in 2002 on the Convention on the Elimination of All Forms of Discrimination against Women (CEDAW), a controversy arose over how provisions of CEDAW applied to *bulubulu*, a form of village reconciliation used in Fiji to settle disputes between parties, including those arising from rape and other sexual violence.

As would be expected, both the country report filed by Fiji—which is produced within an institutional framework that compels certain kinds of responses and precludes others—and the discussion of *bulubulu* by others at the hearing were highly critical of its use in cases of rape and other clear violations of international human rights law. But as Merry explains, there was dissent within the Fijian delegation over how Fijian culture itself was represented within these discussions. So even among a group of elites committed to the international human rights process in general, and its application to gender violence in particular, there was nevertheless concern that certain aspects of Fijian culture were being either ignored or badly misunderstood or both. One official even complained to Merry after the meetings that she was not given time to explain the "centrality of bulubulu to Fijian village life" (2006a:116).

In the next, and final, section, I bring the chapter's different strands together in order to answer the following questions: Why does culture continue to play such a multiply problematic role in relation to human rights? What is really at stake in these debates? And if we do our best to extract ourselves from the rabbit hole of culture, a place where nothing is as it seems, what problems remain for human rights theory and practice?

Surrendering to Utopia

In July 2006 the *New York Times* reported on a one-day meeting between the president and prime minister of Serbia and their counterparts in the breakaway Kosovo Albanian province that has been overseen by UN forces since the end of the NATO bombing campaign in 1999. This meeting by the highest-ranking officials from each side followed six months of failed negotiations by lower-ranking officials on the status of Kosovo. The one-day event was overseen by one of the brightest stars within the UN human rights system, Martti Ahtisaari, the former president of Finland who won the Nobel Peace Prize in 2008 for his work on behalf of human rights and the promotion of peace in postconflict settings in Namibia, Indonesia (Aceh), and Kosovo.

Beyond the fact that the leaders of the two bitterly divided sides had agreed to meet at all, by all accounts the meeting in Vienna was a failure. Fatmir Sejdiu, one of the Kosovar Albanian officials, said that "the ethnic Albanians' desire for an independent Kosovo was 'the alpha and omega, the beginning and the end of our position'" (*New York Times*, July 25, 2006). The Serbian prime minister, Vojislav Kostunica, by contrast, argued that it was "not possible to find even a single precedent in European history which could be used as the argument to deprive Serbia of 15 percent of its territory."

The failure of the talks was, predictably, attributed to hardened political positions following a brutal recent history of ethnic cleansing, international military intervention, and, since 1999, retributive violence against Kosovo's minority Serbian population by Albanians. The commentary by Western politicians and intellectuals in the days following the July meeting was also predictable: both sides were jockeying for political and economic advantage within what was characterized as a complicated regional chess match, one in which strategic calculations were made—and official positions taken—in terms of the rules established by Realpolitik.

This was why negotiations were begun by the United Nations in the first place: if the positions of both sides were merely the result of strategic assessments of political advantage (and disadvantage), then these positions would change as soon as the assessments changed, a process that international actors like the United Nations (and the so-called Contact Group of nations responsible for managing the Serbia-Kosovo conflict) were able to influence. Through mediation, situated compromise, dialogue, and the other tools of diplomacy honed over the centuries, the interests of the "parties to the conflict" could be shifted and thus the conflict transformed.

Yet even as reported by the *Times*, the newspaper of record that has always been a voice of political realism, something other than mere political calculation was apparently behind the failure of the Serbian and Kosovar Albanian sides to dance to the tune of international diplomacy: as the newspaper said, "the divide is enormous"; both sides were "entrenched"; and the Serbs and the Kosovar Albanians took "rigid positions," which did not admit of "even the smallest compromise." In other words, the conventional framework for understanding a conflict like this one is to begin with the thin horizontal layer of political interests, a layer that can, at least theoretically, be transformed through the application of rational techniques of international diplomacy. Anything deeper (and less rational), such as cultural differences between the sides, is refracted through the assumptions of international relations.

But what if the real relationship between the horizontal and the vertical is the other way around? What if the political calculations that occupy the attention of international diplomats and policymakers are in fact refracted by the parties through culture? Even if the different "ethnic groups" (another relatively discursively neutral way of describing cultures) of the former Yugoslavia were brought together under the banner of communism and the promise of world proletarian revolution, this did not change the fact that Serbs and Albanians *saw themselves* from time to time as members of distinct cultures, which were symbolized by all the usual boundary markers that anthropologists and others have identified: language (Serbo-Croatian/Serbian, Albanian), religion (Serbian Orthodox, Islam), different understandings of history (which include the recent conflict), what anthropologists call "origin myths," and many others. Nobody wants to talk about culture and cultural difference in this post–Cold War era of globalization, in which culture is supposed to have suffered a well-earned demise. But as the Serbian-Kosovar Albanian crisis suggests, perhaps the reports of the death of culture were premature.

A world without cultures is a world without conflict, or at least conflict that has its roots in the tensions between (and among) different cultural traditions. But if culture is transformed from a noun into a verb (culture-as-process), then this more peaceful world can at least be imagined. Processes are dynamic, open, the product of ongoing negotiation, and subject to contestation. If cultures-as-systems have evolved into social processes, then it is only a matter of time before the global landscape is filled with overlapping social processes and increasingly blurred lines of demarcation. But who is announcing the transformation—and inevitable death—of those "systems of values, ideas, and behaviors" that have proven so conceptually and politically problematic? Certainly not the Serbian and Kosovar Albanian leaders in Vienna, who must return to their constituencies and demonstrate to them that their actions served the interests of, above all else, the "Serbian people" or "the Albanian nation." And not even the Fijian representative to the CEDAW hearings, someone obviously committed to international human rights, was willing to abandon the idea of Fijian culture. The resulting tension between the trans-cultural imperatives of human rights and the ever-present reality of Fijian "custom" was not, in the end, resolved, as Merry describes so compellingly. So what is happening here?

I think it is not a coincidence that the death of culture in its anthropological sense has been most often promoted by scholars (including anthropologists!), international officials, transnational activists, and other cosmopolitan
elites for whom the idea of culture has never had much personal resonance.
When Erasmus of Rotterdam began visiting Thomas More in London in the
late fifteenth century, the common language was Latin, but the worldview was
essentially the same as it is now for most scholars and others whose community of meaning "transcends" (there's the value judgment) the parochial
boundaries of place, culture, nation. From all accounts, More and Erasmus
had a jolly time together, and they became lifelong friends and collaborators.
On Erasmus's first visit, they produced a Latin translation of the works of Lu-
cian, which was published in Paris. On another extended visit, Erasmus produced his famous *In Praise of Folly*, whose Latin title (*Encomium Moriae*) was
a pun on his friend's name (the book was also formally dedicated to More).

All of this—with certain variations—would be very familiar to any scholar
working in 2009. And can anyone doubt that although More was a lifelong
Londoner (born on Milk Street in 1478), he identified much more closely with
someone like Erasmus than with the English butcher down the street, someone
for whom Latin was gibberish and the transcultural aspirations of humanism
meaningless? But did these aspirations mean that the butcher's English culture was any less real or palpable or consequential? More and Erasmus might
have scoffed at it (if they considered it at all) and spent their lives trying to
conceive of a world in which parochial English culture would have no place,
but all of this did very little to change the terms of English culture, as complicated and diffuse as it was (and still is).

For human rights scholars, activists, and international officials the stakes
are even higher because international human rights represent an attempt to establish real norms for the cosmopolitan future that fifteenth-century human-
ists like Erasmus and More could only dream of. Here the existence of culture
(the source of values that might or might not be consistent with human rights)
is even less desirable. So it is not surprising that, as we have seen, some human
rights scholars have announced the death of culture in one of two ways: by
claiming that the forces of globalization have transformed cultures into mere
locations within transnational flows or by questioning whether there ever were
such things as cultures in the first place, rather than interconnected social
processes—social processes that, from a certain perspective, meant that the
Serbo-Croatian-speaking Orthodox Serbs always had much more in common

with the Gheg-speaking Muslim Kosovar Albanians than they believed, that they were, in effect, simply variations of the same collectivity.

In either case, the death of culture provides a way of surrendering to a Utopia that will be regulated by some version of human rights. It is no coincidence, therefore, that I invoke Thomas More in the way I have, since he is the one who first gave us the idea of Utopia, that fabulous island that cannot, by definition, ever exist, because it serves a different function: to shape human aspirations *despite*, not because of, what people know about the world around them. But is it enough that universal human rights can be willed into existence where they otherwise do not exist, either because they clash with values dear to one cultural tradition or another or because international or transnational institutions are still not powerful enough to shape the world in ways that would make the problem of cultural difference, in a sense, irrelevant?

In other words, can universal human rights come in through the back door, one that is created by the innovative arguments of cosmopolitan elites who cannot but view the idea—and continued reality—of culture with a kind of bemused hostility, even as they treat the idea of it like an exotic conceptual dish—culture on the half shell? Regardless of how we might answer these questions, the stubborn fact of culture remains, even though for populations in diaspora, elites, well-traveled bourgeoisie (whether from the "West" or elsewhere), those regularly on the information superhighway, and others, the world *does* seem to be a smaller, less divided place. But human rights scholars should not be too concerned with these relatively tiny segments of the world's population. Rather, the problems that culture poses for human rights theory and practice will not really be solved until those who have chosen to surrender to utopia come to terms with everyone else.

Chapter 5

Human Rights along the Grapevine

The Ethnography of Transnational Norms

I N CHAPTER 4 I examined the multiple ways in which culture has been understood by human rights scholars, activists, and government officials, and some of the reasons why culture continues to be both an acknowledged and an unacknowledged thorn in the side of human rights. But there was one sense of culture in relation to human rights that I did not discuss, an omission that is admittedly curious because anthropologists of human rights, in particular, have been at the forefront in examining and developing an understanding of it.

Coinciding with the somewhat delayed emergence of neoliberalism in different parts of the developing world—for example, the mid- to late 1980s in parts of Latin America—researchers began to notice the coalescence of networks of human rights actors that connected disparate groups of communities beyond both the nation-state and the international human rights system that had been created in the postwar settlement. These human rights networks—which came to constitute an important part of a new culture *of* human rights (Cowan, Dembour, and Wilson 2001)—were forged by transnational nongovernmental organizations (NGOs) usually working in collaboration with counterparts in different countries, as well as with at least the nominal support of representatives of national ministries or other state agencies charged with human development.

Nevertheless, what was important about the rise of transnational human rights networks was the fact that they interconnected both above and below the radar of an international human rights system that was itself gaining traction in different ways for the first time since 1948. As others have rightly observed (see, for example, Brysk 2002; Cheah 2007; Claude and Weston 2006; Mertus and Helsing 2006; Mutua 2002; Wilson 2001), the seismic shifts that accompanied the crumbling of the Cold War system created openings for what I have described elsewhere as the globalization of sympathetic law (Goodale 2002), including transitional justice tribunals, alternative dispute resolution, and, most consequentially, human rights.

Scholars and others tried to make sense of these developments from a number of different perspectives. Not surprisingly, political scientists and international lawyers made the first contributions. In a series of studies of networks, norms, and institutions, researchers documented what Risse, Ropp, and Sikkink (1999) called the "power of human rights," by which they meant the ways in which international human rights standards were suddenly being considered by (at least some) nation-states as part of the policymaking process. This shift was seen to be the result of a new instrumental and largely political calculus, in which human rights norms could no longer be ignored in light of the demands of newly empowered populations, whose grievances were made public and then made part of the agendas of transnational social movement NGOs. Even though the focus on transnational networks represented a challenge to prevailing theoretical and methodological assumptions, these first sustained attempts to understand the rise of transnational human rights were dominated by the comparative, systems, and policy preoccupations of international relations. So despite the highly suggestive reorientation toward "activists beyond borders" (Keck and Sikkink 1998), this was really a response to what was seen as a new form of international politics (Keck and Sikkink 1998; Khagram, Riker, and Sikkink 2002; Risse, Ropp, and Sikkink 1999).

Somewhat later, others began to track the emergence of transnational human rights networks from what Annelise Riles (2000) described as "the inside out" (see, e.g., Clarke 2008; Englund 2006; Merry 2006a; Speed 2008; Tate 2007; Wilson 2001). This move was partly intentional and partly the result of a kind of serendipity. In my own research in Bolivia, for example, I went to a remote region of the South American altiplano in the late 1990s in order to study dispute resolution and legal subjectivity outside of the boundaries of state law. I found myself, however, firmly anchored within boundaries that I had not even known existed: the boundaries of transnational human rights, in this case in the form of a rural legal services center that had been established in part by European NGOs and that had been working to transform legal and moral consciousness among the region's peasant agro-pastoralists (Goodale 2009a).

But while political scientists were faced with the problem of reconciling macrosystem models of transnational human rights with the data of social practice, anthropologists of human rights were faced with the opposite problem: how to derive the details and, as important, meanings, of transnational networks from the thick descriptions of finely grained ethnographic observations. The accounts of transnational human rights networks framed in the theoretical language of international relations tended to mirror the grand narratives of human rights themselves—they were optimistic, confident in their policy applications, and perfectly comfortable in the company of like-minded internationalists from within the human rights community, whose work they were seen to support. The accounts from the inside out, by contrast, were much less sanguine, agnostic or silent about their relation to policymaking, and often skeptical about the well-intentioned activism of the cosmopolitan elites who worked tirelessly on behalf of victims of human rights abuses in different parts of the world.

The emergence of transnational human rights should not have come as a surprise. In fact, the eventual transnationality of human rights was implicit at the creation of the postwar human rights system itself, although this vision was obscured by the resulting political and legal structures of the international system that were the product of several profound compromises. When Eleanor Roosevelt said that a "curious grapevine" would be the way in which information about human rights "may seep in even when governments are not so anxious for it," she was gesturing toward more than simply the instrumental means through which the set of international norms she helped craft would come to the attention of people living in places without free and open access to information (Korey 1998).[1]

Rather, she was highlighting something much more fundamental about the "statement of basic principles" that was given to the world in 1948: its *anti*-internationalism. The Universal Declaration of Human Rights, in other words, is marked by a set of contradictions at its very core. It is philosophically transnationalist and perhaps even "postnationalist." How else is a normativity that is derived from something as nonpolitical as the fact of common humanness to be understood? Yet despite the basic philosophical transnationalism of human rights, the human rights system that was created in the postwar settlement—with the UDHR as its bedrock—is a quintessential creature of a preexisting *international* system, one that crystallized in the seventeenth century in order to regulate relations between conceptually autonomous and politically sovereign nation-states. This was the same international system—one of treaties, diplomacy, and the dreary calculus of Realpolitik—that had failed so miserably in the first half of the twentieth century (as earlier). Yet when the cosmopolitan elites who took it upon themselves to envision other possibilities for regulating and nurturing social and political relations on a global scale decided upon a universal (*not* international) declaration of human rights, they were forced to embed it within the same political framework that it would seem to transcend.

This history should remind us of at least two things, both of which will be explored at some length in this chapter. First, for both political and philosophical reasons, the position of the nation-state in relation to human rights is ambiguous at best. After all, the Universal Declaration was believed to be a first step toward a future in which nation-states would no longer be able to victimize their own citizens or the citizens of other nations. Yet because the Westphalian system of international law and relations survived World War II intact—though disgraced and in tatters—it was necessary to craft a human rights regime in terms of it, while alluding at the same time to something beyond the hegemony of international relations. If "Westphalian Compromise" can describe the settlement after the Thirty Years' War that created an international system that structures global relations even today, I think one can speak of a Westphalian Compromise in a different sense, one that refers to the postwar Faustian bargain that was necessary to secure agreement on a declaration of norms that were so clearly transnationalist. Nation-states agreed to a statement of principles that suggested a future world in which nation-states would no longer be considered fully sovereign. But because nation-states were the means through which legitimacy for this statement was established (or not, as it turned out), the Universal Declaration was denuded of the very thing that was the source of its greatest potential—its uncomplicated universalism.

And second, if Eleanor Roosevelt did in fact believe that nongovernmental organizations would be the means through which the international system of sovereign nation-states would be eventually breached, this curious grapevine was curious in ways that could only be understood much later. On the one hand, nongovernmental actors had played an important role during the drafting stages, mainly through the comments that had been solicited by UNESCO and then forwarded to the Commission for Human Rights, as we saw in chapter 2 (see also Morsink 1999). But compared with later in the century, NGOs at midcentury were a much more heterogeneous and, more important, less institutionalized set of global actors. The influence they would come to wield within the developing world, in particular, could scarcely be imagined in 1948 by even the most ardent supporters of a post-Westphalian global community. Nevertheless, it would not be until after 1989 that transnational NGOs would begin to really fulfill the mission envisioned by Roosevelt: to serve as a two-way conduit for information about both universal human rights and human rights abuses, carrying the "provisions of the Universal Declaration beyond the censors of totalitarian and authoritarian regimes . . . and perform[ing] the alternative task of bringing out information concerning the nature of repression and discrimination or about violations of human rights," as Korey describes it (1998:48).

But on the other hand, by creating a Frankensteinian monster like the Universal Declaration, a normative hybrid in which a fundamentally transnational set of norms was embedded within a fundamentally international political and legal system, members of the commission like Roosevelt carved out a formal role for a very peculiar set of institutional actors, a move that had unintended consequences. As the constituents of the curious grapevine, transnational NGOs were implicitly given the task of creating networks that would weaken the hegemony of nation-states and, eventually, forge a transnational system in which the Universal Declaration—both in itself and through the follow-on instruments that were meant to actualize its norms—could be both politically and legally effective.

Yet as the recent backlash against the continuing expansion of the European Union by even the most pro-EU member-states demonstrates, sovereign nation-states of whatever political stripe do not voluntarily cede sovereignty easily or without internal resistance. So it was left to institutional actors whose boundaries stretched across and beyond those of nation-states, whose very reason for being was to carry out projects without regard for political borders or the imperatives of nationalism that they symbolized, to do what the Commission for Human Rights or the United Nations could not do: to imbricate the Universal Declaration with moral consciousness one person and village at a time, to plant the seeds from which a thousand (arguably liberal) flowers would bloom.

So who are these transnational actors, these midwives of cosmopolitanism who come bearing both potable water and a radically transformative worldview? They are many things, of course, but they share certain general characteristics. They are institutions staffed by elite cadres of highly dedicated professionals, whose own origins and interests are subsumed in favor of what often becomes the crusading mission of the organization. In their activities they are highly visible and shadowy at the same time; their presence is felt through their good works, but their members do not stay long and often vanish without a trace (indeed, even for their local partners, transnational NGO workers are usually unreachable after the job is done). And in operating beyond the boundaries of the international system, transnational NGOs also operate beyond the boundaries of political accountability, at least as it is understood within dominant theories of legitimacy. Indeed, transnational NGOs are fundamentally undemocratic: they are elite; their power stretches across wide swaths and affects whole populations; their internal operations are a mystery to those whose lives they impact; and criteria for inclusion in this league of transnational actors—in terms of material resources, technocratic knowledge, and human capital—are deeply exclusionary.

For all these reasons—and others—the emergence of transnational human rights has been tightly encased in a paradox: a tiny vanguard of cosmopolitan philosopher-kings, one that is marked above all else by its uniqueness and dedication to fulfilling its extra-ordinary mandate, is the means through which the ideas of universal sameness, ethical and legal equality, and human dignity are being inculcated into the very cells of the global body politic. As Karl Marx, an advocate for a different kind of vanguard, reputedly once said, "I am not of you, but I am for you." In other words, there are times when the work of a small cadre is necessary in order to bring about structural transformations of the kind that something like an actualized Universal Declaration requires. But this depends on the perpetual goodwill and enlightened benevolence of the members of the party, and the hope that the compromises necessary to resolve the paradox will not become insurmountable obstacles on the road to the Kallipolis.

Along the Global Grapevine

Before moving on to consider different dimensions of contemporary transnational human rights, and before I draw out the implications of the recent ethnography of human rights networks, it is important to establish a set of conceptual parameters. If the curious grapevine describes actors, discourse, and practices that are interconnected within the social, political, and legal spaces that open up horizontally both above and below the different strata of the nation-state, then we must be clear about just what kind of interconnections these are. Scholars, government officials, activists, and others often speak of "international" human rights when what they are really referring to is an emergent regime of transnational human rights; or, even more problematic, scholars write about "international" human rights as if these were the (as-yet-unrealized) ideal contemplated by the Universal Declaration. Part of this confusion stems from the fact that the multiple implications of the nation-state for human rights have not been fully appreciated, either because of theoretical or political predispositions among human rights scholars and practitioners or because of the sheer difficulty of "thinking beyond the nation" (Appadurai 1996; Cheah and Robbins 1998).

The "transnational" in transnational human rights invokes a set of connections, social relations, economic networks, and so on, that transcend the boundaries of the nation-state. By "transcend" I mean nothing other than that these relations are not constructed in terms of nation-states, or as expressions of their sovereignty, or on their behalf. Transnational relations encompass a wide range of scales and degrees of expansiveness. They would include something as modest as an interregional peasant trading association, in which members interconnect on the basis of shared interests, language, economic status, and skill set, and something as vast as large-scale financial markets, which can interconnect economies across national boundaries on something approaching a global scale. The key distinction between "transnational" and "international" is the fact that "transnational" describes a set of relations, or networks, or norms, whose legitimacy, function, and ultimate meaning are radically divorced from the nation-state. Of course the shadow of the nation-state still lingers whenever the trans-*national* is invoked, if only because the often dominant presence of the state must be necessarily acknowledged in the course of transcending it.[2]

"Transnational human rights," therefore, should not be used to refer to the postwar human rights system, at least as it has emerged through the international frameworks of the United Nations and the complicated political calculations of inter-state relations that constitute it. But especially since the end of the Cold War, a separate human rights regime has coalesced, one in which human rights consciousness, discourse, and practices (if not law) unfold in terms of starkly different logics.

Transnational human rights have emerged through interconnections of people, or groups of people, rather than states. The transnational human rights system, if we can call it that—"regime" would seem to be the better signifier—lacks all of the political, legal, and institutional features of international human rights, which means, among other things, that one cannot speak, at least formally, of transnational human rights *law*. But the curious grapevine of transnational actors and networks that has grown steadily since 1989 is something that the international human rights system is not, and can never be: an organic, if incipient, expression of the idea of human rights itself. The international human rights system, by contrast, is just another international system, one in which a statement of principles with grander philosophical and ethical aspirations is tightly circumscribed by the set of normative and institutional checks and balances that structures other, essentially political, relations between nation-states.

But to the extent to which a transnational human rights regime interconnects people beyond the boundaries of nation-states, promotes norms that are derived from the apolitical idea of human rights (and not the logics of international relations), and lays the foundation for legitimacy by establishing networks that are organized around *human*, rather than national or political, principles—like the principle of human dignity, or the imperative to protect human rights—it at least has the virtue of cohering with (rather than contradicting) the idea of human rights.

The great value in the idea of human rights is that it implies a set of norms whose legitimacy depends on nothing more complicated than the simple fact of common humanness. Political entities (like the nation-state) will come and go, but the fact of common humanness, if true, both preexists these entities and will remain after they are gone. That is the real genius of the idea of human rights. It is also its greatest weakness, since it is when such a noble (if essentially speculative) idea is converted into the language of social and political practice—as it must necessarily be—that all the problems begin. Nevertheless, we must recognize that to be able to speak meaningfully of *transnational* human rights is to point to evidence that at least some of these problems—like the problem of culture—have so far not proven fatal.

Finally, we must distinguish international and transnational from *postnational*. To invoke the postnational is to suggest some future period in which the nation-state in its current form will have withered away. But if the transnational expresses an organic connection to the idea of human rights, the same cannot be said of the postnational. A future world without nation-states could take different shapes, from a kind of anarchy of collectivities organized around ethnicity, for example, to (at the other extreme) a highly centralized global government without semi-autonomous constituent polities of whatever type. Both of these possibilities are not very likely and, in any event, are not taken seriously by the small and intrepid group of political philosophers who spend their time envisioning postnationality and the role of human rights within it.

Rather, what these scholars and visionaries suggest is that a future post-national world—which is usually described as *cosmopolitan*—would look something like a modern federal nation-state, with any number of semi-autonomous (but not fully sovereign) "states" ultimately subsumed within a single overarching legal and political framework. In fact, the United States makes a good analogy for this future cosmopolitan structure. It has a federal constitution that establishes a set of basic rights that are guaranteed to everyone simply by virtue of citizenship. And this constitution is enforceable—and has, time and time again, actually been enforced—against those within the nation-state's borders who would violate its provisions, or challenge its supremacy, except by procedures that it itself establishes. Yet within this federal structure are (now) fifty semi-autonomous states, with their own constitutions, political traditions, and criminal and civil statutes.[3] The structural relations between the federal level and the states are partly regulated through formal law (in the U.S. Constitution) but also, importantly, through a kind of customary or un-written law, one that expresses what is an evolving and dynamic set of expecta-tions about power, national values, and the highly fraught imperative to forge a common national identity and vision despite regional, class, religious, and other divisions that have repeatedly fractured the not-so-United States.

Yet when there are conflicts between the states and the federal govern-ment, especially when these conflicts involve the failure by the states to apply or enforce basic constitutional rights, or when a challenge to federal suprem-acy has been made, then (assuming the federal government itself has acted properly) there is no question that the subsidiary unit must yield to the larger (as outlined in article VI, paragraph 2 of the U.S. Constitution, the Supremacy Clause).[4]

So here we have a nation-state of almost 300 million people who live within fifty semi-autonomous states, each of which maintains a tremendous amount of legal and political independence from the federal system and, even more important, preserves and fosters its own internal cultural and historical tradi-tions. Despite a tradition of foreign visitors (one going back at least to Toc-queville) remarking on a certain homogeneity across the different regions of the United States, in fact the legal diversity I have already mentioned parallels other kinds of diversity, which can be seen between regions, between urban and rural areas, and between socioeconomic classes. So it cannot be said that cultural richness has been sacrificed in the United States in order to maintain an enforceable federal legal system, one that does demand, at times, the suppression of what can be understood as local norms or ethical imperatives.[5]

What all of this means, I would argue, is that postnationality is certainly not necessary in order for a universal code of human rights to be both enforceable and, more important, effective in regulating social relations among diverse constituencies, in addition to serving as a kind of embodiment of transcultural values (much as the U.S. Constitution does, apart from its legal and political implications).[6] Indeed, *transnational* human rights would seem to strike the right balance, both politically and conceptually when considering a global human rights framework, but only if what remains of the nation-state resembles the state in the current U.S. federal system: independent but not sovereign; free to nurture and encourage distinct traditions but legally and politically bound to accede to superordinate norms when these traditions come into conflict with them; and, to a certain extent, ethically committed—to the extent to which internally diverse political entities can be ethically committed to something—to the values from which such norms are derived.

The Postnational Constellation Comes into View

If it is common for many mainstream human rights theorists and activists to continue to focus—for different reasons—on the role of international human rights institutions, there are other scholars and futurists who are thinking well beyond what is, in essence, a seventeenth-century worldview. In making this comparison, I do not mean to suggest that the work of many human rights scholars embodies a conservative or reactionary approach to global relations. Indeed, international relations, the law of nations, diplomacy, the protection of national sovereignty, the promise to resolve conflicts through negotiation and not war, and so on, have rightly been considered to be enlightened, though essentially unrealized, alternatives to other much worse possibilities, like imperialism, military expansionism, and colonialism (all of which have nevertheless persisted during the Age of International Relations).

But two undeniable facts also persist: first, that the international system is predicated on both the supremacy of the nation-state and its ultimate autonomy as a political, legal, and even moral entity; and second, that the idea of human rights contemplates a global normative framework in which rights are protected without regard to national origin or citizenship. Indeed, regardless of the compromises that were necessary to forge a universal statement of human rights—the first and most important of which is that it emerged from, and was embedded in, the international system—we should remember the calamity that was its most proximate cause. Taken together, the twentieth century's two world wars revealed the essential tragedy at the heart of the international system: when the law of nations cannot manage to peacefully regulate the relations of the world's sovereign nation-states (a law that has been more honored in the breach than in the observance through the centuries), there is nowhere else to go except into the spiral of war and death. As utopian as it has always been, the idea of human rights points toward something more expansive than this—to a time in which an essential and common humanness forms the basis for regulating social, political, and legal relations between people whose cultural identities will come to be nothing other than folkloric variations on a theme, rather than expressions of essential difference.

But the utopianism of human rights has meant that those who are willing to "think and feel beyond the nation" must occupy what anthropologist Michel-Rolph Trouillot (1991) described as the "savage slot": that discursive place reserved for the exotic, the marginal, the Other. There are some surprising members of this savage slot of postnational utopianism, those for whom the nation-state and the international system should be—and, at least theoretically, already are—obsolete. It might seem odd indeed to include a theorist like Jurgen Habermas in this group, but there he is, writing passionately and futuristically about what he calls the "postnational constellation" (a metaphor chosen, it would seem, to emphasize the otherworldly implications of a time without nation-states). Given his preoccupation with political legitimacy, Habermas is most concerned with how a postnational federation would "generate . . . normative cohesion" and a sense of *community*, that all-important, but fragile, entity around which much of the Habermasian lifeworld revolves.

Like most who write on postnationality, Habermas must eventually confront Kant, that prophet of modern cosmopolitanism whose "normative model for a [world] community . . . without any possible exclusions" is what Habermas describes as a "universe of moral persons" (2001:108). Although Habermas can "see no structural obstacles to expanding national civic solidarity and welfare-state policies [the foundations of community in the current international system] to the scale of a postnational federation," he is more agnostic about whether human rights, without more, could generate the kind of "self-referential concept of collective self-determination [that] demarcates [the] logical space" within which a sense of global identity could be forged (107). As he argues, the fact that as a matter of theory human rights are typically made the normative foundation for future cosmopolitan democracy "doesn't predict whether [something like] the UN Declaration on Human Rights, whose wording was agreed on by the comparatively small number of founding members of the United Nations in 1946 [*sic*], could approach a unanimous interpretation and application in today's multicultural world" (108).[7]

This hesitation about making the "moral universalism of human rights" the basis for a future postnational/cosmopolitan world community is not to be seen among the far less visible but much more fervent group of futurists who are to be found mostly on the margins of political philosophy. Although these cosmopolitan theorists can trace their intellectual historical lineage directly back to the sage of Königsberg, the sheer contrast between the fancifulness of their imaginings and the drab concreteness of the prevailing realism that continues to dominate political studies has meant that these spirited visionaries are the SETI astronomers of legal and political theory: no one would deny the importance (in the abstract) of their work, but very few people want to follow them too far into the realm of theoretical fantasy. Nevertheless, as is so often the case, it is from the disparaged margins that real creativity, intellectual courage, and a glimpse into what very well could be the future are to be found.

Take, for example, the writings of the Swedish political theorist Eva Erman. She has been working on the problem of how to reconcile human rights and democratic theory within a more general cosmopolitan framework (2005, 2006).[8] While it has been assumed that "cosmopolitan law demands the subordination of smaller units to an overarching moral and legal framework" (2006:i), Erman argues that what she calls "vertical" approaches to cosmopolitan normativity do not "succeed in offering an appropriate account of the shared intuition that individuals create moral norms within rather than outside of their . . . community" (i). Even more problematic, according to Erman, is the fact that overly political accounts of a postnational global federation framed by human rights "do not recognize the constitutive role of deliberation for agency and the exercise of autonomy" (i).

In order to address these problems, Erman develops a thoroughly "horizontal" account of the mutually constitutive relationship between human rights and democracy within a global system in which identity is based not on "some old absolute sovereignty à la Westphalia" but on what she describes as "sovereignty-as-autonomy" (2006:2). This is a kind of formal principle in which cosmopolitan identity is based on nothing more, but nothing less, than the mutual recognition of equality in terms of human rights. This mutual recognition can never be demanded politically or legally as a condition of belonging or anything else; instead, it must emerge, if at all, through dialogue and the formation of what Erman calls "common deliberation institutions" (3).

In other words, her intensely intersubjective cosmopolitanism is not hostile to political processes as such, which she recognizes are necessary in particular in order to manage conflicts that arise from differing conceptions of exactly *how* sovereignty-as-autonomy as a principle will form the basis for governance on a global scale. But her vision is one in which self-knowledge emerges at the same time as a mutual recognition of basic human equality (she use "intra-" and "interpersonal" to make this distinction) takes root across discrete preexisting units of identity (culture, region, ethnicity, and so on). She even takes aim at Habermas himself in order to show how his account of the role of human rights within the postnational violates his own commitment to intersubjectivity! According to Erman, Habermas "ignores his own insight that deliberation plays a constitutive role for agency and the exercise of autonomy" because he removes moral discourse (which for Erman includes universal human rights) from the level of communicative action in such a way that "morality sneaks its way above politics" (2).

Regardless of what we might think based on this peek into the futuristic world of cosmopolitan/postnational theory, what is most important for my purposes here is how far this is from the preoccupations of scholars and others who continue to problematize different aspects of human rights from within a firmly internationalist paradigm. While the cosmopolitan fringe might be criticized for its gleefully anti-realist and (I would argue) essentially anti-political approach to human rights within a future postnational world, the continued dominance of the nation-state—and thus internationalism—within contemporary political and philosophical debates means that theorists like Erman must, in a sense, keep their eyes firmly focused on what does not yet exist. The hegemony of the international within human rights, the supposedly progressive character of internationalism as an ideology, and the vague utopianism that is associated with cosmopolitanism all conspire to keep the postnational constellation of the future a marginal topic for inquiry.

At the same time, these innovative and necessarily abstracted musings from the margins are most likely a key to how a different, and more organic, human rights framework will regulate a future global political and legal system.

From the Belly of the Benevolent Beast

Perhaps the most significant contribution of the recent anthropology of human rights has been the detailed ethnographic study of transnational human rights networks from within, a perspective that—as we saw above—Annelise Riles describes as the "network inside out." To study transnational human rights networks—or any networks, for that matter—from the inside out is to make at least two key methodological moves. The first is to assume that a network can be apprehended only through multiple encounters with the many nodes or points of articulation through which a network is constituted. The ethnographer tries to get as close as possible to the second-order expressions of the network, which means observing activists during meetings or as they prepare for events and deconstructing the network's artifacts, which for Riles meant statements of organizational goals, copies of international human rights documents, and schematic representations of the network itself, such as the mind-bendingly complex illustration she reproduces that is described as the "Schematic depiction of the Asia and Pacific NGO Working Group" (2000:49).[9]

And second, if the ethnography of transnational human rights networks is the study of essentially transient knowledge practices—and the artifacts that they produce—then the question arises of how we know that these knowledge practices constitute something more, that they can and should be thought of as a kind of consequential sum total. That is, if "networks" come and go with the knowledge practices—including those legal, moral, and political knowledge practices that are encompassed within "human rights"—that constitute them, then how, from a simple methodological perspective, can this something greater be observed and explained?

The short answer is that it cannot be observed, no matter how many nodes of articulation are carefully studied, no matter how many network artifacts are put under the critical microscope. The best solution to this problem is not the one offered by macrosystem theorists, who are forced to deduce the contours of networks from a set of prefigured theoretical assumptions. This approach leads to depictions of transnational human rights networks that are consistent with wider theoretical or political projects, usually conceptually elegant, and even useful to policymakers, but which are disconnected from what we might describe as the practices of transnational human rights networks. Instead, our knowledge of both what transnational human rights networks are and how they might figure in a future system of global governance structured by human rights must emerge from the messier and more contingent experiences through which actual networks are instantiated. But if the sum total cannot be observed, how are we to produce an image "from below" (see Rajagopal 2003) that is not misleading in yet different ways?

Again, we turn to the ethnography of transnational human rights. In her study of the relationship between international law and local justice, Sally Engle Merry (2006a) both provides a view from the inside out and shows how a broader vision of human rights networks can be drawn from the data of ethnographic research. She tracked transnational human rights networks— and parts of the international human rights system that they, at times, support—that have emerged over the last fifteen years to address the problem of violence against women. She managed to study these networks from below across a wide geographical and cultural range: her work took her to India, China, Fiji, Hong Kong, Hawai'i, and Massachusetts. And her work was made more complicated by the fact that the ephemeral transnational networks that crystallize as a response to gender violence are only partly integrated with the branches of the international human rights system that were created to enforce actual human rights law, most notably CEDAW. This means that she was studying two human rights regimes with quite different ontological statuses; even more, these two regimes often interpenetrated each other in terms of a common set of practices (and actors), from patterned human rights activism to the drafting of documents.

Nevertheless, what comes through so clearly in her work is the fact that transnational human rights networks—that is, those that transcend the internation-state system of the United Nations and international relations more generally—can, in fact, be apprehended and then explained through what we can think of as the ethnographic application of both the intellectual and the moral imagination. This is not the kind of orthodox deduction from first principles that we see throughout the literature on human rights networks, in which one begins with something like "networks are a set of interconnected . . ." and then simply overlays this definition on top of whatever actual information about human rights practices and institutions in different places and times is available. Rather, the ethnographer of transnational human rights must project from below in a way that captures the temporality of the sum total—the network—while at the same time accounting for its significance, multiple moral and legal meanings, and impact beyond the local.

The implications of envisioning transnational human rights networks from the inside out are not only, or most importantly, methodological. Take the recent work of the anthropologist Shannon Speed (2006, 2008). She has been focusing on the transnational human rights network that encompasses indigenous social and political struggles in Chiapas, Mexico. This is a network that mobilizes around a set of interconnected issues, some of which are specific to Mexico but others of which open up well beyond the concerns of the historically fraught relationship between the Mexican nation-state and the rural indigenous peoples who have been largely excluded from power by the nation's postrevolutionary elites. By tracking the emergence of norms in a space that I have described elsewhere as *between* the global and the local (Goodale 2007a), Speed's work does much more than simply suggest ways in which our understanding of transnational human rights *networks* must be radically reconceived: her close engagement from within, as it were, the normative practices that constitute these networks points toward a radically different vision of human rights themselves.

This is one in which the specific meanings of human rights remain fluid and essentially plural and depend not on a hypothetical set of principles articulated by a small sliver of the global community but on the social actors for whom human rights come to form part of their contextualized legal, moral, and political practices. So, for example, she shows how indigenous leaders and others who employ human rights discourse as part of a wider long-term struggle for *dignidad* have taken a basic set of international human rights norms—equality, respect for autonomy (both individual and collective), universality—and embedded them within a profoundly unorthodox set of moral and legal principles that are firmly rooted in local cultural tradition. The most far-reaching of these is the notion that the human rights of Mexico's indigenous peoples "exist in their exercise." As Speed explains, "By eliminating the state as the external referent for rights, such conceptual reframings are challenging not only to the state itself, but liberal and neoliberal conceptualizations of rights and their relationship to the law" (2008:37).

At least four major implications for wider (and future) human rights theory and practice can be drawn from the still emergent body of knowledge that is being produced by ethnographers about both transnational networks and human rights. First, regardless of how human rights are associated with the wider system (or, perhaps, network), this linkage, and the wider meanings of human rights, will almost always be reinterpreted in terms of non-cosmopolitan, local, ethnic, and other imperatives that are often inconsistent with those of the international human rights system itself. But as Merry, Speed, and others have shown, this does not mean the inevitable deracination of human rights, because they continue to "work" through a set of core principles, even if these are rendered into the "vernacular," as Merry (2006a, 2006b) describes it.

Second, the ethnography of transnational human rights networks has shown that they open up—even if ephemerally—at two different levels, both of which can be characterized in terms of values. At something like a metalevel, there are values that emphasize social change, evolution, human progress, and so on, values that justify the work it would take to actually constitute a postnational world; these values *might* also include a belief in the network itself as the structural means through which change can be brought about (rather than, say, a global-federal system modeled on modern federal nation-states). But at another, more specific level, there are the values on which this progressive movement into the future will be based. In at least most cosmopolitan visions, these would include—indeed, be dominated by—some version of human rights.

Third, the view from the inside out shows that although human rights will always, to a certain extent, exist in their exercise, there is no question that there are patterns across the many different forms of normative practice that have been documented by legal anthropologists in particular (Cowan, Dembour, Wilson 2001; Goodale and Merry 2007). This means that what Erman and others argue so passionately against—the dreaded "vertical" dimension of global governance—does not have to be inconsistent with cultural autonomy or other forms of self- and collective identity. Indeed, it is difficult to imagine a cosmopolitan system in which a legitimate normative framework based on human rights could not be enforced against those who ignore it, or disagree with it, or would prefer a radical alternative to it. Even scholars who are most committed to intersubjective forms of legitimacy—such as communicative action—agree that, in the end, some overarching enforcement mechanism will be necessary. To the extent that the ethnography of human rights has documented patterns across human rights practices, there is some cause to believe that this vertical dimension can actually be created and legitimated from below.

Finally, and perhaps most provocatively, the study of transnational human rights networks has revealed something else that the system-builders and masters of the cosmopolitan world to come must take very seriously: the tendency of networks based on human rights to become imperial in certain circumstances. There is no question that power is diffused in complicated, and sometimes paradoxical, ways as human rights discourse becomes the dominant means through which moral and legal meanings are constituted by ordinary social actors across a range of contexts. Moreover, the "power of human rights" (Risse, Ropp, and Sikkink 1999) can come to subvert that set of core principles without which human rights discourse becomes something altogether different. There is, of course, a profound irony in the fact that human rights discourse, especially after 1989, functions as a kind of "moral imperialism" (Hernández-Truyol 2002) in certain circumstances.

Yet when transnational NGOs deliver food, equipment, potato seeds, and potable water to hamlets in rural Bolivia, for example, they do so now as part of a broader human rights agenda (see Goodale 2007b, 2009a; Postero 2007). Is it any surprise that local authorities begin solemnly invoking *derechos humanos* not long after, or that everything from gender relations to hamlet dispute resolution begins to shift in light of what locals believe are the imperatives of this radically new worldview? The essence of imperialism is the evacuation of alternative discourses on the basis of what the imperial power believes—earnestly or not—is the correct, or morally superior, or economically more advantageous set of perspectives and practices. Since human rights norms do not emerge fully formed in different parts of the world, whether in rural Bolivia or the planning rooms of the Fijian government, there will always be the problem of how ideas about human rights are accompanied and shaped by political, economic, and other forms of power.

Thinking and Norming Beyond the Nation

In their 1998 manifesto, Pheng Cheah and Bruce Robbins argue that the world of the future, the cosmopolitan world they say will be marked by a prevailing "cosmopolitics," will emerge only when enough people in different parts of the world are willing to *both* think and feel beyond the nation-state and the centuries-old international system that has come to seem almost inevitable. The last century, with its total wars and perhaps hundreds of millions of violently dead upon dead, was a veritable charnel house in which the illusions of internationalism were reduced to ashes. As the political theorist and intellectual historian Isaiah Berlin, a scholar not given to hyperbole, said at one point, "I have lived through most of the twentieth century without, I must add, suffering personal hardship. I remember it only as the most terrible century in Western history" (quoted in Hobsbawm 1995:1).

When Robbins says elsewhere that internationalism—the ideology of international relations as a progressive and realistic solution to managing the world's political and cultural diversity—is in "distress" (1999), he is alluding to the terrible psychological burden of recent history, one that was made possible—even compelled—by an international system whose institutionalization had the effect of validating and even celebrating the apotheosis of the nation state in the mid seventeenth century. And this is why he and Cheah believe that cosmopolitanism and postnationality will never become a reality until people across a wide range are also willing to *feel* beyond the nation, to let go of their attachment to the nation-state as the ultimate unit of identity and agree to reattach themselves to it in a more modest—and structurally reduced—form.

And in both thinking and feeling beyond the nation, it will also be necessary for people to conceive of norms in a radically different way. The essence of cosmopolitanism, according to the political philosopher Martha Nussbaum, is the willingness by social actors and collectivities to see units of identity in terms of a set of nested concentric circles, with the outermost circle given the highest legal, moral, and political value. Even more, cosmo politanism requires global citizens to begin from the outer ring, one that is coextensive with the global community itself, and then "draw the circles somehow toward the center" (Nussbaum 1996:9, quoting from the Stoic philosopher Hierocles). In doing so, of course, all that really remains is one unit of identity—the cosmopolitan. And the normative framework that will encase and, to a certain extent, produce (and reproduce) this cosmopolitan identity will be a version of universal human rights. This will take a real leap of normative faith, one that has not been possible so far because of the obstacles created in large part by the internationalism of the current human rights system.[10]

Finally, I think there needs to be much more honesty about the kind of political system that is either a precondition of or a necessary complement to a truly (I mean fully actualized) global human rights system. This can be at least partly accomplished by shedding those assumptions about international relations and the law of nations that have become a tired and counterproductive mantra, especially over the last fifty years. The creation of the United Nations did not solve the problems of international relations that made the last century the "most terrible century in Western history"; it only suppressed them so that they could reemerge in different, but no less tragic, forms. The cosmopolitan human rights theorists like Erman, who labor away in relative obscurity and flights of imaginative fancy, must be taken seriously if we are to bring the promises of the postnational constellation into sharper focus.

Chapter 6

Rights Unbound

Anthropology and the Emergence of Neoliberal Human Rights

I T HAS BEEN a basic argument of this book that anthropology and anthropologists did not contribute in a significant way to the development of the postwar human rights system, beginning with the framing and then drafting of the UDHR and continuing through the philosophical and institutional refinements of the ideas and practices that slowly crystallized only quite recently into a functioning normative framework with transnational aspirations. As Ellen Messer (1993) has argued, this anthropological absence had the somewhat ironic effect of shaping the way the idea of human rights emerged over the last 50 years, not always for the better.

It is something of a paradox that the discipline that has spent the last 150 years collecting—sometimes under dubious circumstances—empirical data about every facet of the human condition, and developing theoretical frameworks for explaining these data, contributed nothing of significance to the larger set of explanations about what is—if true in any meaningful sense—among the most important facts about human beings: that they are essentially the same by virtue of a common humanness (a moral quality that transcends the mere biological); that this essential sameness has normative implications; and, finally, that these normative implications take a very specific form (rights), one that sets formal limits on the extent to which human rights can coexist with other normativities that might be coherently derived from the same fact of common humanness.

There have been other universalist frameworks throughout history, of course, totalizing idea-systems that claim to encompass and, even more, define people whether or not they believe in the truth of the ideas themselves. But I

111

think the idea of human rights, as it emerged and was refined during the postwar settlement, is the first modern universalism that explicitly recognizes and incorporates all other existing universalisms (especially religions), acknowledges their historic origins and importance for people, even grants them a certain kind of legitimacy, but claims to transcend them in a kind of final, irrefutable assertion of the secular-moral and scientific will. Yet what would the contemporary idea of human rights—not to mention the international legal and political expressions of this idea—have looked like had the methods and forms of knowledge of anthropology been brought to bear on it?

This is a very difficult question to answer, not least because it requires a sustained act of counter-historical and counter-discursive imagining. But to answer—or attempt to answer—it is also a way of looking forward, since contemporary human rights discourse presents itself with no end of seemingly intractable dilemmas. Yet if many of these dilemmas were created by the large hole left when the anthropological voice was diminished in the decades after the promulgation of the UDHR, the fact remains that this voice was not silenced completely.[1]

There is at least one area of human rights in which anthropologists contributed philosophically, institutionally, and politically in ways that gesture toward what might have been, and what could be. Beginning in the 1970s, anthropologists moved to the forefront of theory and practice around different forms of collective rights, a highly contested normative category that might or might not be considered a subcategory of the more general category of human rights.[2] Although the 1970s were already quite late in the historical (and ongoing) development of human rights, this period marked the early stage of what would become a rapid expansion of human rights.

Among other things, this expansion has been distinguished from earlier periods by the fact that arguments for (or against) new categories of rights—indigenous rights, for example—first emerged from the diverse terrains of political and social struggle, rather than primarily from the halls of academia. It was only after new categories of collective rights had become established politically and institutionally—even if only symbolically—that the different (and predictably heated) theoretical battles were joined. This epistemological inversion in the broader intellectual history of human rights had important consequences for the way collective rights were eventually conceptualized and understood in relation to the whole, consequences that can be used as yet another critical lens through which human rights more generally can be examined.

In doing so, we will see that the one dimension of human rights that bears the heaviest mark of anthropology is not, for this reason, without its own contradictions and points of conflict. Indeed, the expansion of human rights to include different categories of collective rights has actually created tensions that did not otherwise exist. Yet as I will argue throughout this chapter, these tensions are also the source of tremendous political and theoretical potential, in part because the later developments in collective rights reflected at least a certain amount of critical internal reflection, if only to the extent that alternative ways of producing human rights knowledge were given serious consideration, in many cases for the first time. And it has only been through the expansion of human rights categories, and the corresponding need for theorists to consider how, if at all, these categories fit within even the most expansive preexisting conceptual frameworks, that the more general idea of human rights itself has been subjected to the kind of critique and reanalysis that it requires.

The Politics and Promise of Rights Unbound

Human rights categories have undergone expansion in several ways since 1948. Two forms of expansion have arguably been the most consequential, and it is the latter of these that I am most interested in here. The first is less a form of expansion, perhaps, than a process through which existing human rights categories were given substance, a process in which the politics of international relations were refracted through the mundane procedural imperatives of international law. The Universal Declaration was followed by (at least theoretically) binding legal instruments that were intended to give effect to specific provisions of the UDHR. For example, both the International Covenant on Civil and Political Rights (ICCPR) and the International Covenant on Economic, Social and Cultural Rights (ICESCR) made most key provisions of the UDHR binding on member-states that had signed and ratified them. And even though it took a full ten years (1966–1976) for each covenant to enter into force, the process by which essential sections of the UDHR were converted into binding law (both international and domestic) did not expand human rights categories so much as give political and legal substance to existing ones.

Take article 6 of the ICCPR, for example. Member-states that have ratified the covenant and thereby made it binding within domestic law are required to recognize and enforce the following: "Every human being has the inherent right to life. This right shall be protected by law. No one shall be arbitrarily deprived of his life." This tracks the UDHR's article 3 ("Everyone has the right to life, liberty and security of person"). So when the ICCPR entered into force in 1976 (and, at least theoretically, acted through domestic law for countries that had ratified it),[3] nothing new was created; the universe of human rights did not experience a sudden increase in normative matter (rather, existing matter underwent an important change in form).

Many other examples of the declaration-to-covenant/convention-to-law process could be given, in which human rights principles articulated (or implied) in earlier human rights instruments were converted into a form through which the normative aspirations embodied in the early instruments were connected to real forms of political, social, and legal practice. Among the most prominent of these would be the following (with the dates when they entered into force): the International Convention on the Elimination of All Forms of Racial Discrimination (1969), the Convention on the Elimination of All Forms of Discrimination against Women (1981), the Convention for the Suppression of the Traffic in Persons and of the Exploitation of the Prostitution of Others (1951), the Convention against Torture and Other Cruel, Inhuman or Degrading Treatment or Punishment (1987), the Convention against Discrimination in Education (1962), and the four Geneva Conventions (1950), whose legal and moral meanings have become such dramatic sources of contention over the last few years because of policies associated with the United States–led invasion and occupation of Iraq and Afghanistan.

But while this process of normative filling-in has been unfolding in terms of the intense politicization of international human rights law, an equally politicized process has been moving down a parallel track, one in which the basic idea of human rights *is* being stretched, challenged, subverted, and (in certain cases) radically transformed. This has been the emergence of what Will Kymlicka has described as "substantive minority rights": special categories of human rights that are both substantive (that is, they articulate specific rights and not just general moral or legal principles) and supra-individual, meaning the rights are ultimately embodied by collectivities of different kinds (minorities, indigenous peoples, First Nations, and so on). As Kymlicka observes:

> Minority rights did receive some international recognition under the "minority protection" scheme of the League of Nations. However, this scheme was badly abused by the Nazis, who encouraged German minorities in Czechoslovakia and Poland to escalate their demands for minority rights. When the Czechoslovak and Polish governments were unable or unwilling to accept these demands, the Nazis used this as a pretext for invasion. As a result, when the United Nations

adopted its Universal Declaration of Human Rights, all references to the rights
of ethnic and national minorities were deleted (1995:18).

Kymlicka's explanation for this is that the drafters of the UDHR believed
that specific articles would more effectively protect vulnerable collectivities
through a kind of misdirection: the UDHR's injunction against discrimination against individuals, for example, would have the cumulative effect of protecting *groups* of individuals, all of whom would enjoy (under article 7) equal
protection of the law. Yet as Kymlicka and others have rightly observed, the
omission of collective rights from the founding instruments of the postwar
international human rights system had unfortunate consequences, in part
because the belief that distinct collectivities would be protected through the
individualist framework of the UDHR proved to be badly mistaken.

But beginning in the mid-1980s, a quite different strategy was pursued
by the rapidly increasing number of international and, even more important, transnational institutions dedicated to the plight of ethnic minorities
and indigenous peoples within the period of economic, political, and military
changes that came to be known as "neoliberalism." The idea was to expand
the framework of human rights so that both individual and collective rights
would receive formal recognition and protection. Of course only certain kinds
of collective rights were believed to be worthy of special recognition—those
necessary to protect groups that had historically been victims of persecution,
oppression, and marginalization.

As Kymlicka explains, these new categories of collective rights-as-human
rights were meant to exclude "artificial or random categories of people who
[had] no shared life together, such as people whose last name [began] with
K" (1995:13). And it was recognized almost immediately that the idea of collective rights presented unique conceptual difficulties, since it represented a
direct challenge to several of the basic assumptions on which the postwar international human rights system was based. Nevertheless, the emergence of
collective rights as a new (or reinvented) category within the international
human rights system—a category that was also picked up within the diffuse
networks that constitute transnational human rights—provides a complicated
window into the way politics intersects with the moral and legal calculus of
human rights and gestures toward an even more transformed way of understanding the idea of human rights itself.

A useful way to begin to understand the implications of collective rights,
I would argue, is to see them as the product first and foremost of a set of

vely recent *political* developments in which the framework of human
s was mobilized in order to address the problem of power as it expresses itself through inequalities in wealth, in the distribution or control of
resources, in the fact of ethnic or racial discrimination, in the historic and
cross-cultural marginalization and abuse of women as part of what Gerda
Lerner (1987) has called "the creation of patriarchy," and so on.

To understand collective rights in this way is to see them as a dynamic
and contingent political response that was articulated in the language of
rights—politics as law (or, perhaps, morality). Although the context in which
the UDHR emerged during the postwar settlement was, of course, profoundly
political in its own way, there are important differences with the much later
development of collective rights. In the immediate aftermath of the Second
World War, the system of international relations was not simply destabi-
lized—it was in ruins. The unimaginable horrors of the Holocaust—and to a
lesser extent the brutalities committed in East and Southeast Asia—led to an
intense disillusionment among even the most committed internationalists, a
disillusionment that expressed itself in the search for an alternative regulatory
framework that could, to a certain extent, transcend politics.

As we have seen at different places throughout this book, those most responsible for the language and structure of the UDHR knew that they were
not creating an instrument that would serve as the foundation for a new international political order. Indeed, as Eleanor Roosevelt in particular acknowledged, what was needed instead was a compelling and unequivocal statement
of principles that would stand apart from even the most enlightened political
framework. And even if the international human rights system soon became
intensely, indeed primarily, political, both its basic conceptual foundations
and normative potential have always been shaped by its origins in the search—
by a small cadre of cosmopolitan elites—for an aspirational discourse that was
apolitical and formally abstracted from the complexities of social practice.
How could it have been otherwise? In 1948 the most chilling recent example
of "social practice" was the one that led to the deaths of millions of people.

Another reason that the edifice of orthodox international human rights
must be contrasted with the more recent development and codification of different categories of collective rights is a natural consequence of the first. It was
no coincidence that the normative framework that emerged from the search
for an aspirational discourse beyond politics was one based in human rights. It
was really the only preexisting, secular, transnational moral-legal framework

available to the members of the Commission on Human Rights, who, gued in chapters 2 and 4, represented a quite limited range of normative ideological interests, despite the official rhetoric both then and afterward. And it is also no coincidence that because the framework that emerged was one based on human rights, it tracked very closely the form and substance of earlier statements of natural/human rights, which themselves bear the heavy imprint of an even longer intellectual history, one that is not difficult to trace along its fairly narrow path into Western antiquity (see, e.g., Herbert 2002; Sweet 2003). (It is no accident of discursive history that the UDHR, along with the ICCPR and the ICESCR, have, taken together, come to be "universally" known as the International Bill of Rights. James Madison would have been proud indeed.)

So what are the implications of this history for my purposes? As we have seen at different points in this book, a natural/human rights framework is grounded in a rigid and immensely consequential epistemology: a set of un-proven (and unprovable) first principles (read: axioms) are asserted, from which any number of implications (read: corollaries) are then deduced. This process of deducing human rights is formally abstracted from the contingen-cies of social practice; indeed, the kind of knowledge that results is intended to both transcend these contingencies and, eventually, control them. As we have seen, there is a long history of this logico-deductive epistemology dominating both legal theory and philosophy, the two intellectual sources that played the most significant roles in the formation and conceptualization of the interna-tional human rights system.

Now I have nothing to say about the value, in some larger sense, of an es-sentially deductive approach to moral or legal or any other kind of knowl-edge. But what must be recognized is that there are consequences to using an approach like this outside of mathematics (and perhaps theology), the most important of which is that it is impossible to know whether there can even be empirical correspondence between the implications deduced from the un-proven first principles and the practice of everyday life. All human beings do (or should) have a right to "leave any country, including [one's] own, and to return to [one's] country" (UDHR, article 13); "Everyone has the right to seek and to enjoy in other countries asylum from persecution" (article 14); "Every-one has the right to own property alone as well as in association with oth-ers" (article 17); and so on. These are among the normative implications that were perfectly reasonably deduced from the basic set of unproven/unprovable first principles: that all human beings are essentially the same and that this essential sameness entails rights. But is there any preexisting correspondence at all between these axiomatic rights and the diversity of normative practices around the world? Or, to put this another way, can anything be said about correspondence from within the UDHR itself? The answer to both of these questions, as I have suggested, is no.

This, I would argue, has been one of the central problems for both the international and the transnational human rights regimes that eventually emerged in the postwar period, even if it has only been over the last twenty years that one has been able to track its effects within the practice of human rights. But if the framework in which the postwar human rights system has unfolded has been marked by this basic disjuncture, the same cannot be said of the much more recent emergence of collective rights, which are grounded in a quite different set of epistemological circumstances. Take the case of indigenous rights. Whether we consider the 1982 formation of the United Nations Working Group on Indigenous Populations, or the efforts of the International Labor Organization to radically revise its 1957 Indigenous and Tribal Populations Convention and Recommendation, or, even more important, the appropriation (or development) of an indigenous rights discourse by collectivities engaged in struggles in different parts of the world over the last twenty years, one thing comes through quite clearly: the idea of indigenous rights, and the political and legal frameworks that eventually emerged to express this idea, were closely associated with (if not derived from) a concrete set of underlying political, economic, and social conditions.

This meant that the international framework of indigenous rights—as fragile and controversial as it is—could not simply be deduced from a set of first principles. If anything, the rights articulated in places like ILO 169 or the 2007 United Nations Declaration on the Rights of Indigenous Peoples represent an attempt to render any number of political-economic problems that beset certain collectivities in terms of a dominant normative language—the language of human rights. This is why, from the perspective of the epistemology that structured an instrument like the UDHR, the concept of indigenous rights (or, as we will see in the next section, cultural rights) is such a mess. But that is exactly the point: how we understand collective rights, and their relation to the broader category of human rights, is conditioned by a kind of meta-discourse of human rights, one that tells us in good Cartesian fashion that only knowledge that is pulled from the Platonic ether—or the smoke of an overheated boiler room—is worth anything.

Now to say that the indigenous rights of instruments like ILO 169 or the 2007 United Nations Declaration—not to mention the rights that are constituted through indigenous political practice—represent an attempt to reframe profound political-economic problems in terms of human rights is *not* to say that these rights are morally or legally dubious or that they represent a weaker conceptual category of rights. Indeed, the fact that they subtly trouble the (Anglo-European liberal) philosophical mind is actually the best evidence that they are stretching what needs to be stretched and shining a critical light on the places that the broader discursive history of postwar human rights had long obscured.

When Shannon Speed (2006, 2008) shows that Zapatistas have come to believe that a certain kind of indigenous human rights is brought into being at the exact moment that they are exercised, and then fade away, in a sense, when they no longer are necessary within existing social struggles, she is describing a theory of human rights that is radically different from the one that frames the UDHR. It is precisely the ontological unassailability and universality that give human rights their special normative power and that distinguish them from many other categories of rights—political, civil, contractual, and so on. But the Zapatistas argue that their legal and political practices bring a category of human rights into being that is neither permanent nor universal, except to the extent that we might say that it is universal among all Zapatistas (or even all indigenous Americans; see Goodale 2006c).

To ask whether this radical stretching of the idea of human rights is *valid* is to be confronted with a set of discursive expectations that have loomed over the entire postwar history of human rights. Validity is a function of epistemology, and as I have already described, the epistemology that structured the creation of the UDHR and most of the postwar human rights system was one with very specific roots within a more general Western intellectual history (yes, I use "Western" here quite deliberately).

It is possible, of course, to argue otherwise: that both the epistemology and what it produced (in the UDHR, for example) reflect a truly pan-cultural (and thus pan-epistemological) consensus. But although many liberal theorists in particular would not admit this, it seems clear (to me at least) that most human rights scholars (not to mention activists) would argue that the major human rights instruments do, in fact, reflect the values of a particular intellectual (and, of course, political) history, but that—here's where the discursive, or meta-normative, dimension becomes apparent—these values[4] are superior to those they confront in the heavily contested domains in which the idea of human rights is imposed (or willingly appropriated, as Wilson reminds us [2006]).

But the diverse emergence of indigenous rights over the last twenty years suggests a different account of validity, one that leads to a system (or systems) of trans-cultural human rights that is derived from the contingency, incompleteness, and multiplicity of cross-cultural normative practice. It is important to underscore the fact that indigenous rights are only a very imperfect example of the kind of alternative human rights framework I have in mind, especially since—at least as expressed in international law—their relationship to cross-cultural normative practice is tenuous at best. (They are embedded, after all, within the existing international human rights system.) But ethnographic examples like Speed's show the tremendous potential in emerging theories and practices of indigenous rights, only some of which find expression in places like ILO 169 and the more recent United Nations Declaration.

Anthropology, Indigenous Rights, and the Right to Culture

As we have seen in different ways throughout this book, the late 1960s and early 1970s were a transformative and contested time for anthropologists. This is not particularly surprising given the fact that many children of the baby boom were railing against an older order that had given the world two catastrophic global wars, genocide, fascism, McCarthyism, and other dark moments in human history. If the United States was a key player on the side of the forces of light in some of these epochal moments, in others it acted like the Prince of Darkness himself. For example, across both Democratic and Republican administrations, the United States developed an ideology of anti-communism that compelled it to use its considerable financial, diplomatic, and military assets to engineer— usually through the CIA—the overthrow of democratically elected governments from Iran (1953) to Chile (1973). By the late 1960s, this same ideology had emerged from the dark places to become the official reason for open war against communists in Southeast Asia, a war that led to the deaths of more than a million people on all sides. Many of the war's victims were indigenous peoples of Vietnam, Laos, and Cambodia, who were bombed, tortured, raped, and forced to serve as irregular soldiers and informants for the U.S. armed forces.

The opposition to U.S. involvement in Southeast Asia within anthropology was, in part, the result of a wider recognition that the discipline itself was embedded in a global political-economic system that depended on the exploitation of many of the world's most marginalized peoples, those very same people whose lives and societies had been the lifeblood of this most peculiar of social sciences. Besides more generalized acts of political protest, this opposition took two more specific forms: first, anthropology drew on sources of theoretical inspiration—Marxism, world-systems and dependence theory, feminism, postcolonial theory, among others—that, more than anything else, sought to anchor academia itself firmly within the world with all of its problems (some of which academics were directly responsible for). Apart from whatever analytical merit they might have had, the infusion of new ideas into anthropology during this time was intended to both explain and critique the discipline itself, to locate it in relation to wider structures of power. But even more important, if the infusion of new ideas had the effect of both relativizing anthropology and shining a skeptical light upon many of its preexisting self-perceptions, it also provided a set of intellectual justifications for using anthropological knowledge for quite different, especially political, purposes.

To acknowledge—and then theorize—the fact that anthropological knowledge was firmly embedded in wider political economies was to open the door for anthropologists to tightly bundle their political commitments with their professional practice; indeed, the line between the two became increasingly blurred. And for anthropologists who had spent their professional lives learning from, and informally advocating for, indigenous peoples, this shift was especially important, because indigeneity had become almost synonymous with historical oppression and systematic victimization.[5]

An important early anthropological intervention on behalf of indigenous peoples was the founding in 1972 of Cultural Survival, Inc., by the anthropologist David Maybury-Lewis and his wife, Pia Maybury-Lewis. Although today Cultural Survival has become one of the leading transnational advocates of indigenous (human) rights, at the time it was founded the discursive context was much different. Even though both the UDHR and the ICESCR had invoked "cultural rights," these were—as I explained at some length in chapter 4—merely additional (and quite vaguely articulated) individual rights that had found their way into these two foundational instruments as a result of both internal negotiations among the small group of drafters and—more speculatively—an attempt to codify a vision of the good life as understood by Western cosmopolitan elites at mid-twentieth century.

And although the ILO had adopted an earlier Indigenous and Tribal Populations Convention and Recommendation (Convention 107), one that formalized the idea of indigenous human rights for the first time within international law, that convention came to be reviled and rejected by both indigenous peoples and their advocates, in large part because of its deeply assimilationist approach to indigenous concerns (see Anaya 1996; de Varennes 1996; Thornberry 2002). The best way to protect the rights of tribal and "semi-tribal" peoples, according to the convention, was to ensure the "progressive integration [of them] into their respective national communities."[6]

Throughout the 1970s, anthropologists developed a rationale for using anthropological knowledge on behalf of indigenous peoples that cut directly against the assimilationist goals of ILO 107. As a new mode of anthropological engagement, the cultural survival movement was shaped by a commitment to self-determination, collective autonomy, the value of cultural difference, and (if necessary) the redistribution of resources in order to ensure the flourishing of vulnerable populations. Despite the different political and intellectual agendas of individual anthropologists (and others) who developed the cultural survival project, it emerged initially as an essentially pragmatic social movement. But into the 1980s, the discursive landscape surrounding indigenous peoples shifted, and anthropologists played a major role in redefining the framework in which the older, more pragmatic goals of the cultural survival movement were pursued. Indeed, the goals were themselves redefined during this period.

Part of this shift was the result of unintended changes within the cultural survival movement itself. As I have said, the idea of cultural survival carried implications that could not have been foreseen. The most important of these was the fact that as time passed, the simple (and perhaps naive) desire to protect indigenous populations merely because survival itself was at stake became more complicated (and perhaps compromised). The reasons for cultural survival were expanded and, even more critically, became instrumental. Even for many original movement leaders, the mere fact of cultural survival was no longer seen as the ultimate goal; rather, the cultural survival of indigenous peoples became a means toward other, much more ambiguous, ends.

For example, during the 1980s transnational actors involved in the wider cultural survival movement began to promote the idea that "indigenous knowledge" was the potential repository of everything from the cure to cancer to the secret to peaceful coexistence.[7] Indigenous cultures should be protected, in other words, in order to preserve knowledge that could have enormous potential well beyond the boundaries of the cultures themselves. But the transformation of at least some branches of the cultural survival movement along these instrumental lines had its dark side: the continued existence of indigenous populations (and their knowledge) was dependent on their usefulness. What would happen if miracle cures were not, in fact, to be found among the Kayapo, or the Coastal Salish, or the indigenous peoples of Australia's Mornington Island? What if developments in synthetic biotechnology eliminated the need to "preserve" the world's biodiversity?

At the same time that the plight of the world's indigenous peoples was being reframed in instrumental terms, a related, but normatively distinct, set of developments was taking place. Within at least some segments of the international human rights community, there was growing support for a bold new approach that would ground the protection of indigenous peoples firmly within a human rights framework. This support eventually came to fruition in two forms: first, the 1989 ILO Indigenous and Tribal Peoples Convention, which entered into force in 1991; and then the 1994 UN Draft Declaration on the Rights of Indigenous Peoples, which was promulgated as a symbolic beginning to the UN's International Decade of the World's Indigenous People (1995–2004).[8]

The renewal of indigenous rights within international human rights law had the effect, among other things, of reestablishing the cultural survival movement on normatively transformed grounds; today, for example, Cultural Survival describes its mission as the promotion of the "rights, voices, and visions of indigenous peoples" and holds itself out as the "leading U.S.-based international indigenous rights organization." Although this shift should not be overstated, the emergence of a formal indigenous rights framework within the broader international human rights system means that it is no longer necessary to ask whether the survival of a particular indigenous population is useful, or beneficial, or calculated to (at least potentially) bring about the greater good for the greater number. Because at least some segments of the international community now view indigenous peoples as bearers of a special subcategory of human rights, they are under at least a moral—and in some cases legal—obligation to protect and reinforce these rights by creating the political, economic, and social conditions in which indigenous peoples can freely pursue their "life projects" (Blaser, Feit, and McRae 2004).

Parallel to the creation of a new indigenous rights framework within international law, anthropologists were also crafting a new rights-based disciplinary orientation to indigenous peoples. The late 1980s and early 1990s were a time in which the problem of indigenous rights became *the* means through which anthropology underwent a radical realignment in relation to human rights more generally; as we have seen, the largest association of professional anthropologists in the world, the American Anthropological Association, had by the mid-1990s reconstituted itself for certain purposes as a transnational human rights NGO. Through its numerous special commissions and (eventually) permanent standing committees, the AAA thrust its members—and thus the discipline—into the forefront of the struggle to have indigenous rights recognized and, more importantly, implemented within the domestic law of countries with vulnerable indigenous populations within their borders.

The most important expression of this radical realignment was the 1999 Declaration on Anthropology and Human Rights, which was ratified by the AAA's general membership through its normal annual voting procedures.[9] This document reflected at least a decade of intellectual and political developments within the association itself, a long process that was intended to both definitively repudiate what was seen as an anachronistic hostility toward human rights (represented by the 1947 statement) and establish a formal basis on which anthropologists could mobilize their expertise in new and politically engaged ways.

As a statement of principles, the 1999 declaration should be read for what it intends to do rather than what it, within its four corners, actually does. In other words, without understanding the broader discursive and historical contexts in which the declaration was forged, it would actually be quite difficult to know how to read it in relation to, for example, the UDHR, not to mention the 1947 Statement on Human Rights. It intends to do several things. Most importantly, the declaration is meant to establish anthropology as a discipline that produces both knowledge of and justifications for human rights that go well beyond those found in existing international law. The most significant of these novel rights is what it calls the "right of people and peoples everywhere to the full realization of their humanity, which is to say their capacity for culture."

The philosophical groundwork for this anthropologically grounded human right was laid most prominently across a number of essays in a 1997 special edition of the *Journal of Anthropological Research*, in which scholars crafted a theoretical scaffolding that could support what Terence Turner described as the promotion of human rights as part of a broader "emancipatory cultural politics." But if the right to realize a capacity for culture was asserted in part as a response to a set of political-economic conditions, it was still necessary to articulate it in the normative language of human rights, rather than in, say, the language of social theory. To do this, the small group of drafters developed what turned out to be an extraordinarily complicated normative principle, one that attempts to innovatively combine the individualism of the foundational international instruments with the more recent concern with collective rights. This was a bold and creative effort, one that—at a conceptual level—continues to be highly suggestive (more below). But the result, as I have implied, was less than satisfactory; the declaration creates more difficulties than it resolves.

For example, one of Melville Herskovits's greatest fears—and a key critique of his (later the AAA's) 1947 statement—was that a statement of universal human rights would not reflect existing diversity in normative practices; in asserting some rights, it would necessarily exclude many others with equal claims to universal legitimacy. The 1999 declaration, however, tries to have it both ways. On the one hand, it asserts that an individual can be fully actualized only through culture and therefore has a right to a *particular* culture.

Yet on the other hand, it implies that this right is merely an addition to the existing body of international law, when in fact a right to culture of this kind would nullify much of it. Consider a hypothetical. A woman in sub-Saharan Africa argues that based on the declaration (or some future legal version of it), she has a human right to realize herself in terms of her culture practices, one of which demands that her daughter undergo female genital circumcision in preparation for marriage. If her daughter does not undergo this procedure—voluntarily or not—the place of the woman and her husband within the wider social network that determines marriage alliances will be compromised, something that could have grave economic consequences for the family, since the relationships established through marriage form the basis for the distribution (and accumulation) of property and other resources.

Now the kind of pressure exerted through cultural expectations in a case like this would compel—in most cases—the daughter to undergo the procedure in a way that would violate any number of provisions within international human rights law (UDHR, articles 3 and 5; Declaration on the Elimination of Violence against Women, article 2, and so on). But if the state were to prevent this procedure from going forward in order to protect the human rights of the daughter, would not the mother's right to culture be violated in the process? She and her husband would be forced to suffer social ostracism, economic penalty, and the possible need to leave the community.

And the classic—Western liberal—limiting language in the 1999 declaration does not help us solve this problem: as it says, the right to culture may be exercised "so long as such activities do not diminish the same capacities of others." This is the language of what Isaiah Berlin (1958) described as "negative liberty," language that could have been lifted directly from *Leviathan*. But if the right to realize oneself through culture is "tantamount to the capacity for humanity," how is it possible to demand that one (like the mother) cede this right (and thus her humanity) in order to protect the rights of another? Is a choice like this inevitable? Necessary?

In the end, the drafters of the 1999 declaration could not resolve this tension between the highly specific individual human rights of instruments like the UDHR and the (largely unarticulated) hybrid and collective human rights that seemed to many anthropologists to be a way out of the normative and political trap of much of the postwar international human rights system. But in its final paragraph, just before exhorting anthropologists to become actively "involved in the debate on enlarging our understanding of human rights on the basis of anthropological knowledge and research," the declaration makes a final key move, one that was intended as a pragmatic recognition that the tension I have just described could not be resolved (at least not within the declaration itself). Yet the implications of this move for wider human rights theory and practice are more profound than the declaration itself seems to realize.

After rejecting what it calls the "abstract legal uniformity of Western tradition," and after a nod to existing international human rights standards, it makes two related assertions: first, that "human rights is not a static concept"; and second, that "our understanding of human rights is constantly evolving as we come to know more about the human condition." Taken together, these represent a radical reinterpretation of both the idea of human rights and its potential expression within international law. They imply that other conceptions of human rights are both theoretically possible and likely to emerge as the historical role of human rights continues to change. An idea of human rights that formally excludes the nation-state and makes a future global federation the source of legitimacy? An idea of human rights that is based on a radically revised understanding of universality? An account of human rights that redefines "human" in a way that subsumes the individual to some global collective? To make the *concept* of human rights itself dynamic is to open the door to these—and many other—possibilities.

Thus, the initial and more circumscribed anthropological preoccupation with indigenous rights led to the development of an alternative vision of human rights with profound implications for wider human rights theory and practice. Although the declaration itself is problematic in many ways, it does manage to outline a framework through which anthropologists (and others, of course) are able to participate in the two-sided project of reframing the idea of human rights itself and at the same time helping to realize the original goals of the postwar human rights system.

Human Rights in an Anthropological Key

BOOKS OF THIS KIND end in different ways. Some end with a final chapter that simply stands alone much as the others did; here the author asks of the reader that she remember the principal arguments and conclusions as they were developed over the course of the book without deigning to formally summarize or restate them. Others end with a concluding chapter that is really more of an introduction, the place where the fullest statement of arguments and structure is to be found. And then there are those in which the author relatively briefly recapitulates the major arguments and implications, not in a way that is meant to substitute for a full engagement with these as they were developed at different points and in different ways, but more in the form of a coda, a conclusion that gives the reader a definite and holistic sense of the book. This last approach is the one I adopt here.

I began by examining the ways in which paradigms have structured our understanding of human rights theory and practice in the postwar period. At an epistemological level, the division of labor into distinct knowledge practices—each with its own mode of engagement, criteria for legitimacy, and set of professional expectations—was perhaps an inevitable response given the historical and political circumstances through which contemporary human rights emerged. But this division of intellectual and institutional labor did not do what it was supposed to do: to more efficiently allocate epistemological resources so as to establish human rights more permanently and legitimately within international political and legal practice. Instead, by breaking down into distinct and exclusionary orientations toward human rights, this historical division of labor has both hardened problems and obscured possibilities.

After a rereading and reinterpretation of the historical relationship between anthropology and human rights, I turned to what have been considered in the wider human rights community the two most anthropological problems facing human rights. In part because of the way the association with relativism, in particular, led to the marginalization of anthropology during the development of human rights theory and practice in the early decades, anthropologists themselves have—as a sort of reaction formation—become its most high-profile and relentless critics. Nevertheless, I showed how the multiple meanings of relativism express dilemmas that continue to bedevil the contemporary human rights project. And apart from the theoretical dimensions of relativism itself, this chapter provided a window into the ways in which key problems within human rights can become politicized beyond all recognition.

The historical understanding of the relationship between culture and human rights has followed a similar trajectory, one in which enduringly pressing issues have been obscured in large part through the way culture itself has been conceived and misconceived. I suggested that to try and examine the relationship between culture and human rights anew is to disappear down a rabbit hole in which nothing is as it appears. As recent ethnographers of human rights have documented in convincing detail, "culture" is often a prism through which broader political, social, and economic imperatives are refracted in ways that have very little to do with the actual relationship between culture and human rights, either conceptually or empirically.

But especially over the last fifteen years, the culture concept has undergone a process of hyper-refinement both in relation to human rights and beyond. This has happened in different ways and for different reasons. Perhaps most telling, and consequential, has been the process through which "culture" has been theoretically complicated in such a way that the traditional opposition between universal human rights and cultural difference appears to vanish into thin air. It is a nice trick and one that is perfectly understandable in light of the stakes involved. The only problem is that it does violence to much of what anthropologists, and others, continue to document about the persistence and even re-entrenchment of culture in its most orthodox and politically unsavory expressions.

I next explored the broader implications of one specialized domain in the recent ethnography of human rights: the study of transnational human rights networks through the actors who constitute them and the artifacts they produce. There is tremendous power and potential in thinking and norming beyond the nation, and the intellectual and moral—if not legal and political—framework of the Universal Declaration was the only real attempt during the postwar settlement to imagine a postnational world, even if it was forced to exist within a broader system in which nation-state sovereignty remained paramount. There is much confusion about what exactly is, or should be, meant by "international" human rights, and the close examination of what has become a truly transnational human rights regime provides a window into a possible future in which citizenship, identity, and translocal affinity might come to approximate the cosmopolitan ideal of human rights.

But despite this momentary burst of futuristic optimism, fueled as it was by the realization that the work of those most grounded of human rights scholars (the anthropologists) had actually converged to a certain extent with the work of those most happily disconnected from reality (the cosmopolitans), the next chapter provided different grounds for skepticism. It is generally acknowledged that anthropologists have contributed the most to human rights theory and practice in the area of collective rights, a contribution that goes back at least to the early 1970s and the founding of Cultural Survival. In particular, anthropologists have worked to advance the cause of indigenous rights politically, institutionally, and, to a lesser extent, theoretically. Yet all of this advocacy on behalf of indigenous populations gave rise, perhaps inevitably, to questions about just what it means to claim human rights based on collective identity. And these questions led to even more basic questions about the nature of identity itself.

The unintended result was that all of the robust political and legal advocacy on behalf of indigenous peoples by anthropologists had the effect of highlighting yet more disjunctures within the broader human rights project. The contemporary and dominant account of human rights relies on both a very specific conception of the person, and (more programmatically) a willingness by people in different times and places to transform identity in terms of this conception. But as it turns out, it is much easier for people to appropriate the idea of human rights for specific legal, political, or social purposes than it is for them to embrace the—at times—radically alternative conception of the person that forms the basis for this idea. In other words, in many cases the coming of human rights demands something of identity that the practice of identity is not prepared (or able) to give.

·   ·   ·

AN ANTHROPOLOGY OF HUMAN RIGHTS makes its contributions as much for what it does not (and cannot) do as for what it does. The implications of anthropology's historical and contemporary engagements with human rights are profound, inspiring, and humbling. This is partly the result of the peculiar combination of ethnographic attention, critical reflection, and (at least for some) sense of ethical commitment through which anthropology has intervened in wider debates over the problems and potential of human rights. An anthropology of human rights underscores a range of basic problems at the heart of the modern human rights project and at the same time points the way toward at least the possibility that transnational (and, perhaps, postnational) normativities can be both conceived and practically constituted in terms of a radically different set of logics.

Yet to make this claim is not to immediately imply what these reformed or alternative normativities are or should be, since at least one of the different logics that emerges from the anthropology of human rights works against the tendency to construct hedgehog-like and totalizing global systems, of which the postwar human rights system is a quintessential example. In other words, one of the implications of these chapters on the relationship between ethical theory and social practice—as this relationship is reflected within human rights—is that the most basic purpose of the postwar international (and, increasingly, transnational) human rights regime is itself problematic. This is the idea that the contemporary world *will be* ultimately unified through a global shift in moral consciousness through which the truth of human rights—and the different ontologies that it implies—will, in the end, be actualized in legal, political, and social practice. Although this teleology was certainly not as hard and fast among the members of the original Commission on Human Rights, who saw their work—as Eleanor Roosevelt's different pronouncements indicate—in aspirational rather than prescriptive terms, the more recent history of human rights simply cannot be understood without it.

It is of course much easier to articulate an alternative account, one that expresses a thoroughgoing skepticism toward several hoary and ethically charged assumptions of the current human rights system, when the ability to count on these assumptions—that the truth of human rights is self-evident, that human rights reflect a conception of the person (based on human dignity, for example) that is universal, that the idea of human rights transcends culture—does not have immediate political or personal consequences. But in answer to the Rortyian, the cynical, the utopian, and the true believers, I can only say that the anthropology of human rights casts a critical light on *both* those who would argue that the pursuit of human rights as currently constituted represents the most effective strategy for realizing concrete (and progressive) reform and those who would argue for the primacy of human rights on metaphysical, neo-Kantian, or other logico-deductive grounds.

If there is a way out of this box, it must be in terms of a practical framework of human rights that critically responds to the historical and political circumstances that gave rise to the postwar international system, and through the articulation of a human rights epistemology that reinscribes the socio-normative in such a way that the idea of human rights emerges from radically different forms of knowledge. I hesitate, in a sense, to make this second claim in precisely this way—that is, in the form of an epistemological critique—because to do so is to draw lines in the sand, lines that also delineate disciplinary boundaries. As we have seen, one of the basic arguments of this book has been that the development—and mis-development—of human rights theory and practice in the postwar period has been shaped in large part in terms of distinct and necessarily competing paradigms, modes of engagement that (less problematically) function as categories of understanding at the same time they (more problematically) work to exclude other possibilities.

So an anthropology of human rights represents, in part, an argument against the disciplinarity of the entire postwar human rights project, a disciplinarity (in both its literal and Foucauldian senses) that has marked the political and institutional dimensions of this project as much as it more obviously has the academic. It is only an apparent paradox that this argument itself emerges from (my own conception of) a discipline, especially when the history of the relationship between anthropology and human rights that I examined in chapter 2 is recalled. Part of what has made contemporary anthropology so innovative and so marginalized at the same time has been the way it has developed and traded in essentially open epistemological frameworks. An anthropology of human rights is thus motivated by both this historical marginalization and commitment to plural approaches (a commitment to pluralism I described in chapter 2 as "ecumenical" in an only partly ironic gesture toward religious history). An anthropology of human rights represents a critical, incomplete, and yet essentially optimistic orientation toward both the current human rights regimes, and, even more, the possibility of different future transnational normativities.

To be optimistic in this sense does not contradict the need to maintain a kind of critical vigilance, especially in light of the wider political economy of human rights that generates a certain amount of positive "power," as Risse, Ropp, and Sikkink (1999) describe it, at the same time it functions as what Laura Nader (1997) would call a "controlling process." As legal anthropologists, comparative legal sociologists, and conflict studies scholars, among others, have shown, to abandon the quasi-religious belief in the need for a tightly circumscribed and narrowly tailored global moral-legal system is not to give in to a Hobbesian vision of a kind of war of all against all, in which no transnational or transcultural norms are empirically possible or morally justifiable. But if there *are* patterns across time and place, patterns that I have described elsewhere as expressing a basic "normative humanism" (2006d), it is doubtful that they have been captured in places like the UDHR or CEDAW, despite sixty years of scholarship, political practice, and earnest activism to the contrary. Yet in documenting the emergence of newly invigorated human rights regimes over the last fifteen years, anthropologists of human rights have shown, among other things, that there *are* good reasons to be hopeful that these patterns do, in fact, exist. What has been lacking is only the intellectual and political will to make sense of these patterns, the willingness to draw out their implications, whatever they might be.

And in doing so, it is entirely possible that we will be led right back, after a fashion, to human rights, although it will be a human rights in a different key, a minor key, one whose tonality does not express the kind of desperate triumphalism and sense of normative certainty that could be heard humming in the background as the postwar international human rights system haltingly emerged over its first five decades, despite the pervasive political opposition, institutional dysfunction, and lack of effectiveness. Instead, an anthropology of human rights envisions a future transnational or postnational normative framework that is based on the imperatives of ethical restraint, humility, and legal pluralism. This does not mean that a human rights in a different and minor key represents a kind of quietism, a capitulation in the face of the ever-present fact of senseless human suffering. It is, rather, a normative response to suffering that reflects a wisdom of a very different and (we might say) anthropological sort: that which comes from an acceptance of the complicated and (to some) endlessly frustrating fact of human multiplicity.

STATEMENT ON HUMAN RIGHTS

SUBMITTED TO THE COMMISSION ON HUMAN RIGHTS,
UNITED NATIONS BY THE EXECUTIVE BOARD,
AMERICAN ANTHROPOLOGICAL ASSOCIATION

The problem faced by the Commission on Human Rights of the United Nations in preparing its Declaration on the Rights of Man must be approached from two points of view. The first, in terms of which the Declaration is ordinarily conceived, concerns the respect for the personality of the individual as such, and his right to its fullest development as a member of his society. In a world order, however, respect for the cultures of differing human groups is equally important.

These are two facets of the same problem, since it is a truism that groups are composed of individuals, and human beings do not function outside the societies of which they form a part. The problem is thus to formulate a statement of human rights that will do more than just phrase respect for the individual as an individual. It must also take into full account the individual as a member of the social group of which he is a part, whose sanctioned modes of life shape his behavior, and with whose fate his own is thus inextricably bound.

Because of the great numbers of societies that are in intimate contact in the modern world, and because of the diversity of their ways of life, the primary task confronting those who would draw up a Declaration on the Rights of Man is thus, in essence, to resolve the following problem: How can the proposed Declaration be applicable to all human beings, and not be a statement of rights conceived only in terms of the values prevalent in the countries of Western Europe and America?

Before we can cope with this problem, it will be necessary for us to outline some of the findings of the sciences that deal with the study of human culture, that must be taken into account if the Declaration is to be in accord with the present state of knowledge about man and his modes of life.

If we begin, as we must, with the individual, we find that from the moment of his birth not only his behavior, but his very thought, his hopes, aspirations, the moral values which direct his action and justify and give meaning to his life in his own eyes and those of his fellows, are shaped by the body of custom of the group of which he becomes a member. The process by means of which this is accomplished is so subtle, and its effects are so far-reaching, that only after considerable training are we conscious of it. Yet if the essence of the Declaration is to be, as it must, a statement in which the right of the individual to develop his personality to the fullest is to be stressed, then this must be based on a recognition of the fact that the personality of the individual can develop only in terms of the culture of his society.

Over the past fifty years, the many ways in which man resolves the problems of subsistence, of social living, of political regulation of group life, of reaching accord with the Universe and satisfying his aesthetic drives has been widely documented by the researches of anthropologists among peoples living in all parts of the world. All peoples do achieve these ends. No two of them, however, do so in exactly the same way, and some of them employ means that differ, often strikingly, from one another.

Yet here a dilemma arises. Because of the social setting of the learning process, the individual cannot but be convinced that his own way of life is the most desirable one. Conversely, and despite changes originating from within and without his culture that he recognizes as worthy of adoption, it becomes equally patent to him that, in the main, other ways than his own, to the degree they differ from it, are less desirable than those to which he is accustomed. Hence valuations arise, that in themselves receive the sanction of accepted belief.

The degree to which such evaluations eventuate in action depends on the basic sanctions in the thought of a people. In the main, people are willing to live and let live, exhibiting a tolerance for behavior of another group different than their own, especially where there is no conflict in the subsistence field. In the history of Western Europe and America, however, economic expansion, control of armaments, and an evangelical religious tradition have translated the recognition of cultural differences into a summons to action. This has been emphasized by philosophical systems that have stressed absolutes in the realm of values and ends. Definitions of freedom, concepts of the nature of human rights, and the like, have thus been narrowly drawn. Alternatives have been decried, and suppressed where controls have been established over non-European peoples. The hard core of *similarities* between cultures has consistently been overlooked.

The consequences of this point of view have been disastrous for mankind. Doctrines of the "white man's burden" have been employed to implement economic exploitation and to deny the right to control their own affairs to millions of peoples over the world, where the expansion of Europe and America has not meant the literal extermination of whole populations. Rationalized in terms of ascribing cultural inferiority to these peoples, or in conceptions of their backwardness in development of their "primitive mentality," that justified their being held in the tutelage of their superiors, the history of the expansion of the western world has been marked by demoralization of human personality and the disintegration of human rights among the peoples over whom hegemony has been established.

The values of the ways of life of these peoples have been consistently misunderstood and decried. Religious beliefs that for untold ages have carried conviction, and permitted adjustment to the Universe have been attacked as superstitious, immoral, untrue. And, since power carries its own conviction, this has furthered the process of demoralization begun by economic exploitation and the loss of political autonomy. The white man's burden, the civilizing mission, have been heavy indeed. But their weight has not been borne by those who, frequently in all honesty, have journeyed to the far places of the world to uplift those regarded by them as inferior.

We thus come to the first proposition that the study of human psychology and culture dictates as essential in drawing up a Bill of Human Rights in terms of existing knowledge:

> 1. *The individual realizes his personality through his culture, hence respect for individual differences entails a respect for cultural differences.*

There can be no individual freedom, that is, when the group with which the individual identifies himself is not free. There can be no full development of the individual personality as long as the individual is told, by men who have the power to enforce their commands, that the way of life of his group is inferior to that of those who wield the power.

This is more than an academic question, as becomes evident if one looks about him at the world as it exists today. Peoples who on first contact with European and American might were awed and partially convinced of the superior ways of their rulers have, through two wars and a depression, come to reexamine the new and the old. Professions of love of democracy, of devotion to freedom have come with something less than conviction to those who are themselves denied the right to lead their lives as seems proper to them. The religious dogmas of those who profess equality and practice discrimination, who stress the virtue of humility and are themselves arrogant in insistence on their beliefs have little meaning for peoples whose devotion to other faiths makes these inconsistencies as clear as the desert landscape at high noon. Small wonder that these peoples, denied the right to live in terms of their own cultures, are discovering new values in old beliefs they had been led to question.

No consideration of human rights can be adequate without taking into account the related problem of human capacity. Man, biologically, is one. *Homo sapiens* is a single species, no matter how individuals may differ in their aptitudes, their abilities, their interests. It is established that any normal individual can learn any part of any culture other than his own, provided only he is afforded the opportunity to do so. That cultures differ in degree of complexity, of richness of content, is due to historic forces, not biological ones. All existing ways of life meet the test of survival. Of those cultures that have disappeared, it must be remembered that their number includes some that were great, powerful, and complex as well as others that were modest, content with the *status quo*, and simple. Thus we reach a second principle:

> 2. *Respect for differences between cultures is validated by the scientific fact that no technique of qualitatively evaluating cultures has been discovered.*

This principle leads us to a further one, namely that the aims that guide the life of every people are self-evident in their significance to that people. It is the principle that emphasizes the universals in human conduct rather than the absolutes that the culture of Western Europe and America stresses. It recognizes that the eternal verities only seem so because we have been taught to regard them as such; that every people, whether it expresses them or not, lives in devotion to verities whose eternal nature is as real to them as are those of Euroamerican culture to Euroamericans. Briefly stated, this third principle that must be introduced into our consideration is the following:

> 3. *Standards and values are relative to the culture from which they derive so that any attempt to formulate postulates that grow out of the beliefs or moral codes of one culture must to that extent detract from the applicability of any Declaration of Human Rights to mankind as a whole.*

Ideas of right and wrong, good and evil, are found in all societies, though they differ in their expression among different peoples. What is held to be a human right in one society may be regarded as anti-social by another people, or by the same people in a different period of their history. The saint of one epoch would at a later time be confined as a man not fitted to cope with reality. Even the nature of the physical world, the colors we see, the sounds we hear, are conditioned by the language we speak, which is part of the culture into which we are born.

The problem of drawing up a Declaration of Human Rights was relatively simple in the Eighteenth Century, because it was not a matter of *human* rights, but of the rights of men within the framework of the sanctions laid by a single society. Even then, so noble a document as the American Declaration of Independence, or the American Bill of Rights, could be written by men who themselves were slave-owners, in a country where chattel slavery was a part of the recognized social order. The revolutionary character of the slogan "Liberty, Equality, Fraternity" was never more apparent than in the struggles to implement it by extending it to the French slave-owning colonies.

Today the problem is complicated by the fact that the Declaration must be of worldwide applicability. It must embrace and recognize the validity of many different ways of life. It will not be convincing to the Indonesian, the African, the Indian, the Chinese, if it lies on the same plane as like documents of an earlier period. The rights of Man in the Twentieth Century cannot be circumscribed by the standards of any single culture, or be dictated by the aspirations of any single people. Such a document will lead to frustration, not realization of the personalities of vast numbers of human beings.

Such persons, living in terms of values not envisaged by a limited Declaration, will thus be excluded from the freedom of full participation in the only right and proper way of life that can be known to them, the institutions, sanctions and goals that make up the culture of their particular society.

Even where political systems exist that deny citizens the right of participation in their government, or seek to conquer weaker peoples, underlying cultural values may be called on to bring the peoples of such states to a realization of the consequences of the acts of their governments, and thus enforce a brake upon discrimination and conquest. For the political system of a people is only a small part of their total culture.

World-wide standards of freedom and justice, based on the principle that man is free only when he lives as his society defines freedom, that his rights are those he recognizes as a member of his society, must be basic. Conversely, an effective world-order cannot be devised except insofar as it permits the free play of personality of the members of its constituent social units, and draws strength from the enrichment to be derived from the interplay of varying personalities.

The world-wide acclaim accorded the Atlantic Charter, before its restricted applicability was announced, is evidence of the fact that freedom is understood and sought after by peoples having the most diverse cultures. Only when a statement of the right of men to live in terms of their own traditions is incorporated into the proposed Declaration, then, can the next step of defining the rights and duties of human groups as regards each other be set upon the firm foundation of the present-day scientific knowledge of Man.

June 24, 1947

Declaration on Anthropology and Human Rights
Committee for Human Rights
American Anthropological Association

Adopted by the AAA membership June 1999

This Declaration on Anthropology and Human Rights defines the basis for the involvement of the American Anthropological Association, and, more generally, of the profession of Anthropology in human rights. Comments and queries from members regarding the Declaration's content are welcome.

Preamble

The capacity for culture is tantamount to the capacity for humanity. Culture is the precondition for the realization of this capacity by individuals, and in turn depends on the cooperative efforts of individuals for its creation and reproduction. Anthropology's cumulative knowledge of human cultures, and of human mental and physical capacities across all populations, types, and social groups, attests to the universality of the human capacity for culture. This knowledge entails an ethical commitment to the equal opportunity of all cultures, societies, and persons to realize this capacity in their cultural identities and social lives. However, the global environment is fraught with violence which is perpetrated by states and their representatives, corporations, and other actors. That violence limits the humanity of individuals and collectives.

Anthropology as a profession is committed to the promotion and protection of the right of people and peoples everywhere to the full realization of their humanity, which is to say their capacity for culture. When any culture or society denies or permits the denial of such opportunity to any of its own members or others, the American Anthropological Association has an ethical responsibility to protest and oppose such deprivation. This implies starting from the base line of the Universal Declaration of Human Rights and associated implementing international legislation, but also expanding the definition of human rights to include areas not necessarily addressed by international law. These areas include collective as well as individual rights, cultural, social, and economic development, and a clean and safe environment.

Declaration on Anthropology and Human Rights

The American Anthropological Association has developed a Declaration that we believe has universal relevance:

> People and groups have a generic right to realize their capacity for culture, and to produce, reproduce and change the conditions and forms of their physical, personal and social existence, so long as such activities do not diminish the same capacities of others. Anthropology as an academic discipline studies the bases and the forms of human diversity and unity; anthropology as a practice seeks to apply this knowledge to the solution of human problems.
>
> As a professional organization of anthropologists, the AAA has long been, and should continue to be, concerned whenever human difference is made the basis for a denial of basic human rights, where "human" is understood in its full range of cultural, social, linguistic, psychological, and biological senses.

Thus, the AAA founds its approach on anthropological principles of respect for concrete human differences, both collective and individual, rather than the abstract legal uniformity of Western tradition. In practical terms, however, its working definition builds on the Universal Declaration of Human Rights (UDHR), the International Covenants on Civil and Political Rights, and on Social, Economic, and Cultural Rights, the Conventions on Torture, Genocide, and Elimination of All Forms of Discrimination Against Women, and other treaties which bring basic human rights within the parameters of international written and customary law and practice. The AAA definition thus reflects a commitment to human rights consistent with international principles but not limited by them. Human rights is not a static concept. Our understanding of human rights is constantly evolving as we come to know more about the human condition. It is therefore incumbent on anthropologists to be involved in the debate on enlarging our understanding of human rights on the basis of anthropological knowledge and research.

Notes

Chapter 1

1. For a more detailed and similarly appreciative discussion of Bowen's study of legal discourse as a form of social reasoning, see my essay "Traversing Boundaries: New Anthropologies of Law," in *American Anthropologist* (2005b).

2. In his book *Postcolonial Liberalism* (2002), the political philosopher Duncan Ivison distills the essence of this bundle in the following way: "[There are] three distinctive liberal values: that individuals and peoples are fundamentally equal; that they are free; and that social and political arrangements should be such as to promote the well-being of individuals and groups in the manner, generally speaking, that they conceive of it" (5). Taken together, these values constitute what Ivison describes as the "liberal register," which acts in the world in order to set boundaries around the "structure of moral experience" (21).

Chapter 2

1. For an excellent overview of the history of the drafting of what became the UDHR, see Johannes Morsink 1999. For a more comprehensive study of the place of human rights within the larger United Nations system, see Alston 2006.

2. To give you a sense of how (un-)representative the UN was at the time the UDHR was being drafted, consider this: only forty-eight countries were able to vote to adopt the Universal Declaration, and there were eight provocative and important abstentions, which included six communist nations and Saudi Arabia and South Africa. Thus, despite the fact that "different cultural, religious, economic, and political systems" (Morsink 1999:21) were indeed present among these forty-eight member-nations, the fact remains that much of the world's cultural diversity simply could not find political expression within the early postwar United Nations.

3. The Statement on Human Rights was published almost exactly one year before the UDHR was adopted by the UN Third General Assembly on December 10, 1948.

4. By *scientific* knowledge I mean to distinguish the anthropological claim to authority at mid-twentieth century from religious, philosophical, creative, and other sources of knowledge—or wisdom—about the human condition that rested on spiritual

or purely theoretical or other grounds. The three major anthropological traditions by the late 1940s were American cultural anthropology and British and French social anthropology.

5. These are currently housed in a Smithsonian Museum Support Center in Suitland, Maryland. I thank the administrator of the NAA for allowing me to conduct research in the archives and for guiding me through the documentary sources of the AAA.

6. The cultural processes studied by American cultural anthropologists both did and did not fit the exotic stereotypes that have been associated with anthropology since the early twentieth century. Margaret Mead's accounts of what the British social anthropologist Bronislaw Malinowski called the "sexual life of savages" are perhaps the quintessential example of this trope, while Melville Herskovits himself produced influential work on America's internal mid-century Other—the culture of the American Negro (see, e.g., Herskovits 1941).

7. For a good discussion of the history of American cultural anthropology and its role in wider political and social currents at different points in the twentieth century, see volumes 7 and 8 of the History of Anthropology series edited by George Stocking (1993, 1996). See also di Leonardo 1998.

8. For a contemporary introduction to the research and politics of public anthropology, see the Web site maintained by Robert Borofsky (www.publicanthropology.org), who is also the editor of the Public Anthropology series published by the University of California Press.

9. For an early analysis of the role of UNESCO in the UDHR drafting process, see Maritain 1949.

10. NAA, Box 23, General File, 1930–1949. The members of the NRC's Committee for International Cooperation in Anthropology at this time were, in addition to Melville Herskovits as chairman, the following: Henry Collins, John Cooper, William Fenton, Henry Field, Frederica de Laguna, Robert Lowie, William Duncan Strong, and Franz Weidenreich.

11. I have not been able to uncover any evidence that other professional anthropological associations were solicited by UNESCO during this time.

12. NAA, Box 192, AAA Executive Board Minutes, March 1946–May 1954.

13. The fact that Herskovits had already submitted the Statement on Human Rights to UNESCO on behalf of the NRC's anthropology committee—and not the AAA—is established definitively in a letter from Herskovits to the AAA Executive Board, in which he says: "Here is the draft of the statement I sent to the UNESCO Committee, revised in accordance with the idea that it would be forwarded to the Commission on Human Rights of the UN, from the Association" (NAA, Box 2, 1947 Presidential Correspondence). Further, there is no correspondence between UNESCO and the AAA about the Commission for Human Rights in the NAA and no official request from UNESCO to the AAA for an advisory opinion.

14. For example, in 1946 there were approximately 600 professional anthropologists in the United States. But there were only 200 AAA members at this time, a majority of which were, remarkably, non-anthropologists. They were, instead, "amateurs, students,

[and] interested persons from other fields, and libraries" (AAA Executive Board Minutes, 1946).

15. Because Canada was not one of the eight members of the Drafting Committee, Humphrey was not actually a voting member of the committee.

16. Morsink describes Santa Cruz as a "professor of criminal procedure and military procedure at various military academies . . . when appointed [a] permanent UN representative" (1999:30).

17. On the day I write this (March 15, 2006—ominously, the Ides of March), the General Assembly of the United Nations voted to disband the Commission on Human Rights (whose ranks had grown to 53 members over the years) and replace it with a new Human Rights Council. Of the 170 member-states, only 4 voted against the new council: Israel, the Marshall Islands, Palau, and the United States. There is obviously a bitter irony in the fact that although an American representative was both the first chair of the Commission on Human Rights, and perhaps the leading (or at least most public) advocate for human rights after the adoption of the UDHR, American officials were, by 2006, among the leading (certainly the most powerful) critics of the international human rights system that the United States did much to create.

18. In fact, this was the point of Julian Steward's short comment on the statement, published in 1949. Interestingly, Steward's invocation of the Holocaust led him to argue *not* that the American Anthropological Association should have supported a declaration of human rights, but that anthropologists should abstain *as scientists* from making any claims whatsoever about human rights.

19. As Bentham famously put it, in his "examination of the Declaration of Rights issued during the French Revolution," "*Natural rights* is simple nonsense: natural and imprescriptible rights, rhetorical nonsense—nonsense upon stilts . . . *Right*, the substantive *right*, is the child of law: from *real* laws come *real* rights" (quoted in Melden 1970:28, 30–34; emphases in original).

20. By October 1946, the Major War Criminals Trial had concluded and ten of the most notorious of the defendants had already been executed (Goering, who had also been given a death sentence, preempted the court by committing suicide).

21. In his brief Comment on the Statement on Human Rights, Steward went even further than Herskovits. As he said, "A declaration about human rights . . . come[s] perilously close to the advocacy of American ideological imperialism" (1948:352).

22. This dual sameness is expressed throughout the UDHR: all "members of the human family" possess an "inherent dignity" and "equal and inalienable rights"; all human beings are "born" with the same capacity for "reason and conscience"; and so on.

23. Indeed, Herskovits's participation in the civil rights movement began much earlier. As Diner explains, Herskovits "spoke frequently at black gatherings and addressed the 1927 Pan-African Congress. . . . He lectured frequently . . . on black contributions to American society and on the history of discrimination against blacks" (1995:146).

24. Whether this divide between civil rights (i.e., those created by the state) and human rights is justifiable is another question. Although the U.S. Constitution does not mention human rights, it is clear that the rights that formed the basis for the civil rights

movements of the 1950s and 1960s (equal protection, due process, etc.) were associated with the natural rights invoked in the Declaration of Independence; indeed, the entire political rationale for government, as understood by the framers, was to create a system for protecting those "inalienable rights" of which all men were "endowed by their Creator." All of this is well known. But what has not been well analyzed is the extent to which the strong *civil* rights language of the U.S. Constitution, and the corresponding absence of human or natural rights language, is part of the reason why the United States has had a persistently ambivalent relationship with the international human rights movement.

25. For example, the Declaration of the Rights of the Child (1959), the Declaration on the Granting of Independence to Colonial Countries and Peoples (1961), the International Covenant on Economic, Social and Cultural Rights (1966), the International Covenant on Civil and Political Rights (1966), and the International Convention on the Elimination of All Forms of Racial Discrimination (1966).

26. I say this with some hesitation because cofounder David Maybury-Lewis gives human rights a more significant role in the origins of Cultural Survival. As he wrote in a 1991 reflection piece in *Cultural Survival Quarterly*, "My wife, Pia, and I founded Cultural Survival in 1972 because we had seen how the human rights of indigenous peoples were being trampled in the name of development. We felt that this was both immoral and unnecessary. But if it was unnecessary, then why did it happen, and what was the alternative? Cultural Survival was launched to investigate the abuses, but also to seek and promote viable alternatives" (1991:1). The dilemma here is that neither "human" nor "indigenous" rights feature prominently in early Cultural Survival publications or statements. For example, in 1982 the six-year-old *Cultural Survival Newsletter* was transformed into *Cultural Survival Quarterly*. Jason Clay, the first editor (who would go on to help develop the concept of "green marketing"), described what the move from a newsletter to a more traditional journal meant. He explained that "the name change reflects the expansion of the format as well as our attempt to provide more in-depth analysis about situations critical to the survival of specific tribal societies or ethnic minorities throughout the world" (1982:1). So even though the cultural survival of "tribal societies" and "ethnic minorities" is obviously the main concern of Cultural Survival as of 1982 (ten years after its founding), this concern had not yet been definitively reframed within an indigenous rights discourse, which was at this time still embryonic. See chapter 5 in this book, which examines anthropology's relationship to the emergence of indigenous and other neoliberal human rights.

27. Dismantling *did* occur in several high-profile cases. For example, in 1988 the Department of Anthropology at Duke University was split into two new units: the Department of Cultural Anthropology and the Department of Biological Anthropology and Anatomy. And somewhat later (1997), Stanford's Department of Anthropology was also dismantled as a result of a "long history of departmental tension" that had its roots in the turmoil of the 1980s (Shenk 2006). What emerged was a new Department of Cultural and Social Anthropology and Department of Anthropological Sciences.

28. Good accounts of developments in contemporary anthropological theory can be found in (among others) Knauft 1996 and Moore and Sanders 2006.

29. The 1993 International Year of the World's Indigenous People had been proclaimed by the UN in a 1990 General Assembly Resolution (45/164). And in the same year (1993), based on a recommendation that emerged from the 1993 UN World Conference on Human Rights in Vienna, the International Year of the World's Indigenous People was converted into the International Decade of the World's Indigenous People (1995–2004).

30. The following is drawn from the *1995–2000 Cumulative 5-year Report* published by the Committee for Human Rights, American Anthropological Association (AAA/CfHR 2001).

31. For an important example of the kind of politically engaged scholarship that expressed this new orientation, see Sanford 2003.

32. The task force was chaired by former AAA president Jane H. Hill. Its members were, besides then-current Committee for Human Rights member Janet Chernela, Fernando Coronil, Ray Hames, Trudy Turner, and Joe Watkins. Ray Hames later resigned from the task force because of the "appearance of bias" (Chagnon had served on his dissertation committee).

33. Before the book was actually published, the *New Yorker* carried an extensive excerpt (October 9, 2000), which laid the critical public foundation for the book and overshadowed the efforts of the AAA to respond to its charges. The two-part reports of the AAA task force can be found at http://www.aaanet.org/edtf/final/preface.htm. A good overview and analysis of the El Dorado controversy can be found in Borofsky 2005.

34. The vote also meant that the AAA had to take several fairly significant corrective actions, including issuing a press release to the national media, reviewing its procedures for internal ethics investigations, and agreeing to maintain the referendum to rescind on the official AAA Web site for as long as the El Dorado Report itself was available there.

35. Important examples would be Sheila Dauer (Amnesty International), Victoria Baxter (Science and Human Rights Program, American Association for the Advancement of Science), and Ida Nicolaisen (UN Permanent Forum on Indigenous Issues).

36. I will be drawing from this body of work throughout this book in different ways. But I am principally thinking about research that has appeared in four edited volumes (Cowan, Dembour, and Wilson 2001; Goodale and Merry 2007; Wilson 1997; and Wilson and Mitchell 2003) and in a number of monographs on different empirical dimensions of human rights, including Clarke 2008; Englund 2006; Goodale 2009a; Merry 2006a; Riles 2000; Slyomovics 2005; Speed 2008; Tate 2007; and Wilson 2001.

Chapter 3

1. *The Defeat of the Mind* was first published in France in 1987. For an insightful and concise intellectual biography of Finkielkraut, see the introduction to Judith Friedlander's 1995 translation. As Friedlander explains more fully elsewhere—in her book *Vilna on the Seine: Jewish Intellectuals in France Since 1968* (1990)—Finkielkraut's attacks on relativism stem very much from his own subject-position as a Jew at a time when the elite left's anticolonial rhetoric against Israel was melding into—in Finkielkraut's opinion—a more general (and insidious) rhetoric of anti-Semitism.

2. Finkielkraut is adapting here for his own purposes what he describes as "the cry against art and thought first expressed by Russian populists in the nineteenth century" (112). But this "cry against art and thought" had its origins in the writings of Dostoevsky, and its use by Finkielkraut is shot through with irony. Dostoevsky has a character say something close to this within the context of a biting *satire* of the growing nihilist movement in mid-century Russia (in a story published in 1864 in Dostoevsky's journal *Epokha*). And instead of being a cry against "world literature" or "universal culture," the original quote has the character comparing the work of the quintessentially Russian poet Pushkin with a pair of boots (although Shakespeare is mentioned in another place, whence the later conflation). To the extent to which the quote was directed against the nihilists, it should be pointed out that they were not "populists" or even "nationalists" (the idea of a Russian "nation" was very much incipient at this period, see Hobsbawm 1987)—as were the conservative Slavophiles, another contemporary movement during this time of ferment in Russian history—but rather took their theoretical and political inspiration as much from Western liberalism as their parents' generation, although they drew radically different conclusions.

3. That is, if "Hopi" can be translated as "the people," this is not because this particular group of Native Americans is locating their identity within a universal class that contains all members of the species *Homo sapiens*, both Hopi and non-Hopi, but because they are doing something quite different: they are defining themselves as fundamentally different from all other beings who might otherwise share some common characteristics. Whether in doing so they also create a hierarchy of being—with Hopis on or near the top—is a different, but also obviously important, question.

4. This rhetorical question is not as odd as it might appear. Johannes Fabian (1983) wrote an entire book on the ways in which the project of Western modernity denies "coevalness," or the privilege of coexisting in the same time and space, to the Other (a category that would include Donnelly's Hopi and Arapahoe, as well as Bolivia's *runa*).

5. As might be supposed based on the last chapter, I fully agree with Donnelly's observation that "anthropologists, right through the Cold War, consistently failed to enter [the relativism and universal human rights] debate with a more sophisticated critique" (2003:87). However, as I have also described, there is still confusion in the historical record over whether or not the 1947 Statement on Human Rights caused anthropologists to exclude themselves en masse from the development of human rights theory and practice in the early postwar period, or (at the other extreme) whether they were the victims of a semi-official campaign by prominent international lawyers to ban them from participating, in part because of what was perceived to be anthropology's essentially subversive commitment to particularity, relativism, and, of course, culture. And, even more significantly, if Donnelly and I are both correct, and anthropologists did not play a key role in the development of human rights—for whatever reason—we certainly diverge in how we understand the implications of this absence.

6. According to Ernesto Laclau, "[An] empty signifier is, strictly speaking, a signifier without a signified" (1996:36). Perhaps more to the point in relation to the uses of "relativ-

ism," an empty signifier is "something which points, from within the process of significa-tion, to the discursive presence of its own limits" (36).

7. I say "suggests" because Spiro draws a distinction between conceptual and histor-ical understandings of relativism, and it is not clear if by a "point of departure" he means that epistemological relativism is related to strong descriptive relativism historically or conceptually (or perhaps both).

8. These are: descriptive ethical relativism, normative ethical relativism, metaethi-cal relativism, and metaevaluative relativism (Peffer 1990). Note that for Peffer "cul-ture" does not constitute a conceptual foundation for any of the four types of relativism. Rather, much more than Dundes Renteln or Spiro, he makes "ethics" the center of the analytical wheel around which the varieties of relativism turn.

9. As Donnelly explains, the "Universal Declaration generally formulates rights at the level of what I will call the *concept*, an abstract, general statement of an orienting value" (2003:94; emphasis in original).

10. I will come back to variations on this intercultural approach to human rights—which seeks to find the basic core of Western human rights within the textual and ritual traditions of different world religions and non-Western cultures—in chapter 4.

11. For example, Donnelly's approach appears in his publication written for the U.S. State Department and intended as a kind of official U.S. position on human rights directed toward foreign audiences. See his "What are human rights?" at: http://usinfo .state.gov/products/pubs/hrintro/donnelly.htm. His overview of human rights is imme-diately followed by an excerpt from a 1978 speech on human rights made by former president Jimmy Carter at an event marking the thirtieth anniversary of the Universal Declaration. It is quite interesting that the current (as of 2008) U.S. State Department gives pride of place to this speech in particular—and not one delivered by subsequent Republican presidents—in order to demonstrate how a "concern for human rights [is] a basic element of the country's foreign policy" (Carter 1978).

12. As he explains, "My fields are political theory and international relations. My strength is conceptual analysis. And I think that the sort of conceptual clarity for which I strive . . . is of both intellectual and political value" (2003:87).

13. This is obviously not the place for a full discussion of this, but it is worth at least reminding ourselves that the core of modern Western epistemology is to be found in Descartes's four ironclad rules of method, among which are to "divide each . . . [prob-lem] . . . into as many parts as possible" and then reassemble them, "commencing with the simplest and easiest to know objects . . . ris[ing] gradually . . . to the knowledge of the most composite things" (*Discourse on Method*, part 2). Descartes was simply taking an approach to knowledge that "geometricians commonly use[d] to attain their most difficult demonstrations" and extending it to everything that could be known by ratio-nal beings. The "long chains of reasoning" that this method produces are—and must be, to be considered valid—entirely conceptual.

14. I invoke phenomenology here as a general way of discussing and highlighting subjective human experience of things beyond the rational or physical. I realize this is an unorthodox usage and one probably not acceptable to professional philosophers.

Nevertheless, as will be seen at different places throughout this book, I find the category useful for capturing the importance of especially mundane encounters with human rights within the vagaries and implicitness of everyday life.

15. I underscore "apparent" as a way of reminding the likely readers of this book that large numbers of people in the world understand the very substance of the body within belief systems that are incompatible with the way the body is understood by modern Western biology and genetics.

16. See Baxi's important discussion of the role of suffering within human rights discourse (e.g., 2002:17–18).

17. It is worth underscoring that the historicization and contextualization of a set of issues associated with both culture and relativism by Cowan, Dembour, and Wilson in and through this 2001 volume was a real turning point for interdisciplinary human rights studies, and also a clear signal that the anthropology of rights was beginning to innovate in key ways.

Chapter 4

1. On the exact day I write this (July 13, 2006), the U.S. House of Representatives voted after a heated debate to renew the 1965 Voting Rights Act, one of the most important symbols of this earlier period in U.S. constitutional history. But as if to give the lie to the dominant idea of that time that the march of progress is unidirectional and inevitable, consider the fact that there even *was* a heated debate in 2006 over the renewal of this most well enshrined of congressional acts from the civil rights era (second only to the Civil Rights Act that preceded it by a year).

2. Hegel's influence on the development of the idea of *Kultur* through *Volksgeist* was a complicated one. For Hegel, the *Volksgeist* was only a specific manifestation of the *Weltgeist*, or World-Spirit, which was the active principle that unified human beings throughout history *across* cultures. But as we will see, it was historical uniqueness (which owes more to Herder than Hegel)—and not the specific expression of an underlying essential unity—that came to define *Kultur* as it was adapted and applied to other contexts.

3. For those interested in a much fuller account of anthropology's intellectual history, see the multiple volumes in the History of Anthropology series edited by George Stocking. For the impact of the German intellectual tradition on American cultural anthropology, see *Volksgeist as Method and Ethic: Essays on Boasian Ethnography and the German Anthropological Tradition* (Stocking 1996).

4. For an excellent more recent anthropological analysis of culture within especially transnational human rights practice, see the introduction to Merry 2006a, 10–19.

5. Other good treatments of the ramifications of German philosophical and ideological currents on twentieth century history can be found in Eric Hobsbawm's multi-volume study of the so-called long nineteenth century, which stretched from the French Revolution to the outbreak of the First World War (1962, 1975, 1987). It should be noted that Hobsbawm's generally skeptical approach to culture—which can be seen in greater detail in both his introduction to, and individual chapter in, Hobsbawm and Ranger

(1983)—was heavily influenced by his own political commitment to Marxism. See also Benedict Anderson's classic study of the development of collective—though not exclusively cultural—imaginaries in the nineteenth century (1983).

6. The chair of the commission, Eleanor Roosevelt, said of article 22 that it was a "compromise between views of certain governments which were anxious that the State should give special . . . recognition to the economic, social and cultural rights of the individual and the view of Governments, such as the U.S. Government, which considered that the . . . obligation of the State should not be specified" (quoted in Morsink 1999:230).

7. I emphasize the significance of the ICESCR to distinguish it from, for example, the earlier Hague Convention for the Protection of Cultural Property in the Event of Armed Conflict (1954), which adopts an even more restricted definition of culture: basically monuments and other cultural "treasures" that may be destroyed during war.

8. The story of the ICESCR has been often told, and lamented, by human rights activists around the world. Although the Commission on Human Rights completed the draft of the ICESCR (and its companion treaty, the International Covenant on Civil and Political Rights) in 1954, it was not until 1966 that the General Assembly "opened it"—as the step is called in the argot of UN legal practice—for signature, ratification, and accession. And a further ten years passed before the ICESCR entered into force after the minimum number (35) of "instruments of ratification or accession" had been received by the UN Secretary-General. As of September 2008, of the 159 parties to the covenant, only 6 have not yet ratified it (http://www2.ohchr.org/english/bodies/ratification/3. htm). The United States, which did not even *sign* the ICESCR until after it had entered into force in 1976, has not yet ratified it and joins a small but diverse list of recalcitrants that includes Belize, Sao Tome and Principe, and South Africa.

9. For an excellent critique of the uses and misuses of culture by UNESCO, see Eriksen 2001.

10. It was not until much later in his career that Rawls formally—if briefly—considered the relationship between his theory of justice and international human rights (1999).

11. See also the work of the Sorbonne's Laboratoire d'Anthropologie Juridique de Paris, in particular the writings on intercultural dialogue, human rights, and law from Christoph Eberhard (2001a, 2001b, 2003).

12. In the interests of full disclosure, I should mention that Professor An-Na'im was a colleague and mentor of mine during the two years I spent as an anthropology faculty member at Emory University (2001–2003), where An-Na'im has been the Charles Howard Candler Professor of Law since 1999.

13. An-Na'im is here citing language from an entry by Preiswerk in *The Year Book of World Affairs* (1978) titled "The Place of Intercultural Relations in International Relations." This definition of culture is interesting for a number of reasons, especially in the way it incorporates the notion of *Weltanschauung* ("worldview"). Like its conceptual cousin *Kultur*, *Weltanschauung* developed within German romanticism as a way of describing the subjective processes through which knowledge of the world emerged

from those hidden recesses of the human spirit that the Romantics valued above reason and intentionality. Here is Dilthey, for example, explaining *Weltanschauung* well after its meaning had been established by Hegel and others: "*Weltanschauungen* [i.e., "worldviews"] are not products of reflection. They are not the fruit of the mere will to know. The perception of reality is an important force in their formation, but only one. They arise from the process of life, from our experience of life, from the structure of our psychic totality. The ascendance of life to consciousness, in the knowledge of reality, the acceptance and appreciation of life, and the accomplishments of the will—this is the slow and difficult work that mankind has performed in the development of its *Weltanschauungen*" (1911).

Chapter 5

1. Korey's study of nongovernmental organizations and the Universal Declaration focuses on the political and institutional implications of Roosevelt's invocation of the "curious grapevine," which first appeared in a 1948 *New York Times* article on the work of the UN Human Rights Commission. As Korey rightly observes, the notion of a curious grapevine of human rights is "pregnant with possibilities" (1998:48).

2. I leave aside the further and important distinction between "nation-state" and "nation"—a distinction that is also frequently ignored—because it is a bit too tangential to the main thrust of the argument here.

3. Although the United States is a relatively young nation-state, there is a surprising level of legal diversity between its different states and regions, a diversity that reflects its complicated political history, especially in the way the official policy of internal imperialism incorporated parts of the legal systems and traditions of Spain, France, and Mexico within the federal structure. This legacy can be seen in the contemporary legal codes of states like of Louisiana, California, and New Mexico. Despite this legal diversity, there has been a powerful countercurrent in the United States since the 1920s, one best represented by the American Law Institute. Led—not surprisingly—by the national equivalent of today's transnational cosmopolitan elites, the ALI's mission has been to foster legal reform throughout the United States by standardizing and clarifying legal principles between different jurisdictions. These efforts have been only partly successful, most notably in the area of commercial law (through the Uniform Commercial Code) and—in collaboration with the American Bar Association—through the standardization of legal education (where ALI's Restatements of the Law are still widely used).

4. "This Constitution, and the Laws of the United States which shall be made in Pursuance thereof; and all Treaties made, or which shall be made, under the Authority of the United States, shall be the supreme Law of the Land; and the Judges in every State shall be bound thereby, any Thing in the Constitution or Laws of any State to the Contrary notwithstanding."

5. A good example was the Civil Rights Act of 1964, a bill passed by the U.S. Congress and signed into law by President Lyndon Johnson. Among other things, this act outlawed, in one dramatic fell swoop, the so-called Jim Crow laws, which were found primarily in the southern part of the country and which had been enacted toward the end

of the nineteenth century in order to counter gains that African Americans had made in the period immediately following the Civil War (a period known as Reconstruction). These laws required segregation by "race" in all manner of public space, from transportation to movie theaters. In my own current state (Virginia), for example, the Civil Rights Act nullified a law that specified the following: "Every person . . . operating . . . any public hall, theatre, opera house, motion picture show or any place of public entertainment or public assemblage which is attended by both white and colored persons, shall separate the white race and the colored race and shall set apart and designate . . . certain seats therein to be occupied by white persons and a portion thereof , or certain seats therein, to be occupied by colored persons" (Cited by U.S. National Park Service 2008).

6. In invoking the case of the United States in this way, I certainly do not mean to suggest that its federal system is not without problems and even glaring contradictions. But I think the analogy between it and a future federal/global political and legal system is suggestive enough to use it in this way, although its many shortcoming are also instructive when thinking about the problems that a global federal system would confront.

7. It is not clear here whether Habermas is saying that the wording of the UDHR was agreed on by the "founding members of the United Nations in 1946" (in which case it would be incorrect) or simply noting the date the UN was founded "by the comparatively small number." There is a syntactic ambiguity here, one most likely the result of what is an unsteady translation (by Max Pensky) from Habermas's notoriously complicated German.

8. I first came across Erman's work on human rights and cosmopolitanism during a spring 2006 international—or transnational?—workshop entitled "Reframing Human Rights: Genesis and Justification," which was sponsored by the Irmgard Coninx Foundation and the Max Weber Center for Advanced Social and Cultural Studies, University of Erfurt. The workshop, which was led by the social theorist Hans Joas, included a provocative keynote speech on torture and human rights by Ronald Dworkin.

9. Riles's study revolved around Fijian government officials and human rights activists who were preparing to attend the United Nations Fourth Conference on Women in Beijing in 1995.

10. For an excellent recent study of the relationship between human rights and cosmopolitanism, see Cheah 2007.

Chapter 6

1. As I mentioned in chapter 4, Ellen Messer has suggested that there was an informal campaign on behalf of at least some international lawyers to exclude anthropologists from the development of human rights in the 1950s and 1960s (and perhaps beyond), because it was felt that the anthropological focus—or, perhaps, obsession—with culture would "destroy the very concept of human rights" (Messer 2006).

2. The literature on collective rights is both contentious and voluminous. Since this book is not intended as a comprehensive survey or introduction to contemporary human rights, as elsewhere I will not burden the reader with a mini-bibliographic essay on

the different debates around collective rights. Nevertheless, I must mention the recent work of one scholar in particular, who has been undertaking a critical historiography of the interwar minority rights treaties, treaties that embodied a quite different doctrine of collective rights (Cowan 2007, n.d.). As she argues, the treaties have been misinterpreted by later scholars, who analyze them *in terms of* much more recent understandings of collective rights. The problem with this, according to Cowan, is that it obscures the more complicated history of collective rights, in which the minority rights treaties were both the expression of a genuine desire to protect vulnerable populations in an earlier new Europe, and an attempt by the great powers to protect their national interests, which were as much moral and ideological as anything else.

3. Costa Rica was the first country to ratify the ICCPR (November 1968); Liberia has been the last (it signed the covenant in 1967 but didn't ratify it until September 2004). The country with about 20 percent of the world's population (China) still has not ratified the ICCPR. The United States, as usual, was a conspicuous holdout: it signed the ICCPR during one Democratic administration (1977), but the U.S. Senate did not ratify it until the next one was about to be elected (June 1992). Although the first President Bush begrudgingly signed the ICCPR's instrument of ratification (the Contract with America was still over two years away), it contained several major reservations, including one that reserved to U.S. states the right to execute juveniles. For a good study of the U.S. reservations to the ICCPR, see Ash 2005.

4. Among which would be the ultimate value of the individual, the value of negative liberty, the value of a system of rights over other normative possibilities, the rejection of group identity (except if by "group" we mean the class "all humans" or, perhaps, "all enlightened liberal humans"), and so on.

5. Indeed, this connection between indigeneity and oppression was later codified in ILO 169, in which indigenous people are "regarded as indigenous on account of their descent from the populations which inhabited the country, or a geographical region to which the country belongs, *at the time of conquest or colonization*" (ILO, art. 1; emphasis added).

6. It is difficult to believe that a policy of assimilationism was considered a progressive advance by some members of the international community as late as 1957. By the end of the century, of course, assimilationism—whether forced or otherwise—had come to be seen as one variation on much darker themes of genocide, ethnic cleansing, and forced migration, among others.

7. For a good overview of this shift, see Greaves 1994, which includes essays of particular interest on efforts to protect indigenous knowledge through the language of intellectual property rights. For a more recent treatment, see Cori Hayden's (2003) ethnographic and critical study of "bioprospecting" in Mexico.

8. ILO 169 has been ratified by only seventeen member-states, twelve of them in Latin America. On September 13, 2007, the UN General Assembly adopted the Declaration on the Rights of Indigenous Peoples. Only four negative votes were cast, but they were all by liberal democracies with large and important indigenous populations (Canada, Australia, New Zealand, and the United States).

9. The 1947 Statement on Human Rights, by contrast, was not ratified by the AAA's general membership. For more on the complicated series of events that led to the statement, and the reasons that these events have been, in general, misconstrued, see the discussions in chapter 2.

Bibliography

Agamben, Giorgio. 1998. *Homo Sacer: Sovereign Power and Bare Life.* Stanford, CA: Stanford University Press.

Alston, Philip, ed. 2000. *Promoting Human Rights through Bills of Rights: Contemporary Perspectives.* Oxford: Oxford University Press.

———. 2005. *Non-State Actors and Human Rights.* Oxford: Oxford University Press.

———. 2006. *The United Nations and Human Rights: A Critical Appraisal.* Oxford: Oxford University Press.

American Anthropological Association (AAA). 1947. Statement on Human Rights. *American Anthropologist* 49 (4): 539–543.

American Anthropological Association, Committee for Human Rights. 1999. Declaration on Anthropology and Human Rights. http://www.aaanet.org/stmts/humanrts.htm, accessed March 18, 2007.

———. 2001. 1995–2000 Cumulative 5-Year Report. http://www.aaanet.org/committees/cfhr/ar95-00.htm, accessed January 20, 2008.

———. 2002. Final report of the El Dorado Task Force, Vols. 1 and 2. http://www.aaanet.org/edtf/final/vol_one.pdf, http://www.aaanet.org/edtf/final/vol_two.pdf, accessed January 20, 2008.

Amit, Vered, ed. 1999. *Constructing the Field: Ethnographic Fieldwork in the Contemporary World.* London: Routledge.

Amnesty International. 2007. About Amnesty International. http://web.amnesty.org/pages/aboutai-index-eng, accessed March 16, 2007.

Anaya, J. 1996. *Indigenous Peoples in International Law.* New York: Oxford University Press.

Anderson, Benedict. 1983. *Imagined Communities: Reflections on the Origin and Spread of Nationalism.* London: Verso.

Anghie, Antony. 2005. *Imperialism, Sovereignty, and the Making of International Law.* Cambridge: Cambridge University Press.

Angle, Stephen C. 2002. *Human Rights and Chinese Thought: A Cross-Cultural Inquiry.* Cambridge: Cambridge University Press.

An-Na'im, Abdullahi Ahmed, ed. 1992. *Human Rights in Cross-Cultural Perspectives: A Quest for Consensus.* Philadelphia: University of Pennsylvania Press.

————. 2006. *African Constitutionalism and the Role of Islam.* Philadelphia: University of Pennsylvania Press.

An-Na'im, Abdullahi Ahmed, and F. Deng, eds. 1990. *Human Rights in Africa: Cross-Cultural Perspectives.* Washington, DC: Brookings Institution.

Appadurai, Arjun. 1996. *Modernity at Large: Cultural Dimensions of Globalization.* Minneapolis: University of Minnesota Press.

Arendt, Hannah. 1951. *The Origins of Totalitarianism.* New York: Harcourt, Brace.

Arnold, Matthew. 2006 [1869]. *Culture and Anarchy.* New York: Oxford University Press.

Ash, Kristina. 2005. U.S. Reservations to the International Covenant on Civil and Political Rights: Credibility Maximization and Global Influence. *Northwestern University Journal of International Human Rights* 3 at http://www.law.northwestern.edu/journals/jihr/v3/7.

Avruch, Kevin. 2006. Culture, Relativism, and Human Rights. In Julie Mertus and Jeffrey Helsing, eds., *Human Rights and Conflict: Exploring the Links Between Rights, Law, and Peacebuilding.* Washington, DC: U.S. Institute of Peace Press.

Barnett, H. G. 1948. On Science and Human Rights. *American Anthropologist* 50:352–355.

Barnhart, Michael. 2001. Getting Beyond Cross-Talk: Why Persisting Disagreements Are Philosophically Nonfatal. In Lynda Bell, Andrew Nathan, and Ilan Peleg, eds., *Negotiating Culture and Human Rights.* New York: Columbia University Press.

Bates, Daniel, and F. Plog. 1990. *Cultural Anthropology.* New York: McGraw-Hill.

Bauer, Joanne R., and Daniel A. Bell, eds. 1999. *The East Asian Challenge for Human Rights.* Cambridge: Cambridge University Press.

Bauman, Zygmunt. 1991. *Intimations of Postmodernity.* New York: Routledge.

————. 1998. *Globalization: The Human Consequences.* Cambridge: Polity Press.

Baxi, Upendra. 1999. Voices of Suffering, Fragmented Universality, and the Future of Human Rights. In Burns H. Weston and Stephen Marks, eds., *The Future of International Human Rights.* Ardsley, NY: Transnational Publishers.

————. 2002. *The Future of Human Rights.* New Delhi: Oxford University Press.

Bayefsky, Anne F. 2001. *The UN Human Rights Treaty System: Universality at the Crossroads.* Ardsley, NY: Transnational Publishers.

Bell, Daniel A., and Jean-Marc Coicaud, eds. 2007. *Ethics in Action: The Ethical Challenges of International Human Rights Nongovernmental Organizations.* New York: Cambridge University Press.

Bell, Lynda S. 2001. Who Produces Asian Identity? Discourse, Discrimination, and Chinese Peasant Women in the Quest for Human Rights. In Lynda S. Bell, Andrew Nathan, and Ilan Peleg, eds., *Negotiating Culture and Human Rights.* New York: Columbia University Press.

Bell, Lynda S., Andrew Nathan, and Ilan Peleg, eds. 2001. *Negotiating Culture and Human Rights.* New York: Columbia University Press.

Bennett, John W. 1949. Science and Human Rights: Reason and Action. *American Anthropologist* 50:329–336.

Berlin, Isaiah. 1953. *The Hedgehog and the Fox: An Essay on Tolstoy's View of History.* London: Weidenfield and Nicolson.

———. 1958. *Two Concepts of Liberty.* Oxford: Clarendon Press.

———. 1969. *Four Essays on Liberty.* Oxford: Oxford University Press.

———. 1990. *The Crooked Timber of Humanity: Chapters in the History of Ideas.* London: John Murray.

Blaser, Mario, Harvey A. Feit, and Glenn McRae, eds. 2004. *In the Way of Development: Indigenous Peoples, Life Projects, and Globalization.* London: Zed Books.

Bloch, Maurice. 1983. *Marxism and Anthropology.* Oxford: Oxford University Press.

Bobbio, Norberto. 1996. *The Age of Rights.* Cambridge: Polity Press.

Borneman, John, ed. 2004. *The Case of Ariel Sharon and the Fate of Universal Jurisdiction.* Princeton, NJ: Princeton University Press.

Borofsky, Robert, ed. 2005. *Yanomami: The Fierce Controversy and What We Can Learn from It.* Berkeley: University of California Press.

Bourdieu, Pierre. 1984. *Distinction: A Social Critique of the Judgement of Taste.* Cambridge, MA: Harvard University Press.

Bowen, John. 2003. *Islam, Law, and Equality in Indonesia: An Anthropology of Public Reasoning.* New York: Cambridge University Press.

Boyle, Elizabeth Heger. 2002. *Female Genital Cutting: Cultural Conflict in the Global Community.* Baltimore: Johns Hopkins University Press.

Brown, Chris. 1999. Universal Human Rights: A Critique. In Tim Dunne and Nicholas Wheeler, eds., *Human Rights in Global Politics.* Cambridge: Cambridge University Press.

Brown, Wendy. 1995. *States of Injury: Power and Freedom in Late Modernity.* Princeton, NJ: Princeton University Press.

Brown, Wendy, and Janet Halley, eds. 2002. *Left Legalism / Left Critique.* Durham, NC: Duke University Press.

Brysk, Alison. 2000. *From Tribal Village to Global Village: Indian Rights and International Relations in Latin America.* Stanford, CA: Stanford University Press.

———, ed. 2002. *Globalization and Human Rights.* Berkeley: University of California Press.

Bush, George W. 2005. President Discusses War on Terror and Upcoming Iraqi Elections. Speech given in Philadelphia, Pennsylvania, December 12. http://www.whitehouse.gov/news/releases/2005/12/20051212-4.html.

Carter, Jimmy. 1978. The U.S. Commitment: Human Rights and Foreign Policy. Speech commemorating the 30th anniversary of the signing of the Universal Declaration of Human Rights. http://usinfo.state.gov/products/pubs/hrintro/carter.htm, accessed August 2, 2008.

Castells, Manuel. 2002. *The Rise of the Network Society.* Oxford: Blackwell.

Chagnon, Napoleon. 1984. *Yanomamo: The Fierce People.* New York: Holt, Reinhart, and Winston.

Chatterjee, Partha. 1993. *The Nation and Its Fragments.* Princeton, NJ: Princeton University Press.

———. 2004. *The Politics of the Governed: Popular Politics in Most of the World.* New York: Columbia University Press.

Cheah, Pheng. 2007. *Inhuman Conditions: On Cosmopolitanism and Human Rights.* Cambridge: Harvard University Press.

Cheah, Pheng, and Bruce Robbins, eds. 1998. *Cosmopolitics: Thinking and Feeling—Beyond the Nation.* Minneapolis: University of Minnesota Press.

Clarke, Kamari Maxine. 2008. *The International Criminal Court and the Micropolitics of Human Rights.* New York: Cambridge University Press.

Clay, Jason. 1982. Editor's Note. *Cultural Survival Quarterly* 6 (1): 1.

Claude, Richard Pierre, and Burns H. Weston, eds. 2006. *Human Rights in the World Community: Issues and Action.* Penn Studies in Human Rights. Philadelphia: University of Pennsylvania Press.

Clifford, James. 1988. *The Predicament of Culture: Twentieth-Century Ethnography, Literature, and Art.* Cambridge: Harvard University Press.

Coicaud, Jean-Marc, Michael Doyle, and Anne-Marie Gardner, eds. 2003. *The Globalization of Human Rights.* Tokyo: United Nations University Press.

Cowan, Jane. 2006. Culture and Rights after *Culture and Rights. American Anthropologist* 108 (1): 9–24.

———. 2007. The Success of Failure? Minority Supervision at the League of Nations. In Marie-Bénédicte Dembour and Tobias Kelly, eds., *Paths to International Justice: Social and Legal Perspectives.* Cambridge: Cambridge University Press.

———. n.d. Were the Minorities Treaties about Justice? In Kamari Maxine Clarke and Mark Goodale, eds., *Mirrors of Justice: Law, Power, and the Making of History.* Unpublished manuscript.

Cowan, Jane, Marie-Bénédicte Dembour, and Richard A. Wilson, eds. 2001. *Culture and Rights: Anthropological Perspectives.* Cambridge: Cambridge University Press.

Cushman, Thomas, ed. 2005. *A Matter of Principle: Humanitarian Arguments for War in Iraq.* Berkeley: University of California Press.

Darian-Smith, Eve, and Peter Fitzpatrick, eds. 1999. *Laws of the Postcolonial.* Ann Arbor: University of Michigan Press.

Dembour, Marie-Bénédicte. 2001. Following the Movement of a Pendulum: Between Universalism and Relativism. In Jane Cowan, Marie-Bénédicte Dembour, and Richard A. Wilson, eds., *Culture and Rights: Anthropological Perspectives.* Cambridge: Cambridge University Press.

———. 2006. *Who Believes in Human Rights? Reflections on the European Convention.* Cambridge: Cambridge University Press.

Dembour, Marie-Bénédicte, and Tobias Kelly, eds. 2007. *Paths to International Justice: Social and Legal Perspectives.* Cambridge: Cambridge University Press.

Descartes, René. 1999. *Discourse on Method and Meditations on First Philosophy.* 4th ed. Indianapolis: Hackett.

de Certeau, Michel. 1984. *The Practice of Everyday Life.* Berkeley: University of California Press.

de Varennes, F. 1996. *Language, Minorities, and Human Rights.* The Hague: Kluwer.

di Leonardo, Micaela. 1998. *Exotics at Home: Anthropologies, Others, American Modernity.* Chicago: University of Chicago Press.

Dilthey, Wilhelm. 1911. Die Typen der Weltanschauung und ihre Ausbildung in den metaphysischen Systemen. In Max Frischeisen-Köhler, ed., *Weltanschauung, Philosophie, und Religion.* Berlin: Reichl.

Diner, Hasia. 1995. *In the Almost Promised Land: American Jews and Blacks, 1915–1935.* Baltimore: Johns Hopkins University Press.

Dionne, E. J., Jr. 2005. Cardinal Ratzinger's Challenge. *Washington Post,* April 19, A19.

Donham, Donald. 1999. *History, Power, Ideology: Central Issues in Marxism and Anthropology.* Berkeley: University of California Press.

Donnelly, Jack. 1985. *The Concept of Human Rights.* New York: St. Martin's.

———. 1997. *International Human Rights.* 2d ed. Boulder, CO: Westview.

———. 2003. *Universal Human Rights in Theory and Practice.* 2d ed. Ithaca, NY: Cornell University Press.

———. 2008. What Are Human Rights? U.S. Department of State, International Information Programs. http://usinfo.state.gov/products/pubs/hrintro/donnelly.htm, accessed August 2, 2008.

Douzinas, Costas. 2000. *The End of Human Rights.* Oxford: Hart Publishing.

Dowdle, Michael. 2001. How a Liberal Jurist Defends the Bangkok Declaration. In Lynda Bell, Andrew Nathan, and Ilan Peleg, eds., *Negotiating Culture and Human Rights.* New York: Columbia University Press.

Downing, Theodore E., and Gilbert Kushner, eds. 1988. *Human Rights and Anthropology.* Cambridge: Cultural Survival.

Dunne, Tim, and Nicholas J. Wheeler, eds. 1999. *Human Rights in Global Politics.* Cambridge: Cambridge University Press.

Dundes Renteln, Alison. 1988. Relativism and the Search for Human Rights. *American Anthropologist* 90: 56–72.

———. 1990. *International Human Rights: Universalism Versus Relativism.* Newbury Park, CA: Sage.

Dworkin, Ronald. 1977. *Taking Rights Seriously.* Cambridge, MA: Harvard University Press.

Dwyer, Kevin. 1991. *Arab Voices: The Human Rights Debate in the Middle East.* Berkeley: University of California Press.

Eberhard, Christophe. 2001a. Human Rights and Intercultural Dialogue: An Anthropological Perspective. *Indian Socio-Legal Studies* 23:99–120.

———. 2001b. Toward an Intercultural Legal Theory: The Dialogical Challenge. *Social and Legal Studies* 10:171–201.

———. 2003. *Droits de l'homme et dialogue intercultural.* Paris: Éditions des Écrivains.

Einstein, Albert. 1965. *Mozart: His Character, His Work.* Oxford: Oxford University Press.

Engle, Karen. 2001. From Skepticism to Embrace: Human Rights and the American Anthropological Association from 1947–1999. *Human Rights Quarterly* 23:536–559.

Englund, Harri. 2006. *Prisoners of Freedom: Human Rights and the African Poor.* Berkeley: University of California Press.

Eriksen, Thomas Hylland. 2001. Between Universalism and Relativism: A Critique of the UNESCO Concept of Culture. In Jane Cowan, Marie-Bénédicte Dembour, and Richard A. Wilson, eds., *Culture and Rights: Anthropological Perspectives.* Cambridge: Cambridge University Press.

Erman, Eva. 2005. *Human Rights and Democracy: Discourse Theory and Global Rights Institutions.* Aldershot: Ashgate.

————. 2006. Cosmopolitanism: A Horizontal View. http://www.irmgard-coninx-stiftung.de/index.php?id=55, accessed March 18, 2007.

Escobar, Arturo. 1995. *Encountering Development: The Making and Unmaking of the Third World.* Princeton, NJ: Princeton University Press.

Fabian, Johannes. 1983. *Time and the Other: How Anthropology Makes Its Object.* New York: Columbia University Press.

Falk, Richard. 1992. Cultural Foundations for the International Protection of Human Rights. In Abdullahi Ahmed An-Na'im, ed., *Human Rights in Cross-Cultural Perspective: A Quest for Consensus.* Philadelphia: University of Pennsylvania Press.

————. 2000. *Human Rights Horizons: The Pursuit of Justice in a Globalizing World.* New York: Routledge.

Finkielkraut, Alain. 1995. *The Defeat of the Mind.* New York: Columbia University Press.

Foucault, Michel. 1972. *The Archaeology of Knowledge.* London: Tavistock.

Fox, Richard G., ed. 1991. *Recapturing Anthropology: Working in the Present.* Santa Fe: SAR Press.

Freeman, Michael. 2002. *Human Rights: An Interdisciplinary Approach.* Cambridge: Polity.

Friedlander, Judith. 1990. *Vilna on the Seine: Jewish Intellectuals in France Since 1968.* New Haven: Yale University Press.

Galipeau, Claude. 1994. *Isaiah Berlin's Liberalism.* Oxford: Oxford University Press.

Galtung, Johann. 1994. *Human Rights in Another Key.* Cambridge: Polity Press.

Geertz, Clifford. 2000. *Available Light: Anthropological Reflections on Philosophical Topics.* Princeton: Princeton University Press.

Gellner, Ernest. 1983. *Nations and Nationalism.* Ithaca: Cornell University Press.

George, Susan. 2003. Globalizing Rights? In Matthew Gibney, ed., *Globalizing Rights: The Oxford Amnesty Lectures, 1999.* Oxford: Oxford University Press.

Gershenhorn, Jerry. 2004. *Melville J. Herskovits and the Racial Politics of Knowledge.* Lincoln: University of Nebraska Press.

Gewirth, Allan. 1996. *The Community of Rights.* Chicago: University of Chicago Press.

Gledhill, John. 2003. Rights and the Poor. In Richard Ashby Wilson and Jon P. Mitchell, eds., *Human Rights in Global Perspective: Anthropological Studies of Rights, Claims, and Entitlements.* London: Routledge.

González, Roberto J. 2007. Phoenix Reborn? The Rise of the "Human Terrain System." *Anthropology Today* 23 (6): 21–22.

Goodale, Mark. 2002. The Globalization of Sympathetic Law and Its Consequences. *Law and Social Inquiry* 27 (3): 401–415.

———. 2005a. Empires of Law: Discipline and Resistance within the Transnational System. *Social and Legal Studies.* 14 (4): 553–583.

———. 2005b. Traversing Boundaries: New Anthropologies of Law. *American Anthropologist* 107 (3): 505–508.

———. 2006a. Ethical Theory as Social Practice. *American Anthropologist* 108 (1): 25–37.

———. 2006b. Introduction to "Anthropology and Human Rights in a New Key." *American Anthropologist* 108 (1): 1–8.

———. 2006c. Reclaiming Modernity: Indigenous Cosmopolitanism and the Coming of the Second Revolution in Bolivia. *American Ethnologist* 33 (4): 634–649.

———. 2006d. Toward a Critical Anthropology of Human Rights. *Current Anthropology* 47 (3): 485–511.

———. 2007a. Locating Rights, Envisioning Law between the Global and the Local. In Mark Goodale and Sally Engle Merry, eds., *The Practice of Human Rights: Tracking Law Between the Global and the Local.* Cambridge: Cambridge University Press.

———. 2007b. The Power of Right(s): Tracking Empires of Law and New Forms of Social Resistance in Bolivia (and Elsewhere). In Mark Goodale and Sally Engle Merry, eds., *The Practice of Human Rights: Tracking Law Between the Global and the Local.* Cambridge: Cambridge University Press.

———. 2009a. *Dilemmas of Modernity: Bolivian Encounters with Law and Liberalism.* Stanford, CA: Stanford University Press.

———. 2009b. Human Rights and Anthropology. In Mark Goodale, ed., *Human Rights: An Anthropological Reader.* Oxford: Blackwell.

———, ed. 2009. *Human Rights: An Anthropological Reader.* Oxford: Blackwell.

Goodale, Mark, and Sally Engle Merry, eds. 2007. *The Practice of Human Rights: Tracking Law Between the Global and the Local.* Cambridge: Cambridge University Press.

Goodhart, Michael. 2003. Origins and Universality in the Human Rights Debates: Cultural Essentialism and the Challenge of Globalization. *Human Rights Quarterly* 25:935–964.

———. 2005. *Democracy as Human Rights: Freedom and Equality in the Age of Globalization.* New York: Routledge.

Greaves, Tom, ed. 1994. *Intellectual Property Rights for Indigenous Peoples: A Sourcebook.* Oklahoma City: Association for Applied Anthropology.

Habermas, Jürgen. 2001. *The Postnational Constellation: Political Essays.* Cambridge, MA: MIT Press.

Hannerz, Ulf. 1992. *Cultural Complexity: Studies in the Social Organization of Meaning.* New York: Columbia University Press.

Hartney, Michael. 1995. Some Confusions Concerning Collective Rights. In Will Kymlicka, ed., *The Rights of Minority Cultures.* Oxford: Oxford University Press.

Hatch, Elvin. 1983. *Culture and Morality: The Relativity of Values in Anthropology.* New York: Columbia University Press.

———. 1997. The Good Side of Relativism. *Journal of Anthropological Research* 53 (3): 371–381.

Hayden, Cori. 2003. *When Nature Goes Public: The Making and Unmaking of Bioprospecting in Mexico.* Princeton, NJ: Princeton University Press.

Hayner, Priscilla. 2002. *Unspeakable Truths: Facing the Challenges of Truth Commissions.* New York: Routledge.

Held, David. 1995. *Democracy and the Global Order: From the Modern Nation-State to Cosmopolitan Governance.* Cambridge: Cambridge University Press.

Herbert, Gary B. 2002. *A Philosophical History of Human Rights.* New Brunswick, NJ: Transaction Publishers.

Hernández-Truyol, Berta Esperanza, ed. 2002. *Moral Imperialism: A Critical Anthology.* New York: NYU Press.

Herskovits, Melville. 1941. *The Myth of the Negro Past.* New York: Harper and Brothers.

Hobsbawm, Eric. 1962. *The Age of Revolution, 1789–1848.* New York: New American Library.

———. 1975. *The Age of Capital, 1848–1875.* London: Weidenfeld and Nicolson.

———. 1987. *The Age of Empire, 1875–1914.* New York: Pantheon.

———. 1992. *Nations and Nationalism since 1780: Programme, Myth, Reality.* Cambridge: Cambridge University Press.

———. 1995. *Age of Extremes: The Short Twentieth Century, 1914–1991.* London: Abacus.

Hobsbawm, Eric, and Terence Ranger, eds. 1983. *The Invention of Tradition.* New York: Cambridge University Press.

Hood, Steven. 2001. Rights Hunting in Non-Western Traditions. In Lynda Bell, Andrew Nathan, and Ilan Peleg, eds., *Negotiating Culture and Human Rights.* New York: Columbia University Press.

Horkheimer, Max, and Theodor W. Adorno. 2002. *Dialectic of Enlightenment: Philosophical Fragments.* Ed. Gunzelin Schmid Noerr. Stanford, CA: Stanford University Press.

Howard, Rhoda E. 1995. *Human Rights and the Search for Community.* Boulder: Westview.

Ignatieff, Michael. 1998. *Isaiah Berlin: A Life.* New York: Metropolitan Books.

———. 2001. *Human Rights as Politics and Idolatry.* Princeton, NJ: Princeton University Press.

———, ed. 2005. *American Exceptionalism and Human Rights.* Princeton, NJ: Princeton University Press.

Ivison, Duncan. 2002. *Postcolonial Liberalism.* Cambridge: Cambridge University Press.

Jackson, Jean. 1995. Culture, Genuine and Spurious: The Politics of Indianness in the Vaupes, Colombia. *American Ethnologist* 22 (1): 3–27.

Kahn, Joel. 1989. Culture: Demise or Resurrection? *Critique of Anthropology* 9 (2): 5–25.

Kazin, Michael. 2006. The Gospel of Love. Review of *The Most Famous Man in America: The Biography of Henry Ward Beecher,* by Debby Applegate. *New York Times Book Review* (July 16).

Keck, Margaret, and Kathryn Sikkink. 1998. *Activists Beyond Borders: Advocacy Networks in International Politics.* Ithaca, NY: Cornell University Press.

Khagram, Sanjeev, James V. Riker, and Kathryn Sikkink, eds. 2002. *Restructuring World Politics: Transnational Social Movements, Networks, and Norms.* Minneapolis: University of Minnesota Press.

Kleinman, Arthur, Veena Das, and Margaret Lock, eds. 1997. *Social Suffering.* Berkeley: University of California Press.

Klug, Heinz. 2000. *Constituting Democracy: Law, Globalism, and South Africa's Political Reconstruction.* Cambridge: Cambridge University Press.

Knauft, Bruce. 1996. *Genealogies for the Present in Cultural Anthropology.* New York: Routledge.

Korey, William. 1998. *NGOs and the Universal Declaration on Human Rights: "A Curious Grapevine."* New York: St. Martin's.

Kuper, Adam. 1999. *Culture: The Anthropologists' Account.* Cambridge, MA: Harvard University Press.

Kymlicka, Will. 1995a. *Multicultural Citizenship: A Liberal Theory of Minority Rights.* Oxford: Oxford University Press.

————, ed. 1995b. *The Rights of Minority Cultures.* Oxford: Oxford University Press.

Laclau, Ernesto. 1996. *Emancipation(s).* London: Verso.

Langlois, Anthony J. 2001. *The Politics of Justice and Human Rights.* Cambridge: Cambridge University Press.

Lazarus-Black, Mindie, and Susan Hirsch, eds. 1994. *Contested States: Law, Hegemony, and Resistance.* New York: Routledge.

Lerner, Gerda. 1987. *The Creation of Patriarchy.* Oxford: Oxford University Press.

Likosky, Michael. 2005. *Privatising Development: Transnational Law, Infrastructure, and Human Rights.* Leiden: Martinus Nijhoff.

————. 2006. *Law, Infrastructure, and Human Rights.* Cambridge: Cambridge University Press.

Lutz, Ellen L. 2005. Cultural Survival: A Human Rights Organization. *Cultural Survival Quarterly* 28 (2): June 15.

Malkki, Liisa. 1995. *Purity and Exile: Violence, Memory, and National Cosmology among Hutu Refugees in Tanzania.* Chicago: University of Chicago Press.

Mamdani, Mahmood, ed. 2000. *Beyond Rights Talk and Culture Talk: Comparative Essays on the Politics of Rights and Culture.* New York: Palgrave.

Marchetti, Raffaele. 2005. Human Rights as Participatory Elements within a Global Democratic System. http://www.irmgard-coninx-stiftung.de/index.php?id=48, accessed March 18, 2007.

Marcus, George, and James Clifford, eds. 1986. *Writing Culture: The Poetics and Politics of Ethnography.* Berkeley: University of California Press.

Maritain, Jacques. 1949. Introduction to *Human Rights: Comments and Interpretation.* New York: Columbia University Press.

————. 1996. *Integral Humanism, Freedom in the Modern World, and A Letter on Independence.* Rev. ed. South Bend, IN: University of Notre Dame Press.

Marx, Karl. 1978 [1844]. On the Jewish Question. In Robert C. Tucker, ed., *The Marx-Engels Reader.* New York: Norton.

Mattei, Ugo, and Laura Nader. 2008. *Plunder: When the Rule of Law Is Illegal.* Oxford: Blackwell.

Maybury-Lewis, David. 1991. The Decade Ahead. *Cultural Survival Quarterly* 15 (1): 1.

Mayer, Ann Elizabeth. 1991. *Islam and Human Rights: Tradition and Politics.* Boulder: Westview.

Melden, A. I., ed. 1970. *Human Rights.* Belmont, CA: Wadsworth Publishing.

Merry, Sally Engle. 2001. Changing Rights, Changing Culture. In Jane Cowan, Marie-Bénédicte Dembour, and Richard A. Wilson, eds., *Culture and Rights: Anthropological Perspectives.* Cambridge: Cambridge University Press.

———. 2006a. *Human Rights and Gender Violence: Translating International Law into Local Justice.* Chicago: University of Chicago Press.

———. 2006b. Transnational Human Rights and Local Activism: Mapping the Middle. *American Anthropologist* 108 (1): 38–51.

Mertus, Julie. 2005. *The United Nations and Human Rights: A Guide for a New Era.* New York: Routledge.

Mertus, Julie, and Jeffrey Helsing, eds. 2006. *Human Rights and Conflict: Exploring the Links Between Rights, Law, and Peacebuilding.* Washington, DC: U.S. Institute of Peace Press.

Messer, Ellen. 1993. Anthropology and Human Rights. *Annual Review of Anthropology* 22: 221–249.

———. 2002. Anthropologists in a World with and without Human Rights. In Jeremy MacClancy, ed., *Exotic No More: Anthropology on the Front Lines.* Chicago: University of Chicago Press.

———. 2006. Comment on "Toward a Critical Anthropology of Human Rights." *Current Anthropology* 47 (3): 502–503.

Midgley, Mary. 1999. Towards an Ethic of Global Responsibility. In Tim Dunne and Nicholas Wheeler, eds., *Human Rights in Global Politics.* Cambridge: Cambridge University Press.

Mills, Kurt. 1998. *Human Rights in the Emerging Global Order: A New Sovereignty?* New York: Palgrave/St. Martin's.

Mills, Martin. 2003. This Turbulent Priest: Contesting Religious Rights and the State in the Tibetan Shugden Controversy. In Richard A. Wilson and Jon P. Mitchell, eds., *Human Rights in Global Perspective: Anthropological Studies of Rights, Claims, and Entitlements.* London: Routledge.

Moore, Henrietta L., and Todd Sanders, eds. 2006. *Anthropology in Theory: Issues in Epistemology.* Oxford: Blackwell.

Morsink, Johannes. 1999. *The Universal Declaration of Human Rights: Origins, Drafting, Intent.* Philadelphia: University of Pennsylvania Press.

Mutua, Makau. 2002. *Human Rights: A Political and Cultural Critique.* Philadelphia: University of Pennsylvania Press.

Nader, Laura. 1997. Controlling Processes: Tracing the Dynamic Components of Power. *Current Anthropology* 38 (5): 711–737.

———. 1999. In a Women's Looking Glass: Normative Blindness and Unresolved Human Rights Issues. *Horizontes Antropológicos* 5 (10): 61–82.

Nickel, James. 2007. *Making Sense of Human Rights*. 2d ed. Oxford: Blackwell.

Norris, Christopher. 1996. *Reclaiming Truth: Contribution to a Critique of Cultural Relativism*. Durham, NC: Duke University Press.

Nussbaum, Martha. 1996. Patriotism and Cosmopolitanism. In Joshua Cohen, ed., *For Love of Country*. Boston: Beacon.

———. 1997. Kant and Stoic Cosmopolitanism. *Journal of Political Philosophy* 5 (1): 1–25.

———. 2000. *Women and Human Development: The Capabilities Approach*. Cambridge: Cambridge University Press.

Ong, Aihwa. 1999. *Flexible Citizenship: The Cultural Logics of Transnationality*. Durham, NC: Duke University Press.

Ong, Aihwa, and Stephen Collier, eds. 2005. *Global Assemblages: Technology, Politics, and Ethics as Anthropological Problems*. Oxford: Blackwell.

Ortner, Sherry. 1973. On Key Symbols. *American Anthropologist* 75:1338–1346.

Panikkar, Raimon. 1979. *Myth, Faith, and Hermeneutics: Cross-Cultural Studies*. New York: Paulist Press.

———. 1982. Is the Notion of Human Rights a Western Concept? *Diogenes* 120:75–102.

Peace Brigades International. 2007. http://www.peacebrigades.org/, accessed March 16, 2007.

Peffer, Rodney. 1990. *Marxism, Morality, and Social Justice*. Princeton, NJ: Princeton University Press.

Perry, Michael J. 1998. *The Idea of Human Rights: Four Inquiries*. Oxford: Oxford University Press.

———. 2006. *Toward a Theory of Human Rights: Religion, Law, Courts*. Cambridge: Cambridge University Press.

Postero, Nancy. 2007. *Now We Are Citizens: Indigenous Politics in Postmulticultural Bolivia*. Stanford: Stanford University Press.

Povinelli, Elizabeth. 2002. *The Cunning of Recognition: Indigenous Alterities and the Making of Australian Multiculturalism*. Durham, NC: Duke University Press.

Preis, Ann-Belinda. 1996. Human Rights as Cultural Practice: An Anthropological Critique. *Human Rights Quarterly* 18:286–315.

Preiswerk. 1978. *The Place of Intercultural Relations in International Relations*. In *The Year Book of World Affairs*. London: Stevens and Sons.

Provost, René. 2005. *International Human Rights and Humanitarian Law*. Cambridge: Cambridge University Press.

Rajagopal, Balakrishnan. 2003. *International Law from Below: Development, Social Movements, and Third World Resistance*. Cambridge: Cambridge University Press.

Rapport, Nigel. 1998. The Potential of Human Rights in a Post-Cultural World. *Social Anthropology* 6 (3): 381–388.

Ratzinger, Joseph Cardinal. 1996. Relativism: The Central Problem for Faith Today. http://www.ewtn.com/library/curia/ratzrela.htm.

Rawls, John. 1971. *A Theory of Justice.* Cambridge, MA: Belknap Press of Harvard University Press.

———. 1993. *Political Liberalism.* New York: Columbia University Press.

———. 1999. *The Law of Peoples.* Cambridge: Harvard University Press.

Riles, Annelise. 2000. *The Network Inside Out.* Ann Arbor: University of Michigan Press.

———. 2006a. Anthropology, Human Rights, and Legal Knowledge: Culture in an Iron Cage. *American Anthropologist* 108 (1): 52–65.

———. 2006b. Comment on "Toward a Critical Anthropology of Human Rights." *Current Anthropology* 47 (3): 503–504.

Risse, Thomas, Stephen C. Ropp, and Kathryn Sikkink, eds. 1999. *The Power of Human Rights: International Norms and Domestic Change.* Cambridge: Cambridge University Press.

Rorty, Richard. 1979. *Philosophy and the Mirror of Nature.* Princeton, NJ: Princeton University Press.

———. 1993. Human Rights, Rationality, and Sentimentality. In Stephen Shute and Susan Hurley, eds., *On Human Rights: The Oxford Amnesty Lectures.* New York: Basic Books.

Rosen, Lawrence. 1989. *The Anthropology of Justice: Law as Culture in Islamic Society.* Cambridge: Cambridge University Press.

Ross, Fiona. 2003. Using Rights to Measure Wrongs: A Case Study of Method and Moral in the Work of the South African Truth and Reconciliation Commission. In Richard Ashby Wilson and Jon P. Mitchell, eds., *Human Rights in Global Perspective: Anthropological Studies of Rights, Claims, and Entitlements.* London: Routledge.

Sanford, Victoria. 2003. *Buried Secrets: Truth and Human Rights in Guatemala.* New York: Palgrave.

Sanjek, Roger, ed. 1990. *Fieldnotes: The Makings of Anthropology.* Ithaca, NY: Cornell University Press.

Santos, Boaventura de Sousa. 1995. *Toward a New Common Sense: Law, Science, and Politics in the Paradigmatic Transition.* New York: Routledge.

Santos, Boaventura de Sousa, and César A. Rodríguez-Garavito, eds. 2005. *Law and Globalization from Below: Towards a Cosmopolitan Legality.* Cambridge: Cambridge University Press.

Sarat, Austin, and Thomas Kearns, eds. 2002. *Human Rights: Concepts, Contests, Contingencies.* Ann Arbor: University of Michigan Press.

Schmidt, Paul F. 1955. Some Criticisms of Cultural Relativism. *Journal of Philosophy* 70:780–791.

Sharma, Arvind. 2006. *Are Human Rights Western? A Contribution to the Dialogue of Civilizations.* New Delhi: Oxford University Press.

Shenk, Mary. 2006. Models for the Future of Anthropology. www.aaanet.org/press/an/0106/shenk.html, accessed March 18, 2007.

Skeel, David A., Jr. 2007. The Unbearable Lightness of Christian Legal Scholarship. *University of Pennsylvania Law School, Scholarship at Penn Law.* Paper 126. http://lsr .nellco.org/upenn/wps/papers/126.

Slaughter, Anne-Marie. 2004. *A New World Order.* Princeton, NJ: Princeton University Press.

Slyomovics, Susan. 2005. *The Performance of Human Rights in Morocco.* Philadelphia: University of Pennsylvania Press.

Smith, David Woodruff. 2005. "Phenomenology." In Edward N. Saltz, ed., *The Stanford Encyclopedia of Philosophy.* URL=http://plato.stanford.edu/archives/win2005/ entries/phenomenology/.

Speed, Shannon. 2006. At the Crossroads of Human Rights and Anthropology: Toward a Critically-Engaged Activist Research. *American Anthropologist* 108 (1): 66–76.

———. 2008. *Rights in Rebellion: Indigenous Struggle and Human Rights in Chiapas.* Stanford, CA: Stanford University Press.

Spiro, Melford. 1986. Cultural Relativism and the Future of Anthropology. *Cultural Anthropology* 1 (3): 259–286.

———. 1996. Postmodernist Anthropology, Subjectivity, and Science. A Modernist Critique. *Comparative Studies in Society and History* 38 (4): 759–780.

Steward, Julian. 1948. Comment on the Statement on Human Rights. *American Anthropologist* 50:351–352.

Stocking, George, ed. 1989. *A Franz Boas Reader: The Shaping of American Anthropology, 1883–1911.* Chicago: University of Chicago Press.

———. 1993. *Colonial Situations: Essays on the Contextualization of Ethnographic Knowledge.* History of Anthropology, Volume 7. Madison: University of Wisconsin Press.

———. 1996. *Volksgeist as Method and Ethic: Essays on Boasian Ethnography and the German Anthropological Tradition.* History of Anthropology, Volume 8. Madison: University of Wisconsin Press.

Svensson, Tom G. 1992. Right to Self-Determination: A Basic Human Right Concerning Cultural Survival. The Case of the Sami and the Scandinavian State. In Abdullahi Ahmed An-Na'im, ed., *Human Rights in Cross-Cultural Perspective: A Quest for Consensus.* Philadelphia: University of Pennsylvania Press.

Sweet, William, ed. 2003. *Philosophical Theory and the Universal Declaration of Human Rights.* Ottawa: University of Ottawa Press.

Tate, Winifred. 2007. *Counting the Dead: The Culture and Politics of Human Rights Activism in Colombia.* Berkeley: University of California Press.

Theidon, Kimberly. 2004. *Entre projimos: El conflicto armado interno y la politica de la reconciliacion en el Peru.* Lima: Instituto de Estudios Peruanos.

Thornberry, P. 2002. Minority and Indigenous Rights at the "End of History." *Ethnicities* 2 (4): 515–537.

Tierney, Patrick. 2000. *Darkness in El Dorado: How Scientists and Journalists Devastated the Amazon,* New York: Norton.

Trouillot, Michel-Rolph. 1991. Anthropology and the Savage Slot. In Richard Fox, ed.,

Recapturing Anthropology: Working in the Present. Santa Fe: School of American Research.

Turner, Terence. 1997. Human Rights, Human Difference: Anthropology's Contribution to an Emancipatory Cultural Politics. *Journal of Anthropological Research* 53:273–291.

United Nations Educational, Scientific, and Cultural Organization. 1969. *Four Statements on the Race Question.* Paris: UNESCO.

———. 2001. Universal Declaration on Cultural Diversity. http://unesdoc.unesco.org/images/0012/001271/127160m.pdf.

United Nations, Statistics Division. 2005. *The World's Women 2005: Progress in Statistics.* http://unstats.un.org/unsd/Demographic/products/indwm/ww2005_pub/English/WW2005_Annex1_Statistical%20tables.pdf), accessed March 19, 2007.

Unnithan-Kumar, Maya. 2003. Reproductions, Health, Rights: Connections and Disconnections. In Richard Wilson and Jon P. Mitchell, eds., *Human Rights in Global Perspective: Anthropological Studies of Rights, Claims, and Entitlements.* London: Routledge.

U.S. National Park Service. 2008. Jim Crow Laws. http://www.nps.gov/malu/forteachers/jim_crow_laws.htm.

Waltz, Susan. 1995. *Human Rights and Reform: Changing the Face of North African Politics.* Berkeley: University of California Press.

Washburn, Wilcomb. 1987. Cultural Relativism, Human Rights, and the AAA. *American Anthropologist* 89:939–943.

Wilson, Richard A. 2001. *The Politics of Truth and Reconciliation in South Africa.* Cambridge: Cambridge University Press.

———. 2006. Afterword to "Anthropology and Human Rights in a New Key": The Social Life of Human Rights. *American Anthropologist* 108 (1): 77–83.

———, ed. 1997. *Human Rights, Culture, and Context: Anthropological Perspectives.* London: Pluto Press.

———. 2005. *Human Rights in the "War on Terror."* New York: Cambridge University Press.

Wilson, Richard Ashby, and Jon P. Mitchell, eds. 2003. *Human Rights in Global Perspective: Anthropological Studies of Rights, Claims, and Entitlements.* London: Routledge.

Wiredu, Kwasi. 1990. An Akan Perspective on Human Rights. In Abdullahi Ahmed An-Na'im and Francis M. Deng, eds., *Human Rights in Africa: Cross-Cultural Perspectives.* Washington, DC: Brookings Institution.

———. 1996. *Cultural Universals and Particulars: An African Perspective.* Bloomington: Indiana University Press.

Index

AAA. *See* American Anthropological Association

Afghanistan: U.S. intervention in, 52, 114

Ahtisaari, Martti, 86

Alston, Philip, 143n1

Amants, Les, 65–66

American Anthropological Association (AAA): Committee for Human Rights (CfHR), 34–35, 36, 45; "Declaration on Anthropology and Human Rights," 34–35, 36–37, 44–45, 124–27; El Dorado Task Force, 35–36, 147nn32–34; membership of, 144n14; and right to culture, 34–35, 44, 124–27; and "Statement on Human Rights" in *American Anthropologist*, 19–21, 22–29, 34, 124, 125, 143n3, 144n13, 145nn18,21, 148n5, 155n; and UNESCO, 20–21, 22, 144n11; Web site, 35, 36; and Yanomami, 33–34, 35–36

Amit, Vered, 32

Anaya, J., 122

Anderson, Benedict, 151n5

Anghie, Antony, 14

An-Na'im, Abdullahi Ahmed, 151n12; on culture and human rights, 81, 82–83; on *Weltanschauung*, 83, 151n13

anthropology: American historical particularism in, 21–22, 31; attitudes toward culture in, 13, 16, 21–22, 34–35, 44–45, 68–72, 74, 79–80, 83–84, 129, 148n5, 153n1; British social anthropology, 31, 144nn4,6; and collective rights, 17, 33–34, 112–13, 120–27, 130, 146n26; dismantling of anthropology departments, 146n27; ethnographic research on human rights practices, 11, 12–13, 14, 15, 16, 37–38, 59, 104–8, 129–30, 147n36; exclusion/marginalization regarding human rights, 10, 13, 16, 18–19, 25–26, 29–31, 33, 111–12, 129, 132, 148n5, 153n1; fieldwork, 32, 44; French social anthropology, 31, 144n4; and indigenous rights, 33–34, 120–27; major traditions in, 20, 144n4; and marginalized/subaltern populations, 22, 28–29, 31, 32–37, 70, 71, 120–27, 130, 146n26; and Marxism/neo-Marxism, 30–31, 32; and politics, 11, 19, 29–31, 32–33, 36–37, 38; public anthropology, 22, 29, 144n8; re-engagement with human rights, 11, 19, 31–39, 44–45, 46, 123–27, 129–33; and relativism, 14, 16, 21–22, 26, 27, 39, 44–45, 46, 49, 56–59, 62–63, 129, 148n5; scientific expertise in, 18–19, 20, 32, 33, 61, 143n4, 145n18, 146n27. *See also* American Anthropological Association (AAA)

Appadurai, Arjun, 97

Appiah, K. A., 14

Arendt, Hannah: on Nazi Germany, 74

Arnold, Matthew: *Culture and Anarchy*, 67, 68, 70

Ash, Kristina, 154n3

Asian Human Rights Charter, 54

Asian values debate, 52–54, 55–56, 149n10

Australia, 154n8

Bardot, Brigitte: in *And God Created Woman*, 65
Barnett, H. G., 25
Bates, Daniel, 68
Bauman, Zygmunt, 8
Baxi, Upendra, 14, 150n16; on relativism, 43, 48, 50
Baxter, Victoria, 147n35
Beals, Ralph, 23
Beecher, Henry Ward, 72
Belize, 151n8
Bell, Lynda S., 52–54
Benedict, Ruth: on patterns of culture, 21
Benedict XVI: on relativism, 40
Bennett, John W., 25
Bentham, Jeremy: on natural rights, 27, 145n19
Berlin, Isaiah, 13, 26; on hedgehogs and foxes, 60; on negative liberty language, 126; on the twentieth century, 108–9
Bhabha, Homi, 14
biodiversity, 122–23
Biolsi, Thomas, 14
Blaser, Mario, 123
Boas, Franz, 21, 22, 68, 69
Bolivia, 108; rural legal services in, 92; self-identity as *runa* in, 43, 148n4
Borofsky, Robert, 144n8, 147n33
Bourdieu, Pierre, 77
Bowen, John: on Indonesia, 5–7, 8, 9; on liberal political and legal theory, 5–6, 7, 8, 143n1; on pluralism of values, 5–7, 8, 9; on public reasoning, 6
Brazil: Yanomami in, 33–34, 35–36
Breckenridge, Carol, 14
Brennan, William, 65
Brysk, Alison, 92; *Globalization and Human Rights*, 84–85
Bush, George H. W., 154n3
Bush, George W.: on human rights, 51–52, 53, 54; Philadelphia speech on Iraq, 51–52

Cambodia, 120
Canada, 154n8
capitalism and multinational corporations, 10

Carter, Jimmy, 149n11
Cassin, René, 24
CEDAW. *See* Convention on the Elimination of All Forms of Discrimination against Women
Chagnon, Napoleon, 35–36
Chang, Peng-chun, 24
Cheah, Pheng, 92, 97, 108, 109, 153n10
Chernala, Janet, 147n32
Chiapas, 106
China, 53, 154n3; Tiananmen Square, 52
Christian God and human rights, 52
civil rights vs. human rights, 29–30, 145n24
Clarke, Kamari Maxine, 37, 92, 147n36
Claude, Richard Pierre, 38, 92
Clay, Jason, 146n26
Clifford, James, 32
Cold War, 29; end of, 10–11, 12, 30, 37, 39, 42, 45, 71, 83–84, 92, 97
collective rights: and anthropology, 17, 33–34, 112–13, 120–27, 130, 146n26; cultural rights, 34–35, 36–37, 44–45, 118, 121–22, 124–27; indigenous rights, 17, 31, 32–34, 36–37, 112, 114–15, 118–19, 120–27, 130, 146n26, 154n5; literature on, 153n2; and neoliberalism, 115, 146n26; relationship to individual rights, 114–15, 125, 126; relationship to normative practice, 118–20, 126–27, 130; relationship to politics, 116–17, 118–20, 121, 124–25, 130; and UDHR, 114–15, 116–18
collectivities: and culture, 68–69, 74; as exclusionary, 43, 71; self-identity in, 13, 43, 74, 130, 148nn3,4
Collier, Stephen, 7
Collins, Henry, 144n10
colonialism, 11, 20, 26, 28, 30, 32, 55–56, 69, 100, 154n5
conceptual analysis, 47–51, 54–55, 58, 59, 61–62, 149nn12,13
constructivism, social and ethical, 14
Convention against Discrimination in Education, 114
Convention against Torture and Other Cruel, Inhuman or Degrading Treatment or Punishment, 114

Convention Concerning the Protection of the World Cultural and Natural Heritage (World Heritage Convention), 78

Convention for the Suppression of the Traffic in Persons and of the Exploitation of the Prostitution of Others, 114

Convention on the Elimination of All Forms of Discrimination against Women (CEDAW), 86, 88, 105, 114, 133

Cooper, John, 144n10

Coronil, Fernando, 147n32

cosmopolitanism: and culture, 73–74, 84–85, 89–90; and globalization, 84–85, 89–90; and human rights, 14, 93–94, 107–10, 116, 130, 153n10; of Kant, 101, 102; as postnational, 14, 93, 99–104, 107, 109–10; and United States Federal System, 99–100, 152nn3,4, 153n6. *See also* transnational human rights networks; utopianism regarding human rights

Costa Rica, 154n3

Cowan, Jane, 37; on Asian values debate, 53–54; *Culture and Rights*, 14, 45, 85, 91, 107, 147n36, 150n17; on German Romanticism, 59; on interwar minority treaties and collective rights, 154n2

Cultural Survival, Inc./cultural survival movement, 31, 44–45, 121, 122–23, 130, 146n26

Cultural Survival Newsletter/Cultural Survival Quarterly, 146n26

culture: and anthropology, 13, 16, 21–22, 34–35, 44–45, 68–72, 74, 79–80, 83–84, 129, 148n5, 153n1, Arnold on, 67, 68, 70; and cosmopolitanism, 73–74, 84–85, 89–90; culture-as-process vs. culture-as-system, 70–71, 88, 89–90; definitions of, 67–80, 83–85, 88; extent of specific cultures, 72–73, 76; and globalization, 42, 70–72, 73–74, 83–85, 88, 89–90; high vs. low, 67, 70, 77, 78, 89; and judgments of relative worth, 69; *Kultur*, 67, 68, 73, 74, 150n2, 151n13; local vs. society at large, 65–67; overlap of cultural traditions, 80–84, 88; relationship to human conflict, 88;

relationship to human diversity, 69, 79–80; relationship to human rights, 67, 72, 73, 74–86, 89–90, 91, 129, 131, 150n4, 153n2; relationship to political calculations, 88; similarities in, 27–28; spokespersons for, 73–74; as transnational, 70–72, 84, 89, 90; and UDCD, 79–80; and *Volksgeist*, 68, 150nn2,3; and *Weltanschauung*, 151n13. *See also* right to culture

Cuvier, Georges, 41

Czechoslovakia: German invasion of, 114

Das, Veena, 13

Dauer, Sheila, 147n35

Davidson, Donald, 47

De Certeau, Michel, 14

"Declaration on Anthropology and Human Rights," 34–35, 36–37, 44–45, 124–27

De Laguna, Frederica, 144n10

Dembour, Marie-Bénédicte: on Asian values debate, 53–54; *Culture and Rights*, 14, 45, 91, 95, 107, 147n36; on German Romanticism, 59; on human rights claims, 16; on relativism and universalism, 62–63

democracy, 70, 102–3

Deng, F., 83

Descartes, René, 47, 55, 62, 118, 149n13

De Varennes, F., 122

Dewey, John, 47

Di Leonardo, Micaela, 144n7

Dilthey, Wilhelm, 152n13

Diner, Hasia, 145n23

Dionne, E. J., Jr., 40

Donnelly, Jack: on Asian values debate, 53, 55–56; on cultural differences, 72, 73–74; on human nature, 43; and Preis, 44, 72; on relativism and universal human rights, 43, 55–56, 148nn4,5, 149nn9,12; on UNDHR, 53

Dostoevsky, Fyodor, 148n2

Dundes Renteln, Alison: on cross-cultural legitimacy for human rights, 82; on relativism, 48–49, 55, 149n8

Dunne, Tim, 39

Dworkin, Ronald, 153n8

Eberhard, Christophe, 151n11
Engle, Karen, 19, 25
Englund, Harri, 92, 147n36
Enlightenment, the, 16, 40–41, 51; in
    France, 59
Erasmus, Desiderius: relationship with
    More, 89
Eriksen, Thomas Hylland, 16, 37, 151n9
Erman, Eva: on cosmopolitanism, 102–3,
    110, 153n8; on democracy and human
    rights, 102–3; on Habermas, 103; on
    "vertical" dimension of global gover-
    nance, 102, 107
European Court of Human Rights, 63
European Union, 8; membership in, 95
exploitation, economic and scientific, 28, 32

Fabian, Johannes, 148n4
Falk, Richard, 38, 82
Feit, Harvey A., 123
female genital circumcision, 125–26
feminism, 121
Fenton, William, 144n10
Field, Henry, 144n10
Fiji, 108, 153n9; village reconciliation
    (bulubulu) in, 86, 88
Finkielkraut, Alain: The Defeat of the Mind,
    40–41, 147n1, 148n2
First Nations, 17, 114
first principles: and human rights, 105,
    117–18; in liberal political and legal
    theory, 7–9, 117; in philosophy, 61, 117
500 Years Observances in 1992, 33
Foucault, Michel, 132; on archaeology of
    knowledge, 13; on conditions of exis-
    tence, 13
foundationalism, 8–9, 44, 46–47, 117
Fox, Richard G., 32
France: Collège de France, 41; cultural rela-
    tivism in, 41; the Enlightenment in, 59;
    Revolution, 28, 145n19; rights of man
    in, 28; social anthropology in, 31, 144n4;
    structuralism in, 31
Frazer, Sir James, 11
Friedlander, Judith: Vilna on the Seine,
    147n1
Friedman, Thomas, 42

gender violence, 85–86, 105, 125
Geneva Conventions, 114
German Romanticism, 59
Gershenhorn, Jerry, 29
Giddens, Anthony, 5
Gledhill, John: on anthropologists as
    observers, 5, 6; on regimes of truth, 7
globalization: and cosmopolitanism, 84–85,
    89–90; and culture, 42, 70–72, 73–74,
    83–85, 88, 89–90; of sympathetic law, 92
Greaves, Tom, 154n7
Gregor, Thomas, 36
Gross, Daniel, 36

Habermas, Jürgen: on community, 101–2;
    on human rights, 102, 103, 153n7; on the
    postnational constellation, 101–2
Hague Convention for the Protection of
    Cultural Property in the Event of Armed
    Conflict, 151n7
Hames, Ray, 147n32
Hatch, Elvin: on relativism, 62
Hayden, Cori, 154n7
Hegel, G. W. F.: on the Volksgeist, 68, 150n2;
    on Weltanschauung, 152n13
Helsing, Jeffrey, 92
Herbert, Gary B., 117
Herder, Johann Gottfried von, 150n2
Hernández-Truyol, Berta Esperanza, 38,
    108
Herskovits, Melville, 144nn6,10; and civil
    rights movement, 29, 145n23; "Statement
    on Human Rights," 21, 22–29, 34, 124,
    125, 143n3, 144n14, 145nn18,21, 148n5,
    155n9
Hierocles, 14, 109
Hill, Jane H., 147n32
Hobbes, Thomas: Leviathan, 126, 133
Hobsbawm, Eric, 148n2, 150n5
Holocaust, the, 28, 41–42, 116, 145n18
Hopi, 148nn3,4
human autonomy, 106
human difference vs. human sameness, 43,
    57–59, 61, 63, 79, 148n3
human dignity, 40, 79–80, 96, 98, 106, 131,
    145n22
human diversity, 69

human equality, 96, 103, 106, 143n2, 145n22

human freedom, 143n2

human reason, 145n22, 149n13

human rights: case-study approach to, 81–82; vs. civil rights, 29–30, 145n24; and cosmopolitanism, 14, 93–94, 107–10, 116, 130, 153n10; as dynamic concept, 106, 119, 126–27; epistemological division of labor regarding, 129–30, 132; hedgehogs and foxes regarding, 60–61, 62; hermeneutical approach to, 81; intercultural/crosscultural approach to, 80–84; language of, 39; optimism regarding, 14, 39, 130, 132–33; paradigmatic approach to, 12, 13; relationship to human sameness, 11, 15, 29, 43, 52, 57–58, 93, 96, 98, 101, 111–12, 117–18, 131–33, 145n22; relationship to human suffering, 58–59; relationship to natural rights theory, 27, 146n24, 150n16; relationship to ontological status of individuals, 11; relationship to relativism, 21–22, 41–45, 46, 48, 49, 50–59, 129; relationship to Western intellectual history, 7–9, 10–11, 16, 28–29, 41, 42–43, 46–47, 52, 53–54, 117–20, 121, 126, 145n21, 154n4; since end of Cold War, 10–11, 12, 30, 37, 39, 42, 45, 71, 83–84, 92, 97; synthetic approach to, 12–13; theory vs. practice of, 10–11, 12, 13–15, 17, 98, 104–8, 116–18, 131–33. *See also* collective rights; cosmopolitanism; international human rights system; right to culture; transnational human rights networks; utopianism regarding human rights

Human Rights in Cross-Cultural Perspectives, 81

human rights violations, 34, 38, 95; in former Yugoslavia, 42

human sameness: as first principle, 116–17; vs. human difference, 43, 57–59, 61, 63, 79, 148n3, 150n15; and race, 29; relationship to ethical norms, 18–19, 57–58, 101, 111; relationship to human rights, 11,

14–15, 29, 43, 52, 57–58, 93, 96, 98, 101, 111–12, 117–18, 131–33, 145n22

human suffering and human rights, 58–59

Humphrey, John P., 24, 76–77, 78, 145n15

ICCPR. *See* International Covenant on Civil and Political Rights

ICESCR. *See* International Covenant on Economic, Social, and Cultural Rights

Ignatieff, Michael: on relativism and human rights, 42–43

imperialism, 46, 64, 70, 100, 108, 145n21

indigenous peoples: assimilation of, 122, 154n6; and biodiversity, 122–23; indigenous rights, 17, 31, 32–34, 36–37, 112, 114–15, 118–19, 120–27, 130, 146n26, 154n5; knowledge possessed by, 122–23, 154n7; and UN, 33, 123, 147n29

Indonesia: Aceh, 86; pluralism of values in, 5–7, 8, 9

International Convention on the Elimination of All Forms of Racial Discrimination, 114, 146n25

International Covenant on Civil and Political Rights (ICCPR), 146n25, 151n8; article 6 of, 113–14; ratification of, 154n3; and UDHR, 113–14, 117

International Covenant on Economic, Social, and Cultural Rights (ICESCR), 77–78, 146n25, 151n7, 151n8; article 15, 121; and UDHR, 77–78, 113, 117

international human rights system, 109, 131–32, 133; vs. transnational human rights networks, 14, 91–92, 93–96, 97–99, 105–6, 107, 118, 130. *See also* Convention on the Elimination of All Forms of Discrimination against Women; International Covenant on Civil and Political Rights; International Covenant on Economic, Social, and Cultural Rights; United Nations; Universal Declaration of Human Rights

International Labor Organization (ILO): Convention 107, 121–22; Convention 169, 118, 119, 120, 154nn5,8; Indigenous and Tribal Peoples Convention, 123,

133; Indigenous and Tribal Populations Convention and Recommendation, 118
Iraq: Constitution of 2005, 52; human rights in, 51–52; George W. Bush on, 51–52; U.S. invasion of, 114
Islam: and human rights, 81, 82; the Qur'an, 81
Israel and Human Rights Council, 145n17
Italian fascism, 74
Ivison, Duncan: *Postcolonial Liberalism*, 143n1

Jacobellis, Nicol, 65–67
Joas, Hans, 153n8
Journal of Anthropological Research, 36, 124–25

Kant, Immanuel, 13, 52, 132; cosmopolitanism of, 101, 102
Kayapo, 36
Kazin, Michael, 72–73
Keck, Margaret, 92
Khagram, Sanjeev, 92
Kim Il-sung, 56
Kleinman, Arthur, 13
Kluckhohn, Clyde, 23
Knauft, Bruce, 146n28
Korey, William, 29, 93, 95, 152n1
Kosovo and Serbia, 86–88, 89–90
Kostunica, Vojislav, 87
Kymlicka, Will, 7; on substantive minority rights, 114–15

Laclau, Ernesto, 148n6
Laguna, Frederica de, 22
Laos, 120
Latin America: and ILO Convention 169, 154n8; neoliberalism in, 33
League of Nations, 114
legal pragmatism, 47
Lerner, Gerda: on patriarchy, 116
Lévi-Strauss, Claude, 29, 41
liberal political and legal theory: first principles/foundationalism in, 7–9, 117; and human rights, 10–11, 119–20, 126, 154n4; Ivison on, 143n2; vs. social science, 5–8
Liberia, 154n3

linguistic minorities, 17
local communities vs. society at large, 65–67
Lock, Margaret, 13
Lowie, Robert, 22, 144n10

Madison, James, 117
Malaysia, 53
Malik, Charles Habib, 24
Malinowski, Bronislaw, 144n6
Malle, Louis: *Les Amants*, 65–66
Marcus, George, 32
Maritain, Jacques, 144n9
Marshall Islands and Human Rights Council, 145n17
Marxism, 30–31, 96, 121, 151n5
Maybury-Lewis, David and Pia, 31, 121, 146n26
McRae, Glenn, 123
Mead, Margaret, 144n6
Merry, Sally Engle, 92, 147n36; on human rights and gender violence, 85–86, 88; on human rights in the vernacular, 13–14; on transnational human rights networks, 105–6, 107, 150n4
Mertus, Julie, 38, 92
Messer, Ellen, 19, 20, 25, 36, 75, 111, 153n1
Métraux, Alfred, 29
Mitchell, Jon P., 19, 147n36
Montagu, Ashley, 29
Montaigne, Michel de: *Essais* of, 11
Moore, Henrietta L., 146n28
More, Thomas: relationship with Erasmus, 89; on Utopia, 90
Morsink, Johannes, 94, 145n16; on AAA Statement on Human Rights, 23–24; on UDHR, 20, 23–24, 76–77, 143nn1,2
multinational corporations, 10
Mutua, Makau, 14, 92

Nader, Laura, 133
Namibia, 85
Nathan, Andrew, 52
nationalism, 74–75, 95
National Research Council (NRC): Committee for International Cooperation in Anthropology, 21,

22–23, 24, 144nn10,13; relations with UNESCO, 21, 22–23

nation-states/international system, 103–4, 108–10, 126; international human rights law, 39, 78, 79–80, 85–86, 113–14, 120, 121–22, 123–24, 125; national sovereignty, 93–94, 95, 97, 100–101, 103, 130; nation-states vs. nations, 152n2; and right to culture, 75–76; and Treaty of Westphalia, 94, 103

Nazi Germany: Arendt on, 74; the Holocaust, 28, 41–42, 116, 145n18; invasion of Czechoslovakia, 114; Nuremberg trials, 28, 145n20; and relativism, 26

Neel, James, 35–36

negative liberty, 126, 154n4

neoconservatism, 52

neoliberalism: and collective rights, 10, 17, 115, 146n26; in Latin America, 33, 91

New Approaches to International Law movement, 38

New York Times, 86–88

New Zealand, 154n8

Nicolaisen, Ida, 147n35

Nietzsche, Friedrich, 41

nihilism, 14

nongovernmental organizations (NGOs), 5, 15, 38; as elitist/un-democratic, 95–96, 108; and Eleanor Roosevelt, 93, 94, 95, 152n1; and transnational human rights networks, 91, 94–96, 108. *See also* Cultural Survival, Inc.

North Korea, 56

Northwestern University Dept. of Anthropology, 21

NRC. *See* National Research Council

Nuremberg trials, 28, 145n20

Nussbaum, Martha: on cosmopolitanism, 14, 109

obscenity, 65–66, 67

Ong, Aihwa, 7

orientalism, 32

Ortner, Sherry: on relativism, 63

Palau and Human Rights Council, 145n17

Panikkar, Raimon, 81

patriarchy, 116

Pavlov, Alexie P., 24

Peffer, Rodney: on relativism, 50, 149n8

Peleg, Ilan, 52

Perry, Michael, 47, 63; on relativism, 42

Plog, F., 68

pluralism of values: Bowen on, 5–7, 8, 9; in Indonesia, 5–7, 8, 9

Poland: German invasion of, 114

Pollock, Jackson: *Number One 1948*, 77

Posner, Richard, 47

postcolonial theory, 14, 43, 121

Postero, Nancy, 108

postnational human rights systems, 14, 98–104, 107, 109–10, 130, 131, 133

power, 18, 39, 64, 69, 83, 116

pragmatism, 8, 47

Preis, Ann-Belinda, 44, 45, 72

Preiswerk, 151n13

Principe, 151n8

property rights, 76, 117

Quine, W. V. O., 47

Qur'an, the, 81

racism, 26, 29, 64

Rajagopal, Balakrishnan, 14, 39, 105

Ranger, Terence, 150n5

Rawls, John: on justice, 80, 151n10; on overlapping consensus, 80–81; *Political Liberalism*, 80–81

Raz, Joseph, 7

reason, 40–41, 52; and social organization, 6, 11

relativism: and anthropology, 14, 16, 21–22, 26, 27, 39, 44–45, 46, 49, 56–59, 62–63, 129, 148n5; and Asian values debate, 52–54, 55–56; categories/types of relativism, 45–46, 48–56, 57–64, 129, 149n8; and conceptual simplification, 62; cultural vs. ethical relativism, 48–49; epistemological relativism, 48; as fundamental issue, 62–64; phenomenological/intuitive approach to, 57–59, 62, 149n14; philosophical approach to, 47–51, 54–56, 57, 58, 59, 61–62; political approach to, 51–56, 57, 58, 59; relationship to human rights, 21–22, 41–45, 46, 48, 49, 50–59, 129; "relativism" as empty signifier, 46, 148n6; and "Statement on Human Rights," 26, 30; vs. universalism, 40–45, 52–64, 65–67

right to culture: and AAA, 34–35, 36–37, 44–45, 124–27; and nation-states, 75–76; and UDHR, 74–78, 80, 121, 125–26; UN Declaration on the Rights of Indigenous Peoples, 118, 119, 120. *See also* International Covenant on Economic, Social, and Cultural Rights

right to life, 113–14

right to social and economic development, 17

Riker, James V., 92

Riles, Annelise, 15–16, 38, 147n36; on transnational human rights networks, 92, 104, 153n9

Risse, Thomas: on power of human rights, 92, 108, 133

Robbins, Bruce, 97, 108, 109

Roosevelt, Eleanor: and Commission for Human Rights/UDHR, 19, 24, 29, 93, 94, 95, 116, 131, 151n6; and NGOs/the "curious grapevine," 93, 94, 95, 152n1

Ropp, Stephen C.: on power of human rights, 92, 108, 133

Rorty, Richard, 55, 131; on foundations, 8–9, 46–47; "Human Rights, Rationality, and Sentimentality," 8–9; on philosophy as mirror of nature, 46–47

Russian nihilism, 148n2

Russian revolutionaries, 26, 28

Sanders, Todd, 146n28

Sanford, Victoria, 147n31

Sanjek, Roger, 32

Santa Cruz, Hernán, 24, 145n16

Sao Tome, 151n8

Saudi Arabia, 143n1

Schmidt, Paul F., 49

Sellars, Wilfred, 47

Serbia and Kosovo, 86–88, 89–90

Shenk, Mary, 146n27

Sikkink, Kathryn: on power of human rights, 92, 108, 133

Singapore, 53

Skeel, David A., Jr., 47

slavery, 28

Slyomovics, Susan, 147n36

social anthropology: in Britain, 22; in France, 22

social contract theory, 52

social theory and anthropology, 5–7

Sorbonne: Laboratoire d'Anthropologie Juridique de Paris, 151n11

South Africa, 143n1, 151n8

Speed, Shannon, 92, 147n36; on transnational human rights networks, 106–7; on Zapatistas, 119

Spiro, Melford, 32; on relativism, 49, 50, 55, 149n7

"Statement on Human Rights" (AAA), 21, 22–29, 34, 124, 125, 143n3, 144n14, 145nn18,21, 148n5, 155n9

Steward, Julian, 25, 145nn18,21

Stewart, Potter: on obscenity, 66, 67

Stocking, George, 21, 144n7; *Volksgeist as Method and Ethic*, 150n3

Strong, William Duncan, 144n10

Sweet, William, 117

Tate, Winifred, 92, 147n36

Thirty Years' War: Treaty of Westphalia, 94, 103

Thornberry, P., 122

Tiananmen Square, 52

Tierney, Patrick: *Darkness in El Dorado*, 35–36, 147n33

Tocqueville, Alexis de, 99–100

Todorov, Tzvetan, 16

transnational human rights networks, 10, 11, 15, 17; and collective rights, 115; ethnography of, 92, 104–8, 129–30, 150n4; vs. international human rights system, 14, 91–92, 93–96, 97–99, 105–6, 107, 118, 130, 131; and local human rights discourse, 106–7, 108; vs. nation-states, 91, 92, 93, 94–95, 96, 97–98, 100–101, 106, 107; and NGOs, 91, 94–96, 108; vs. postnational systems, 98–104

Treaty of Westphalia, 94, 103

Trouillot, Michel-Rolph, 101

truth: coherence theory of, 47; correspondence theory of, 47
Turner, Terence, 33, 36–37, 124
Turner, Trudy, 147n32

UDCD. See Universal Declaration on Cultural Diversity
UDHR. See Universal Declaration of Human Rights
UNESCO. See United Nations Educational, Scientific, and Cultural Organization
United Nations: adoption of ICESCR, 77, 151n8; adoption of UDHR, 20, 143n2; charter of, 29; Commission on Human Rights, 19–21, 23–24, 26–27, 28–29, 93, 94–95, 116–17, 131, 144n13, 145nn15,17, 151nn6,8, 152n1; creation of, 109–10; Draft Declaration on the Rights of Indigenous Peoples, 33, 123; founding of, 26; General Assembly, 24, 145n17, 151n8; Human Rights Council, 145n17; International Decade of the World's Indigenous People, 123, 147n29; International Year of the World's Indigenous People, 147n29; and Kosovo, 86–88; membership of, 143n2, 153n7; Working Group on Indigenous Populations, 118. See also Universal Declaration of Human Rights
United Nations Declaration of the Rights of the Child, 146n25
United Nations Declaration on the Elimination of Violence against Women, 125
United Nations Declaration on the Granting of Independence to Colonial Countries and Peoples, 146n25
United Nations Declaration on the Rights of Indigenous Peoples, 118, 119, 120, 154n8
United Nations Educational, Scientific, and Cultural Organization (UNESCO), 151n9; and AAA, 20–21, 22, 144nn11,13; and NRC, 21–22, 22, 144n13; relations with NRC, 21, 22–23; statement on race, 29; and UDHR, 19–21, 22, 94; Universal Declaration on Cultural Diversity

(UDCD), 79–80; World Heritage Committee, 78
United States: American Bar Association, 152n3; American Law Institute, 152n3; anti-communism in, 120; CIA covert operations, 120; Civil Rights Act of 1964, 150n1, 152n5; civil rights movement in, 29, 145n23, 150n11, 152n5; Declaration of Independence, 28, 146n24; and Declaration on the Rights of Indigenous Peoples, 154n8; federal system in, 99–100, 152nn3,4, 153n6; foreign policy, 30, 120–21; and Human Rights Council, 145n17; and ICCPR, 154n3; and ICESCR, 151n8; Jim Crow laws, 152n5; legal jurisdictions in, 152n3; national identity in, 99; racism in, 29; Uniform Commercial Code, 152n3; Vietnam war, 30, 120–21; Voting Rights Act of 1965, 150n1
United States Constitution, 52, 100, 145n24; Bill of Rights, 28; due process in, 146n24; equal protection in, 146n24; First Amendment, 66–67; Supremacy Clause, 99, 152n4
United States National Anthropological Archives, 20–21, 144nn5,13
United States Supreme Court: obscenity and Jacobellis v. Ohio, 65–67; Warren Court, 67
Universal Declaration of Human Rights (UDHR), 30, 34, 39, 53, 73, 82, 97, 111, 133, 149n11; article 3, 113–14, 125; article 5, 125; article 13, 117; article 14, 117; article 17, 117; article 22, 75–76, 77; article 27, 76–77, 78; and collective rights, 114–15, 116–18, 124, 125–26; and cultural rights, 74–78, 80, 121, 125–26; and domestic law, 113–14; ethnic and minority rights absent from, 114–15; Habermas on, 102, 153n7; and human sameness, 145n22; and Humphrey, 24, 76–77, 78, 145n15; and ICCPR, 113–14, 117; and ICESCR, 77–78, 113, 117; Morsink on, 20, 23–24, 76–77, 143nn1,2; and nation-states, 75–76, 77, 93–94, 95, 130, 151n6; and NGOs, 93, 94–95, 152n1; vs. the Qur'an, 81; relationship to

social practices, 116–18, 131–32; right to asylum in, 117; right to leave/return to any country in, 117; right to life in, 113; right to property in, 117; and Eleanor Roosevelt, 19, 24, 29, 93, 94, 95, 116, 131, 151n6; and "Statement on Human Rights," 22–25, 26–29; as transnationalist, 93–95; vs. UDCD, 79–80; and UNESCO, 19–21, 22, 94; and Western intellectual history, 10–11, 42, 52, 117–20, 121, 145n21, 154n4

Universal Declaration on Cultural Diversity (UDCD), 79–80

universalism in human rights, 9, 39, 111–12; and foreign policies, 51–52; George W. Bush on, 51–52; vs. relativism, 40–45, 52–64, 65–67; vs. universality of human rights, 14–15. *See also* human sameness

utopianism regarding human rights, 14, 86–90, 101, 103–4, 131–32. *See also* cosmopolitanism

Vietnam War, 30, 120–21

violence against women, 85–86, 105, 125

Voltaire, 41

Waltz, Susan, 38

Warren, Earl, 67

Watkins, Joe, 147n32

Weidenreich, Franz, 144n10

Weston, Burns H., 38, 92

Westphalian Compromise, 94, 103

Wheeler, Nicholas J., 39

Wilson, Richard A., 19, 38–39, 91, 92, 120; on Asian values debate, 53–54; *Culture and Rights*, 14, 45, 85, 107, 147n36; on German Romanticism, 59

Wittgenstein, Ludwig, 47

World Heritage Convention, 78

world-systems and dependence theory, 121

World War II, 26, 28, 94, 101, 116

Yanomami, 33–34, 35–36

Yeats, William Butler, 16, 60

Zapatistas, 119

About the Cover Image

The photograph on the back cover provides a wider view of the mural from which the detail on the front cover was taken. This extraordinary political painting was commissioned by Bolivia's Ministry of Justice in 2008 and was meant to serve as a discursively charged panorama of Bolivian history inspired by the works of earlier Latin American muralists like Diego Rivera and José Clemente Orozco. The Bolivian-American artist Gonz Jove and his team of local artists drew from diverse aesthetic and ideological sources in order to depict the moments of both tragedy and resistance that have marked Bolivia's complicated historical trajectory.

The cover image shows a portion of the mural that represents the turmoil surrounding Bolivia's 1952 National Revolution. The artist explained that he chose to vernacularize Eugène Delacroix's famous painting *Liberty Leading the People* because he believes that, like the French Revolution, both the 1952 National Revolution and the contemporary revolution of Evo Morales (elected in 2005) are struggles for universal human rights.